KEY
to the
CITY

KEY
to the
CITY

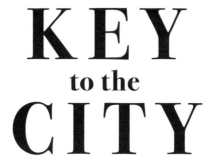

How Zoning Shapes
Our World

SARA C. BRONIN

W. W. NORTON & COMPANY
Independent Publishers Since 1923

For information about special discounts for bulk purchases, please contact
W. W. Norton Special Sales at specialsales@wwnorton.com or 800-233-4830

Manufacturing by Lakeside Book Company
Book design by Chris Welch
Production manager: Devon Zahn

ISBN: 978-0-393-88166-0

W. W. Norton & Company, Inc.
500 Fifth Avenue, New York, N.Y. 10110
www.wwnorton.com

W. W. Norton & Company Ltd.
15 Carlisle Street, London W1D 3BS

10 9 8 7 6 5 4 3 2 1

To the people of the city of Hartford

Contents

PART III. DESIGNING FOR DELIGHT

KEY
to the
CITY

Introduction

Eighty-nine degrees and no breeze meant that the smell of oil and
chicken permeated the air. The unshaded asphalt took on the cloy-
ing essence of the fryer. We had stopped in front of Popeyes, part-
way through our tour of the Upper Albany neighborhood.

It was the summer of 2014, and neighborhood leader Denise Best had
been kind enough to spare a few hours to take me around. A few weeks
earlier, I had become chair of the city's planning and zoning commission,
the public body that determines what can be built where in Connecticut's
capital city, Hartford. As a law professor deeply enmeshed in land use
research, I had spent years studying how zoning shapes our lives, but this
was the first time I had the chance to apply that knowledge. Our family
had lived in Hartford's South Downtown for four years, and I knew that
neighborhood well. But I hadn't explored other parts of the city nearly
enough. So I asked Denise and other residents across our fifteen neighborhoods to show me what they loved about the places they called home, and
what they wanted to change.

Denise's tour started with some highlights: Scott's Jamaican Bakery, a mainstay for our West Indian community, one of the largest in the United States. The Albany Avenue branch of the Hartford Public Library, a well-maintained haven for neighborhood families. The Artists Collective, offering training in the performing and visual arts with a focus on the African diaspora. She also showed me areas that promised big development opportunities: the Bravo shopping plaza, slated for a cosmetic facelift; two acres of cleared land at a prominent intersection; and a one-acre lot with a deteriorated former police substation that could be transformed for new public use.

And then there was the Popeyes. There had been a fast-food joint on the site since at least 1970, but in the years since 1986, when Denise bought her home—a charming century-old two-family—conditions had deteriorated. She was fed up with the cars idling and honking in the drive-through line and the trash routinely deposited in her yard around the corner. She also pointed out the wide curb cuts, which put pedestrians at risk of careless drivers—a fear confirmed by statistics, as Albany Avenue topped the state's pedestrian casualty charts. All in all, the Popeyes was an eyesore for the neighborhood. Neither Denise nor I had anything against fried chicken. But it was easy to see why this place detracted from the community's day-to-day quality of life.

As Denise pointed out, the restaurant was just one of many such less-than-optimal places lining the commercial spine of her once-thriving neighborhood. So was the Mr. Sparkle Car Wash, a wholly asphalted corner lot with six wash-it-yourself stalls, a jarring contrast to a handsome home with a two-story porch next door. And so were the four gas stations within about a dozen blocks, each producing toxic smells and too much traffic.

Exploring the avenue that summer day, it was hard not to feel anguish over what might have been—in fact, over what once *was*. At the beginning of the twentieth century, Hartford had ranked as one of the richest cities in the country. The insurance industry, innovative manufacturers like Elizabeth Colt and Albert Pope, and literary illuminati like Mark Twain and

Harriet Beecher Stowe had given the city economic and cultural promi-
nence. Back then, Hartford was renowned both for its commercial bustle
and for its stately elegance. "Of all the beautiful towns it has been my for-
tune to see, this is the chief," Twain enthused upon his first visit. "You do
not know what beauty is if you have not been here."

The past half-century-plus, however, had been unkind. The dawn
of the automobile led to the rise of the suburbs and a shift at multiple levels of policy priorities that favored those suburbs over cities. In
Hartford as in other American cities, civil-rights protests in 1968 after
the death of Martin Luther King created lacerating images of inner-city
damage, images that accelerated White flight, leaving behind neighborhoods that were increasingly segregated. Banks refused to lend. Businesses closed. More people moved away. Urban residents suffered from
decisions that favored commuters. On Albany Avenue, property owners demolished three- and four-story ornate brick or wood buildings
with abandon, putting gas stations, car washes, strip malls, and drive-
throughs in their places. These types of businesses were convenient for
drivers speeding to and from the wealthy western suburbs. Indeed, anyone visiting Albany Avenue today might quake a bit wanting to cross
the avenue in certain places. However, these businesses generated little
tax revenue for the city, and they tended to be owned by out-of-towners
who neglected the needs of the community. (The owner of the Popeyes
lot lives in a million-dollar home in another state.) Just a mile south,
Mark Twain's neighborhood has fared a little better, managing to retain
a greater share of the architecture he admired. Still, across the street
from his old home sits a one-story strip mall with a run-down parking
lot running three hundred feet along Farmington Avenue. And following Farmington Avenue to the city line, you'd see a few gas stations
and fast-food chains interspersed among the older buildings. The down-
grading of Hartford is not just a matter of subjective perception, but a
quantifiable reality. Connecticut's capital is now one of the poorest cities in the country—an island of concentrated poverty in one of America's wealthiest regions.

Of course, Hartford is not alone. Versions of its same story were play-ing out across the postwar United States, with such conspicuous similar-ity that one could be forgiven for thinking of urban decline as reflecting some natural process, ineluctable and inevitable. To be sure, the story does reflect broad evolutions and transformations in technology, demography, and industry. But that's not the whole picture—and it would be wrong to view the changes in Hartford and other such cities fatalistically.

The devolution of Albany Avenue was not happenstance. It was dic-tated in large part by zoning laws that changed in the 1950s and 1960s and were then accepted for decades. Arcane zoning rules still in place the day I toured Upper Albany, for instance, would have prevented a property owner from rebuilding one of those gracious four-story brick buildings torn down a half-century ago, even if she had wanted to. Zon-ing set onerous parking requirements that resulted in more asphalt, less building and green space, and too many paved-over lots like the one we were sweltering in that July day. Zoning rendered impossible the lovely townhomes and apartment buildings that had graced the avenue in its heyday.

Even worse was the impact on health. In prioritizing cars and drivers, our city's zoning code had effectively mandated the air pollution that made Hartford the asthma capital of Connecticut, and Upper Albany its neighborhood with the highest asthma rate. And as food options worsened—there is neither a sit-down restaurant on the avenue nor a grocery store selling fresh food—obesity rates skyrocketed. Today, Upper Albany has the highest rates of adults with diabetes (17 percent) and high blood pressure (44 percent) of any neighborhood in the city, which has some of the worst such health outcomes in the state. Overall, Denise's neighbors have a life expectancy six years below the residents of Avon, a suburb just eight miles away. If you're familiar with health disparities in America, it will not surprise you to learn that Upper Albany is predominantly Black and just 1 percent White, with a median household income of about $23,000, while Avon is 7 percent Black and Latino, with a median household income of about $131,000. And while zoning alone can't account for this disparity entirely, it has demonstrably worsened it.

Why did Hartford condemn its own residents to this fate? Why did it adopt zoning policies that proved not only discriminatory but in some senses deadly? Looking back at the fractious events of the 1960s, one imagines city officials' panicked efforts to keep major companies downtown and to cater to the White office workers who had fled to the suburbs. Yet by prioritizing the desires of those who had left the city, Hartford officials neglected the needs of the residents who remained. In the decades after, inertia may have resulted simply from inattention. Perhaps decision-makers felt reluctant to upend the settled expectations of property owners. At any rate, zoning changes, once made, went unexamined for decades. So even as attitudes toward central cities changed, and the standards and priorities of community planning evolved, Albany Avenue did not.

The history of zoning in the United States is rife with instances of racially invidious mischief. But one doesn't have to assume malice or intent to explain the persistence of bad outcomes in the way we organize our cities. The paradox of zoning—the tragedy of zoning—is that it often starts out in a hopeful attempt to improve our cities and the lives we live in them. Then, all too often, it fails; it even does the opposite. Yet, when done right, zoning has the power to make all the difference for a community. Because zoning for good—for more vibrant economies, for greater household security, for more delightful experiences—is both achievable and necessary.

By and large, people think of zoning as an often-bewildering set of rules enshrined in inscrutable maps and regulations. Except for those relatively rare instances in which some controversy comes to the fore, zoning discussions can be pretty stultifying—and as I know well from my years chairing Hartford's commission, attending a zoning meeting doesn't rank high on most people's list of fun for an evening. Yet properly understood, zoning is much more than a mere bureaucratic nuisance.

The urge and need to differentiate uses in one's surroundings—where to farm; where to build fires; where to locate waste; where to situate the sacred and conduct business and heal the sick, and so on—have shaped human society from the beginning. The earliest maps we've discovered, from China and Mesopotamia and Egypt, depict walls, temples, parks, plazas, and housing, as do later maps of the city-planning-obsessed Greeks and Romans. These maps not only showed what existed. Many also showed what could be, ancient graphics forming the template for growth to come.

Zoning codes are simply a modern means of codifying and enforcing our fundamental desire for ordering our world. Zoning as we know it today in the United States has a modern-day origin story. In part, it grew out of garden-variety municipal ordinances adopted in the late nineteenth and early twentieth centuries in the hope of making development more orderly and protecting people from harms, known or perceived. Some pre-zoning land use regulations targeted potentially hazardous uses, like tanneries and slaughterhouses, separating these uses from residences and from nonhazardous commercial businesses. Cities passed ordinances shaping the design of signage, billboards, and theater marquees, an attempt to declutter the streetscape. Others established spacing requirements for new multifamily "tenement" dwellings, which aimed to reduce overcrowding and provide light and air to occupants. The prehistory of zoning is also rife with semicovert, racially invidious action, an excellent example of which is late-nineteenth-century laundry regulation in California, motivated by anti-Chinese sentiment.

Both the order-promoting and the discriminatory rationales behind pre-zoning land use ordinances were reflected in New York City's 1916 comprehensive zoning code, the country's first. At the turn of the twentieth century, explosive growth in that city—growth both reflected in and exacerbated by the construction of the underground subway system—yielded a built environment broadly viewed as chaotic. Business leaders became convinced that the city needed to adopt rules to guide ever-proliferating new construction, especially of skyscrapers, which were unrestricted in height and bulk. At the same time, they felt that the right rules might also curb the spillover social effects of haphazard city planning, including the mixing of different classes of people—such problems as the factory workers daring to use Fifth Avenue sidewalks, disturbing wealthy ladies out shopping.

In 1914, the state legislature granted the city zoning authority. Over a two-year period, the city drafted and enacted the Building Zone Resolution, consisting of a map and a thirteen-page-long text dividing the entire city into use, height, and area districts. That resolution received national attention, and other cities started to study whether to adopt zoning themselves. A zoning wave swept the country, and more large cities began to adopt their own codes.

Federal officials, including then–Commerce Secretary Herbert Hoover, took notice. Hoover and others came to believe that zoning could improve the economy by making development patterns more predictable. He convened an advisory committee, charging it with drafting a model state law for zoning, so that more legislatures could do what New York State had done for its biggest city. The resulting State Standard Zoning Enabling Act of 1924 gave broad powers to local governments to regulate the uses of buildings and land, and to regulate structures, too. These powers expressly allowed local governments to divide all land in their jurisdiction into districts—zones—and then to regulate land uses, structures, and lots in each of the districts. The act charged zoning with achieving the "purpose of promoting health, safety, morals, or the general welfare of the community." Embedded in these words are the community-minded rationales used to justify pre-zoning land use regulation: to separate noxious uses, develop aesthetic standards, and promote public health. At the same time, it would be wrong to overlook the more sinister interpretations of the word "morals" in particular, given that so much zoning was deployed to maintain or promote racial and economic segregation through seemingly race-neutral provisions. As we will see, all of these motivations have had significant impacts on the way our cities look and work today.

The State Standard Zoning Enabling Act proved popular among state legislators and the political elite. By 1925, nineteen states had adopted the act, and by 1926 there were at least 425 municipalities with zoning. State legislators were further emboldened by the 1926 Supreme Court decision in *Village of Euclid v. Ambler Realty*, which upheld as constitutional a comprehensive local zoning ordinance dividing land into use-based districts. Within a few short years, all fifty states adopted state enabling acts, delegating zoning powers to local governments. Local governments could exercise these powers to adopt and administer zoning codes, consisting of text and a corresponding, color-coded map showing the district assigned to each lot (each piece of land, also called a parcel). Under those codes, which remain largely similar today, districts have a variety of names and purposes, but the most common are commercial, residential, industrial, open space, and mixed districts. Local governments can also create special districts for a specific kind of building or neighborhood, such as a hospital or museum district. Single-family homes are usually assigned to residential districts, while skyscrapers might be part of a commercial or downtown district. While these rules of thumb sound straightforward, most zoning codes are not. Using terms and jargon often difficult to decipher, code texts typically run about a hundred and fifty pages long. Maps, too, often lack legibility, with a smorgasbord of colors, hatch marks, and borders explained sometimes only by abbreviations for the names of zoning districts. To the layperson, zoning must seem impenetrable.

Yet its workings are everywhere around us. Zoning has become the most significant regulatory power of local government, and a central means by which cities attempt to shape their future. It dictates where and how we can build housing, factories, restaurants, parks, and shops. It limits how tall buildings can be. It defines how big a lot must be. It specifies tree plantings, stormwater management systems, parking, and sidewalks. Although zoning rules can't ordinarily be applied retroactively, when they do apply, they are binding. You cannot open a new restaurant, expand your factory, or occupy your house unless you have first complied with zoning laws. Given this immense power, zoning has a huge influence on our economy, and on the very structure of our society. Hidden in plain sight, it governs the places we occupy and, by extension, our health, wealth, and happiness.

What struck me most about my meeting with Denise, and my walks and talks over the years with so many other neighborhood leaders and local activists in Hartford, was how hard they had all worked to beautify their neighborhoods. They had identified problems and goals, and they had shown up at public meetings to fight for improvements in infrastructure and services. These were intelligent and thoughtful people, fierce advocates and defenders of their communities. Yet none of them had fully understood that Hartford's zoning code was at least partly responsible for many of the structural problems they had identified over the years. Whether intentional or not, the code was cloaked in a shroud of mystery that obscured its culpability for and its contributions to these problems.

This book represents my effort to lift that shroud—because you have a right to know what it's all about. The people of Hartford did, too. In the six years that followed my meeting with Denise, I recruited a new slate of commissioners who were committed to listening and working for change. Together, we engaged anyone who cracked the door open to a conversation, including business groups and religious organizations, individual property owners and children. We heard tremendous frustration with the way the city was developing. Dusting off the zoning code, we decided it was not only the culprit, but that it was irredeemable: we threw it out and wrote a completely new code. We redrew the zoning map to create districts that would transition Hartford from its industrialized past. We enshrined neighborhood priorities while fast-tracking the equitable, sustainable development that Hartford continues to need. We hired consulting planners who catalogued every parcel in the city and created a clear and user-friendly visual guide to the rules. In Denise's neighborhood, we banned new fast-food joints, expanded two-family zoning to enable a revenue stream from rent for homeowners, required tree plantings for shade-starved heat islands, and ensured that new buildings would be compatible with historic architecture. In Twain's old neighborhood, we blocked new drive-throughs—to the dismay perhaps only of an out-of-town landowner who wanted to build a McDonald's so badly he sued the city five times before finally giving up. Citywide, we modernized outdated rules and pioneered innovations, including eliminating minimum parking requirements and freeing all housing from burdensome public hearings—both firsts for a city of Hartford's size.

The effort to refresh stagnant codes is crucial, and yet in making these changes, Hartford is unfortunately rare. In the 2010s, when many American zoning codes had already endured at least a semicentennial without major revision, only two dozen large cities tossed out their old codes in favor of new ones. The institutional inertia and reluctance to change that typified Hartford for half a century is all too common, leaving antiquated concepts about city planning and society embedded in local laws almost everywhere. As a result, there's a lot of bad zoning out there, and plenty of well-founded critiques about its demerits. Understanding these critiques can help us steer clear of, and replace, the problematic parts.

And so this book considers what zoning can achieve, and how. The first part examines how zoning can help create communities that foster vibrant economies. It shows how zoning strategies can support a lively mix of uses and generate a platform for the creative arts. It also tackles age-old questions about how to best integrate nightlife. The second part addresses zoning's ability to provide households with the essentials they need to thrive. It covers the affordability and accessibility of housing, transportation options, and the often-overlooked issue of food security. The third part tackles zoning's role in creating delightful experiences and meaningful places. It covers zoning's potential to integrate natural features in our neighborhoods and to improve our streets, upending the conventional notion that zoning is just about buildings. And it highlights zoning's emerging role in building design and historic preservation, and in helping to make signage a delight rather than blight. In each of these chapters, I focus on the values and priorities that zoning can help us realize, weaving in examples from the boardwalks of Delray Beach and the red-light district of Baltimore to the flashy Las Vegas Strip and the deserts of Tucson.

Done wrong, zoning can yoke us to past mistakes, acting as an invisible drag on our aspirations. But done right, zoning can be a revolutionary vehicle for transforming place. Properly wielded, the zoning power can give us the built environments that we yearn for and deserve. It can facilitate equitable and sustainable cities and neighborhoods. And it can help shape our economic, experiential, sociopolitical, and environmental evolution for the better. Good zoning can bring tremendous benefits, promoting communities' values and aspirations. That's why we must demand more of zoning as it enters its second century. It is, in many ways, the key to our cities.

Part I

VIBRANT ECONOMIES

The Goldilocks Zone

El Principe Azul nightclub was a perfect place to park, because the strip-mall lot was empty. Standing in the dumpster area behind the club, I looked right: a check cashing place and a gas station. Left: a self-storage facility covered in chain-link fence. After crossing the street, I found myself in front of the building on Westward Street where my parents had bought a three-bedroom place just before I was born, in 1978. It was smaller than I remembered, but the two-story brick façades remained unchanged. The chlorine from the complex pool where I learned to swim wafted over the locked gates.

The Gulfton neighborhood, where I stood, sits in the heart of Houston, the only large city in the United States without zoning. In the 1950s, the neighborhood had just one small residential subdivision. But when Houston's population exploded—attracting about 1,000 new residents every day between 1965 and 1980—Gulfton, just off the Southwest Freeway, beckoned. Developers saturated the area with new apartments, about 15,000 of them, during this period. They geared their advertisements toward young professionals, offering recreational amenities like clubhouses and pools and adopting "adults-only" policies.

My parents, recent college graduates who worked as a civil engineer and a special-education teacher, bought their condo toward the end of this optimistic boomtime. My mom's parents moved to the same complex, bringing my aunt and two uncles with them. Revolution had forced my grandparents to flee Nicaragua, where my grandfather had worked as a ship broker importing and exporting cotton, and to come join their children in Houston. Ever entrepreneurial, they started a restaurant in Gulfton, naming it U.S. Submarine Sandwiches. Later they traded subs for hamburgers, opening Romy's Hamburgers. After putting in full days at their jobs, my mom and dad would work at the restaurants, manning the cash register, stepping in as waiters or busboys—whatever needed to be done. My younger sister and I were in playpens and side rooms, looking on.

Then came the 1980s, when the oil markets tanked and boomtown went bust. Houston's professional population was rattled, and the flood of new residents diminished to a trickle. Seeking a new clientele, owners of Gulfton condos and apartment complexes jettisoned adults-only policies, advertised in Spanish, and slashed rents. Over the next few years, Gulfton quickly shifted from a neighborhood of young professionals to an immigrants' gateway and a haven for low-income families. Such changes signaled the advent of a welcoming and inclusive community, one offering affordable housing to those who needed it. Contemporaneous commentators believed these shifting demographics brought deleterious consequences, including a rise in crime, and soon dubbed the neighborhood the "Gulfton Ghetto." The truth is that Houston's deteriorating economic conditions made crime skyrocket citywide, and to whatever extent Gulfton experienced more crime than other areas, it may have much to do with the vulnerability of people with fewer resources—in particular immigrants wary of reporting crimes to police.

These conditions directly impacted my family. My mom got held up at gunpoint, with me beside her, at the cash register in one of the restaurants.

In another incident, a tattooed gunman ordered my dad and one of the cooks who had been closing up for the night to lie facedown on the ground—positioning them like the victims of the quadruple homicide at the Malibu Grand Prix, which had just happened a few blocks away. At some point, my parents decided enough was enough. Along with my grandparents, we decamped to Crosby, an hour northeast.

After we left, Gulfton continued to struggle. The churn in the types of land uses present in the neighborhood presented a puzzle: Why was haphazard development so pronounced in Gulfton, if the rest of the city lacked zoning, too? For one simple reason: permanent deed restrictions, or covenants, written into deeds to dictate the use and nature of the property. Most other Houston neighborhoods relied on covenants to constrain unwanted development. Gulfton lacked such restrictions.

As a legal matter, covenants have been available to American property owners since colonial times, centuries before zoning. They can be traced back to English common law, on which our legal system is based. A covenant embeds some kind of written promise—usually, a promise to use (or not use) land in particular ways, or to allow other people to do so—into a property deed. Covenants became popular in the United States at the end of the nineteenth and beginning of the twentieth century, with the rise of residential "planned communities" with large lots and green space outside downtowns. Tracking the broader trends of American covenant use, Houston neighborhoods built during this period almost universally employed covenants to bar all uses except single-family housing.

Alongside single-family residence-only provisions, many older deed provisions restricted sales to Whites, barring Blacks, Jews, Hispanics, "Mongolians," and others from residency. The 1922 deed for a historic house my uncle Rich owns in central Houston demands both perpetual residential use and that "[t]he premises herein described shall never be sold, conveyed or demised to any person except of the Caucasian race." As a Mexican American, like me, Rich could not have owned the property if that provision retained its legal validity. Fortunately, it does not, because the Supreme Court deemed racially restrictive covenants unenforceable in 1948. However, problematic covenants like these usually remain on the land records. A covenant "runs with the land" forever, unless a court strikes it down, or most or all of the property owners bound by it agree to release it.

Even where covenants are not so blatantly problematic, their inflexibility can hurt people seeking to adapt to changing conditions. My uncle Rich, a veterinarian, was faced with this unfortunate reality when he tried to rehab that house to open a second location for his clinic. He actually had to file a lawsuit against the city to lift the residence-only covenant before the city would issue a building permit. His bid for a new clinic should have been a slam dunk. Commercial conversions of neighboring homes built at the same time and subject to the same covenant had lined the street for decades, including law offices, a "med-spa," and a hair salon on the same block as the proposed clinic, along with a real estate office, a gift shop, and a wellness studio across the street. What's more, the previous owner of my uncle's property had used it for commercial purposes. So Rich's proposed clinic would not have changed the commercial character of West Alabama Street or even his specific property. The city's issuance of a building permit would have had other benefits, too: supporting a minority-owned business, creating new jobs, offering a valuable amenity to the many pet owners in the neighborhood, and increasing property tax receipts. But city attorneys would not budge, and my uncle spent tens of thousands of dollars on legal fees and lost several years of potential profits to erase the legal fiction that the property was and would be residential forever.

A zoned city would have recognized those West Alabama blocks as part of a commercial district. If the property had been zoned commercial, Rich might have only needed to file a simple permit application and pay a $150 fee before proceeding to build his clinic. But in the unzoned city, private rules fill the regulatory vacuum left by zoning's absence. The preferences enshrined in covenants lock in choices, some rooted in discrimination, made sometimes over a century ago. Over time, covenants become legal straitjackets that prevent a community from adapting to modern needs.

For all their problems, covenants do create a sense of order—one that Gulfton lacks. Unfettered by land use controls, El Principe Azul blasts music into the night. As I saw that day visiting my first home, gas stations and self-storage facilities are randomly strewn about, and industrial warehouses sit right next to housing. While there is always some uncertainty, even with zoning or covenants, in Gulfton truly anything can spring up next door. This degree of uncertainty lowers property values: median home value is the second lowest of Houston's 143 neighborhoods, and Gulfton has the highest percentage of renter-occupied units (96 percent). Overcrowding has become severe. The population grew by three-quarters between 1980 and 2015, even though there were about two hundred fewer housing units. The real population is likely much higher than Census counts, which tend to see low rates of participation by non-English speakers and immigrants.

It may seem counterintuitive to start a book about zoning with a scene from the poster child for land use anarchy. But the difficulties Gulfton faces illustrate exactly why and how communities can benefit from zoning. The statistics I cited above highlight the neighborhood's continuing role in affordably housing diverse and immigrant populations. But they also demonstrate that the consequences of neglectful policymaking fall on low-income people and people of color. Gulfton developed rapidly, with neither public nor private controls on the use of land, and its residents suffer because the nonresidential land uses around them impose serious costs on their quality of life.

Moving from Gulfton to Newport, a residential subdivision in Crosby at the northeastern edge of Houston's sprawl, was whiplash for my second-grade self. The bustle, noise, danger, and excitement of the city vanished, replaced by sleepy, meandering streets. My grandparents bought a four-bedroom house, and we all squeezed in: grandparents, aunt, uncle, my parents, my sister, and me. That home sat at the end of a cul-de-sac, amid three houses with exactly the same design as ours, and with a mile of

houses fanning out in every direction. The subdivision's layout—the
result of residence-only covenants—guaranteed that it would be a car-
centered place. Walking to school, church, or restaurants was out of the
question. We drove everywhere, including an hour each way to gym-
nastics and piano lessons. My sister and I did our homework in the car,
trained out of car sickness.

Newport was my only brush with living in the kind of development
that typifies large swaths of the country—thanks to zoning decisions
made by thousands of city councils and local boards. While each entity
in charge of zoning makes decisions independently, the vast majority
follow a common formula. They start by sectioning cities into different
districts and allowing specific uses in each one, sometimes through a
"use table" that puts these allowances in graphic form. A typical code
exercises so-called "Euclidean" zoning, named not for the famed math-
ematician of antiquity, but rather for the Ohio city that figured in the
pivotal 1926 Supreme Court case, *Euclid v. Ambler*, which affirmed the
legitimacy of the new, local land use ordinances adopted in the years
after World War I. In the zoning world, Euclidean refers to zoning that
establishes districts that primarily differ from each other on the basis
of the uses allowed. Residential districts allow for single-family homes,
apartments, duplexes, or some combination of these; commercial districts might allow retail stores, offices, and medical clinics; industrial
districts might allow factories, warehouses, and storage; open-space districts might only allow parks and conservation land; and so on. Cities
also have established special districts and "overlay" districts with highly
tailored provisions.

Euclidean zoning offers certainty, but it often pulls the use reins too
hard, creating one-dimensional neighborhoods like the one my family
moved to in Newport. Indeed, of all the single-purpose districts planners have dreamed up, the most common is the exclusively single-family
district—districts that exclude multifamily housing. That type of exclusion was ratified in the *Euclid* decision itself, which espoused a brazenly
anti-apartment sentiment, with the justices opining that "very often the

apartment house is a mere parasite" on single-family neighborhoods, one whose predation will persist "until, finally, the residential character of the neighborhood and its desirability as a place of detached residences are utterly destroyed." Embracing this sentiment, zoning codes assign not just the largest share of land to single-family homes, but an overwhelming share of land. Based on my and others' work mapping zoning codes across the country, I estimate about 75 percent of urban and suburban zoned land requires single-family, detached houses, and allows no other kinds of housing. If any nonresidential uses are allowed, they are usually limited to religious institutions and schools, as long as they comply with specific development parameters. Shops, restaurants, and offices do not appear in these neighborhoods. Neither do medical clinics, hair salons, or coffee shops. Or much of anything else. And so we have the standard-issue American single-family neighborhood—the home, the religious facility, and the school—designed to separate people from almost all the activities and amenities they find useful and interesting and fun, and inconveniencing people going about their daily lives.

People who cannot drive (like my second-grade self), or who do not need or want to drive, suffer most from this approach. But we all suffer, really. Economists agree that overregulation of land use can hinder a strong economy and can result in a less productive workforce. That's probably because people waste so much time getting from home to work. Separating uses also increases our demand for fossil fuels, because we end up driving so much. In turn, it reduces the opportunity to create the kind of dense neighborhoods that support robust public transportation. Separating uses also makes us less healthy because we can't build walking into our daily routines. And it disconnects us physically from each other, diminishing our well-being. It would be hard to exaggerate the downside of this kind of zoning. Yet it's ubiquitous.

To the rest of the world, this use-based separation is bizarre and entirely alien. The United States is unique internationally in its devotion to single-family housing, and in its conviction that such housing must be protected from nonresidential uses, and even from apartments. But in rejecting these uses, American zoning codes also deny the country's past—namely, the organic mixing existing in many neighborhoods at the dawn of zoning. A century ago, in urbanized areas, corner stores abounded every few blocks, hawking a variety of dry and fresh goods. Homes themselves contained space for making and selling: residents could can vegetables, bake bread, or fashion clothes, and then sell these goods from their front porches or parlors. Others might have offered haircuts, tailoring, and shoe repair. Some homeowners added one-story additions along the sidewalk to establish a more permanent outpost. Instead of driving to secure these goods and services, residents could walk to a nearby location. This natural mixing made life more convenient and fostered informal connections between people. It also helped to incubate small businesses, which could expand to more established commercial areas as they grew.

When officials laid zoning over existing residential neighborhoods, they often deemed "nonconforming" the home-based businesses, small-batch manufacturing, retail shops, and service providers that existed at the time of the code's adoption. So while these legacy businesses were legally allowed to endure, they could not be expanded, nor could the buildings themselves be modified to further accommodate them. Once abandoned, they could not be resurrected. Over time, most were naturally phased out. In many places even today, those same strict codes make it impossible to re-create the interconnected neighborhoods that organically emerged in the pre-zoning era. That's the tide against which cities engaging in mixed-use zoning continue to swim. The good news is that even though zoning has often embedded into public laws the same principles behind private-covenant-bound neighborhoods, zoning codes—unlike covenants—can be changed. And they should change.

State laws governing zoning don't *require* such stringent separation. Neither do they prohibit a mix-and-match approach, which has been chosen for many urban downtowns and small-town main streets. Both historically and today, we expect downtowns and main streets, where offices and residences have always mingled with stores and entertainment venues, to give residents a range of choices. Mixed-use zoning must expand beyond these areas at a more rapid clip.

One approach is just to bring back what was. Some legacy cities have made corner stores—legacy stores—legal again in residential neighborhoods. In 2016, the postindustrial upstate New York city of Buffalo did just that, allowing restaurants, retail spaces, taverns, artisan spaces, and offices in buildings built before 1953 "to incubate small businesses and artisans in order to serve as catalysts for neighborhood revitalization, as a tool for economic development, and as an important component of the walkability of a neighborhood." Why 1953? That's the year the city adopted a zoning code with stringent use-based provisions that strangled once-vibrant businesses. Many other places around the country made the same dumb decision. Fortunately, seventy years later, this regulatory reversal in Buffalo has allowed immigrants, entrepreneurs, and other dreamers to bring dozens of old gems—including shops smaller than 1,000 square feet—back to life. It's a small but important win, one other cities can copy by amending just a few lines of code.

Other places have found other strategies to reverse past mistakes. Some have proven inventive in creating entirely novel districts: commercial-industrial, residential-office, open space–residential, transit-oriented multiuse, and other zoning combos. In doing so, they eschew stringent use separation to better integrate living, making, shopping, learning, and working.

One city imagining new combinations is San Diego, where planners are rectifying the outcomes of a city council meeting in the summer of 1958. The fourth item on the agenda that long-ago day involved a petition to rezone four large empty lots in rural Mission Valley—an eighty-acre combined parcel that sat between the highway and the San Diego River, four miles north of the city's bustling downtown. City officials had placed them in a residential zone, with the hope they might be subdivided to satisfy pressing housing needs. In the preceding two decades, the city had more than doubled in population. This rapid growth tracked along with military investments in camps, training facilities, hospitals, an air station, and a major naval base.

That morning in June, proponents of the rezoning made the case that these eighty acres should be assigned to a zone permitting a limited array of commercial uses. Speaking first for the property owners, attorney Walter Ames stated that his client, the May Company, hoped to build a shopping center on the land. He presented a list of supporters and stated that the mall—one of the first in the country—would draw tourists, benefit the economy, and generate employment opportunities. A vice-president of the May Company reinforced this message, adding that the company planned to spend $35 million on improvements and that it had thoroughly accounted for traffic and flood impacts. Commercial property owners and the labor council also testified in favor of the rezoning.

Not everyone agreed that it would be a good idea. The meeting became so contentious that the mayor of San Diego, who was running the meeting, ordered the bailiff to remove objectionable signs. Once order was restored, the testimony continued. Opponents noted that the rezoning would irreversibly change the river channel and destroy open space. But the most prescient words came from Guilford H. Whitney, a downtown five-and-dime merchant who argued that the new mall would hurt downtown businesses. He pointed to the decline of Fresno's downtown after the development of a similar shopping center, predicting, "If we build another central city only four minutes away from downtown, we may end by having a slum business district in what is now our central area." Hamilton Marston, a downtown department store owner, apologized for sounding as if he wished to stifle competition but, like Whitney, urged city leaders to punt on this decision until they could finalize a comprehensive land use plan.

These concerns notwithstanding, excitement about the proposed mall carried the day, and the city council unanimously approved the rezoning. The decision changed San Diego's trajectory. More malls followed, including Fashion Valley, which came up next door to the May Company complex in 1969. Vast parking lots encircled the stores, creating complete separation from the residential areas nearby. Driving became the only way to reach the shops. As Walter Ames had predicted, many of the malls' patrons were tourists, including some who drove in from Mexico. Meanwhile, downtown suffered. Whitney's department store fell in 1965, while the handsome, six-story Marston building was demolished in 1969.

Fifty years later, trends have reversed. Many urban downtowns have roared back, and San Diego's downtown has attracted new businesses and housing, along with entertainment in the historic Gaslamp neighborhood popular with residents and tourists alike. Meanwhile, several of the outlying malls have aged poorly, falling from novel attraction to generic big-box sprawl. The departure of Saks Fifth Avenue in 2010 was a blow for Fashion Valley, while in the original May Company parcel, the last true department store, Macy's, shuttered in 2017, leaving only its home goods division and an outlet. Even 75-percent-off bargains in its final days reportedly attracted only a few shoppers.

Spurred by that closure and other events, members of the San Diego City Council—the very body that rezoned for single-use retail sprawl back in 1958—decided to take a closer look at the city's outdated shopping centers. Reviewing neighborhood plans calling for a mixed-use rezoning, they explored how "infill" development—making use of the empty space occupied by parking lots—could knit the community together. They solicited more public input. Finally, in 2019, the council adopted a new section of the zoning code, unanimously undoing what its predecessor body had done sixty-one years prior.

The new code established two mixed-use districts and mapped them on many large, underutilized sites, including the malls of Mission Valley. It articulated the purpose for these districts: to offer a mix of housing and jobs, to reduce automobile dependency, to increase transit use, and to encourage a walkable environment. To achieve these aims, the code streamlined permitting, allowing for speedier approvals of proposed construction.

The mixed-use district assigned to the May Company site allows for office, industrial, and retail uses as the primary land use, with housing as a secondary use. While the previous version of the code allowed some mixed-use buildings, the permitting process was costly and time-consuming, requiring many stages of review and public hearings. The new code freely permits most mixed-use projects, so long as developers abide by certain guidelines. Many of these guidelines relate to the building "frontage," or the façade of the building abutting the street. The guidelines require that frontages be active and transparent, meaning entrances belong on the ground floor, must be oriented toward a public sidewalk, and must include some combination of arcades, porches, balconies, awnings, trellises, or other "activation elements." The code also requires pedestrian entrances, paths, and connections, as well as buffers (like landscaping) shielding parking spaces from view. It breaks up megablocks, calling for *paseos*—defined as pedestrian accessways connecting streets, plazas, alleys, parks, and other amenities—and bicycle accessways for every two acres of lot. Together, these guidelines better connect buildings to the street, and create a walkable and bikeable environment in an area previously designed for drivers alone.

Councilwoman Vivian Moreno helped lead the charge for these changes. Rather than trying to downplay the impact of rezoning, as some politicians do, she made a compelling public case for them. The website for her last reelection campaign explained how the San Diego upzonings—changes to code designed to foster more development—will help to address the housing crisis, which she called "one of the central challenges of our generation." As chair of the city council's land use and housing committee, she also led efforts to eliminate parking mandates near transit infrastructure so developers do not have to build expensive parking garages in areas where people don't need them.

As she and others keep a watchful eye, these neighborhoods are already being remade. Perhaps most significantly, the rezonings have spurred a $290 million sale of two Mission Valley mall parcels to an investment firm eager to build a mixed-use development. While plans have yet to be released as of this writing, the city's code will ensure that the new development fills in vast, unsightly parking lots and integrates into surrounding neighborhoods better than the single-use retail that came before.

Excitement about the economic value created by the rezonings has generated activity on neighboring properties, too. The owners of a two-hundred-acre former golf course site straddling the San Diego River, recognizing the spillover value created by the rezonings, successfully petitioned the city council to approve a site-specific master plan for an integrated live-work community centered around a riverwalk that will restore water access to the community. The council granted zoning approval for the construction of 4,300 housing units (10 percent of them affordable), a million square feet of office space, and over 150,000 square feet of retail space, all connecting to transit and bike and pedestrian paths. The first phase of the project broke ground in 2023, a strong signal that San Diego's rezonings will generate big returns—not just financial, but social, too.

Pressures to loosen use-based regulations keep coming, helping usher in a new age of zoning. The latest challenge to single-use communities was the COVID-19 pandemic, which revealed the adaptive power of greater flexibility in zoning. To cope with demand for emergency housing, shelters, and health clinics, public health emergency declarations superseded zoning rules that prevented such facilities from being in shopping malls, sports stadiums, and parking lots. Ensuring that zoning explicitly anticipates such emergency needs could allow for more nimble responses in the future.

During the pandemic, when restaurants and shops all over the country saw customers disappear, their owners petitioned officials to suspend regulatory barriers to expanding to adjacent outdoor spaces. I worked with a few attorneys advising the Connecticut governor on the issuance of an executive order that suspended local zoning constraints on outdoor dining and retail, lifted minimum parking requirements to allow parking lots to be repurposed for outdoor extensions of indoor uses, and streamlined permitting for liquor sales. The order also created an expedited process for local governments to amend their zoning codes to address issues raised by COVID-19. Around the country, many local governments responded to the pandemic by adopting similar emergency zoning measures to ensure businesses could keep serving customers. While all these temporary measures ended with the expiration of official public health emergency declarations, many communities realized that these experimental measures had value. Several Connecticut towns amended their codes to permanently enable outdoor dining and shopping.

In the wake of the pandemic, another shift is putting continued pressure on outdated codes: the widespread adoption of remote work among white-collar workers, which seems to be here to stay. That has meant that office buildings in downtowns and suburban office parks now sit empty, and more people are spending their time in what previously might have been called "bedroom" communities (places used primarily for sleeping). Zoning can help cope with the changes that shift has brought. Downtowns can be rezoned to fast-track housing conversions by lifting procedural hurdles (like public hearings), while suburban districts previously limited to offices can add housing to the list of allowable uses. In residential areas, new code provisions can expressly legalize home-based offices and allow small shops to bring amenities to homebound workers. Cities with regulatory flexibility are best prepared to enable everyone, including workers and business owners, to adapt to the circumstances.

Coping with the exigencies of an unexpected public-health calamity required regulatory improvisation, underscoring that zoning is as much art as science. Flexibility is essential to our economic and social vitality, but codes should not allow anarchy. What's needed in our zoning codes is the perfect Goldilocks balance. The Gulfton-Newport contrast reveals that while there is such a thing as too much mixing, there is also such a thing as too little mixing—in other words, too much homogeneity. Ill-conceived zoning can create lopsided realities that may take decades to correct, but a well-fashioned code, updated to address new challenges, can ensure just the right kind of porridge.

(2)

The Magic of Makers

When I hear mention of Baltimore, the first thing I think of is Charm City Cakes, a bakery famed for its novelty fondant cakes—colorful delights encased in a silky, rigid layer of sugar paste and crafted into everything imaginable, from lions to vintage gasoline pumps to Converse sneakers. Beginning in 2006, the shop was the focus of the popular Food Network show *Ace of Cakes*, which I was hooked on for a couple of seasons. The show's appeal rested in the creative process of the motley crew of tattooed bakers led by owner Duff Goldman, but for me a strong secondary attraction was the way the show conveyed the life of the city. Many cakes resembled local sites, including Baltimore's iconic rowhouses, its Washington Monument, and the baseball stadium of Camden Yards. Deliveries traveled through neighborhood streets and ended at community events like the city's tree lighting ceremony. The cakes themselves were baked in a 1930s-era one-story brick building that had been a former sewing factory. All very tasty for an urbanist.

While *Ace of Cakes* ended in 2011, the bakery's headquarters remain located in the Remington neighborhood, which offers a thick slice of Baltimore history and development. The area, about two miles north of downtown, nestles between Druid Hill Park and the Baltimore Art Museum, and sits east of what used to be Jones Falls. Jones Falls flowed from northwest of Baltimore all the way to the city's inner harbor, and by the 1850s the Northern Central Railroad was built along its east side. River and railroad helped make Baltimore one of the busiest trade hubs on the East Coast. In Remington, stone quarries producing a granite-like rock called gneiss (used on the Charm City Cakes building façade) had been operating since the late eighteenth century, and they continued to expand throughout the nineteenth century. Enterprising settlers built mills—mostly grist mills for flour—and factories that produced sailcloth and other textiles, harnessing the river's current for hydropower. Eventually, Remington became a stop on the streetcar line, and in the 1880s, small, two-story rowhouses in a variety of colors were built for the factory, quarry, and railroad workers. The City of Baltimore annexed the neighborhood, previously considered a part of Baltimore County, in 1888. In subsequent decades, Remington's prospects waxed and waned. Around World War I, the quarries and mills started to slow down, and by the 1930s they were working half-time, if at all.

It was amidst these economic shifts, in 1923, that the city of Baltimore—embracing the national trend—adopted its first comprehensive zoning ordinance. Enforcement followed, and when police arrested a resident whose home business fixing sewing machines violated zoning, he sued, claiming that the ordinance infringed upon his constitutional rights to due process. Maryland's supreme court agreed, holding in 1925 that the ordinance takes "from the property owner the right to use his property for any purpose not sanctioned by the letter of the ordinance or allowed by the practically unfettered discretion" of city officials. Far from the deference that would be shown the next year by the U.S. Supreme Court in *Euclid*, Maryland's court balked at what it viewed as a ban on legitimate businesses. In response, the city adopted another ordinance in 1925—only to be challenged again, by a property owner denied a permit to build a stable. Again, the state supreme court struck down the law, ruling that the powers exercised by local officials were "arbitrary, undefined, and unreasonable." Within days of that decision, the persistent city enacted still another new ordinance, more carefully delineating constraints on officials' decision-making powers. This one survived the same stable-seeker's second challenge. For zoners in Charm City, the third time proved the charm.

And so zoning took hold in Baltimore, using Euclidean techniques that created strictly defined use-base districts. Unlike San Diego, where zoning mapmakers mostly started from scratch, Baltimore's mapmakers had to contend with existing, fully built-out neighborhoods like Remington. In these cases, mapmakers matched districts to existing uses, zoning industrial sites as industrial and residential sites as residential. On the one hand, this approach guaranteed that existing uses could continue—technically speaking, that they would not be rendered "nonconforming" and thus be at risk of having to phase out. On the other, it based a regulatory framework on what happened to exist in 1925. The resulting citywide map looked like an imaginative child's color-by-number drawing, especially in neighborhoods like Remington where very different uses existed side by side.

The code and its hodgepodge map stayed more or less the same for their first nine decades—even as the neighborhoods around mills and other industrial sites evolved, and even as Baltimore's population significantly declined. Scholars have observed the effects of regulatory stagnation in residential neighborhoods, including the suburbs whose built form has never evolved from the 1950s ideal of nearly identical homes with two-car garages and grassy lawns. But a frozen zoning code has had equally detrimental impacts in commercial and mixed contexts. In Remington, the code's continued assignment of historical industrial sites into industrial districts reflected a stubborn detachment from the reality that heavy industry would not be returning. It made the reuse of these places for other things nearly impossible. Meanwhile, the city's population continued to dwindle. By the time Duff Goldman launched his business in 2002, Baltimore had just two-thirds of its 1950 population. Remington had fallen on particularly hard times, with a serious drug problem and vacancies not just in the commercial properties, but also in the rowhouses once filled with factory workers.

Charm City Cakes's popularity no doubt drew people into the neighborhood, and over the next decade, low start-up costs (especially cheap rents) attracted a few new businesses, like coffee shops and retail, in old industrial spaces. The corner stores sprinkled throughout the neighborhood continued to operate, some with fresh coats of paint and new murals. The rate of homeownership improved slightly, and property values rose—always a double-edged sword in a working-class community. And two neighborhood improvement organizations began doing community cleanups, gardening, and other beautification and bridge-building activities. Yet, despite Remington's central location and proximity to Baltimore's largest park, vacancies endured, along with crime.

An inflection point came in 2013, when researchers from Johns Hopkins University drew public attention to the role of zoning in fostering healthy, interconnected communities with vibrant and growing economies. The researchers published a health impact assessment finding that mixed-use zoning would benefit Baltimore by improving residents' well-being in three big ways: increasing physical activity, reducing obesity, and lowering violent crime rates. All three were especially important for Baltimore, whose residents suffer from more excess deaths from cardiovascular disease and violent crime than residents elsewhere in Maryland. The Hopkins researchers zeroed in on the ways in which zoning decisions affect these outcomes, writing: "Mixed-use districts may positively impact health by increasing the likelihood that residents walk to daily services (e.g., restaurants, banks, and other retail). Pedestrian-friendly design elements incorporated in the zoning code, such as transparent ground-floor windows, may also positively impact health by creating an environment that is more inviting and safer; as a result, residents may be more likely to be physically active in these areas."

Spurred in part by this report, the city undertook a comprehensive rezoning that incorporated the researchers' recommendations. The new code that resulted, adopted in 2016, assigned about ten blocks in Remington to the industrial mixed-use zone, which legalizes a healthy mix of industrial and nonindustrial uses, including light industrial uses that have little noise, odor, or vibration effects outside of the building where they transpire. The zone enables food processing facilities like breweries and, yes, large bakeries, to operate. It also allows multifamily and live-work housing, schools, shops, art galleries, restaurants, banks, health clinics, offices, and even agriculture. Significantly, the code permits all these uses "as of right," meaning that a simple staff review to verify compliance can expedite the permitting of a project. No public hearing is required.

While allowing Remington's history of making things to continue, the code also recognized that neighborhoods must evolve—and thus addressed the "frozen-neighborhood" syndrome that sets in when zoning fails to keep pace with change. Sure enough, in the years since the code was adopted, the neighborhood has seen diverse businesses pop up, including a bookstore, a clothing store, and a CrossFit training studio. A whiskey distillery offers tours and tastings. Rowhouses and apartments in rehabbed factories—no longer damned to vacancy—offer options for residents at different income levels. Between 2010 and 2020, the number of housing units in Remington increased by 10 percent, while residential vacancies dropped as the number of Remington residents increasing by 9 percent. And with a "walk score" of 91 and a "bike score" of 89 (both out of 100) according to Redfin (a national real estate company), it clearly is becoming a place where people get around with ease. Above and beyond these heartening particulars is the sense that life in Remington is becoming fundamentally better. A plan developed by one of the neighborhood-improvement organizations lauds the area's regeneration and foresees its benefits in the form of a more diversified neighborhood economy, continued residential rehabilitation, lower crime, and reclaimed public space.

Charm City Cakes perfectly suits Remington's modern incarnation, even as its reliance on flour—the very product that helped boost the neighborhood's fortunes over a century ago—is a nod to Remington's history. While many factors contribute to neighborhood vitality, the city's

revamped zoning code, with its more permissive approach to makers
and mixers, has helped catalyze Remington's neighborhood-wide revitalization. Other neighborhoods with former factories and vacant worker
housing should take note. Mixed-use zoning offers flexibility, forging a
neighborhood where people can eat their cake—and make it, too.

———

While Charm City Cakes was able to run Baltimore's zoning gauntlet
and emerge flourishing, zoning codes in other places don't always easily
handle the artisanal manufacture of goods by small-scale, often family
owned, producers. Policymakers haven't quite caught up to the fact that
this type of manufacturing differs from the larger-scale industrial manufacturing that partly prompted zoning in the first place, a century and
more ago.

Consider the example of craft brewers. Small-scale artisanal beermak-
ing has exploded in the United States, now numbering more than 10,000
brewers nationwide. They are emblematic of the smaller enterprises that
can run up against restrictive zoning rules. Although these businesses
do not operate like such industrial megabrewers as Budweiser or Coors,
zoning often treats them the same, lumping all manufacturers into the
all-encompassing "industrial" category. It is a longstanding mainstay of
zoning that industrial uses must generally be located far from the action,
along the unattractive edges of towns. If you've seen the kind of place
where Budweiser is produced—as I have, when driving between Crosby
and Houston, passing the colossal and smelly factories on the city's eastern
fringes—you might agree that this isolation makes sense. But it is not necessary for the kind of small, craft breweries that thrive on foot traffic and
are optimally located in walkable areas near a variety of activities. Tasting
rooms and tours of brewery facilities generate crucial revenue for a business where distribution can be hit-or-miss. But brewers won't see on-site
sales if guests have a hard time finding their brewhouse—or enjoying the
ambiance once they *do* find it.

Finding the right location meant a lot to Curt Cameron, president of

Thomas Hooker Brewery. Naming his brewery after a noted seventeenth-century preacher and one of Hartford's founders, Cameron originally opened in a semi-industrial section of an inner-ring Hartford suburb. All the while, he yearned for the symbolic arrival of the brewery in its namesake's colonial hometown. When he started looking for sites, however, he learned that the city's zoning code limited breweries to industrial zones. Would patrons prefer to sip their blonde ale by a capped landfill, a sewage treatment facility, or a trash burning plant? Cameron opted for none of the above. He waited.

Our overhaul of Hartford's zoning code in January 2016 offered hope. As part of the revamped code, our commission defined a new category of "craftsman industrial" uses to include "small scale production, assembly, and/or repair with little to no noxious by-products." We rezoned the city to allow these craftsman industrial uses in virtually every neighborhood that isn't exclusively residential. In doing so, we aimed for an expansive vision of what those uses might be—and so the code counts filmmaking, woodworking, taxidermy, and the making of beverages including beer, wine, liquor, soft drinks, and coffee among many allowable uses. Calling all taxidermists! The point is that we chose to make the range as wide as possible, to allow for all kinds of small-scale creative endeavors that make places interesting and rewarding.

With this change in place, Curt Cameron's search for a site could begin. After inspecting several sites, he found the perfect spot on the ground-floor level of the Colt Armory—the factory, tucked in alongside the interstate in Hartford, where Sam and Elizabeth Colt started making their revolvers in 1855. Titans of industry and generous philanthropists, this husband-and-wife team has been heralded for their contributions to manufacturing and culture (and criticized for their role in popularizing guns in America). After about 140 years, their company left its old factory complex, including a sprawling five-story brick structure capped with a landmark onion-shaped blue dome adorned with a gilded equine figure of the "Rampant Colt." For some years, the complex was left to decay, its size deterring conversion. But in 2006, a visionary developer finally started

its rehabilitation, working piece by piece, resulting in hundreds of apartments, as well as offices and cultural venues, plus a brand-new soccer stadium next door. Cameron knew that all this activity could translate into
hundreds of potential beer-drinking residents and visitors. There was just
one problem: part of the Colt Armory had been converted into a school—
and the new zoning code barred bars within two hundred feet of schools.
Hooker Brewery could not open without first securing that perpetual bane
of the zoning process: a variance.

Tracing its roots back to the 1920s-era State Standard Zoning Enabling
Act, a variance is a local-government approval that allows a property
owner to deviate from the terms of the zoning code. While each zoning
code lays out the criteria that would enable granting of a variance, the
general rule is that to receive one, a property owner has to demonstrate
that she would suffer a hardship if the zoning code were applied as written. For Cameron, the hardship clause made the variance option a dead
end—because with large portions of Hartford zoned to allow craftsman
industrial uses, Hooker Brewery could have easily been located elsewhere
within city limits.

And so Cameron sought a rezoning, or a change to the code itself,
instead. He approached the planning and zoning commission to suggest
that the dispersion requirement of a 200-foot radius was unnecessarily
strict in the mixed-use Colt neighborhood—pointing out that the code
already exempted downtown, where several schools were located, from
the requirement. After discussing various options, in October 2016 the
planning and zoning commission extended that exemption to the mixed-
use district in which the Colt factory was located. Hooker Brewery could
now open in Cameron's dream location.

With this zoning change, and its Colt Taproom doing brisk business,
Hooker Brewery has thrived. In thriving it is contributing to a larger
revitalization. The brewery has become the perfect all-season after-work
watering hole for residents of the Colt complex, as well as for the architects, U.S. Senate staff, teachers, and assorted others who make up the
highly varied workforce toiling under the complex's iconic blue onion

dome. Game days for the Hartford Athletic, the minor-league soccer team that plays in the new stadium next door, bring good crowds. Their stadium was another piece of the revitalization project, replacing a long-neglected stadium with a storied history that included a 1966 concert by the Rolling Stones and a strutting Mick Jagger, whose rendition of what the *Hartford Courant* terms "something called 'Satisfaction'" drove teenage girls to rush the stage in a good old-fashioned riot. For me, sitting outdoors on the Hooker Brewery patio with a beer, watching soccer fans and others stroll by, brings, well, satisfaction: a gratifying recognition of the positive effect a zoning decision had on our community.

One of the boons of zoning reform is that the good things that happen in its wake tend to multiply. Since the relocation of Hooker Brewery to Hartford, we have added two other breweries and a distillery within our eighteen square miles. I particularly love the story of Hartford Flavor Company, a distillery run by Lelaneia Dubay, a former landscape designer who made her first raisin wine in eighth grade and now grows the lavender, dandelions, and roses for the organic botanical liqueurs she and her husband produce right in Hartford. Originally operated out of Lelaneia's garage, it's a true mom-and-pop shop whose hard-won success has led to significant expansion. Hartford Flavor now has a manufacturing facility and a tasting room in a former pay-phone factory (talk about defunct!) that mixes lots of artistic tenants in a buzzing hive of creativity. Combined with the breweries, these new producers are creating jobs, enlivening their immediate surroundings, and collectively writing a new chapter in Hartford's history of makers.

As planning commissioners presented with the brewery's dilemma in Hartford, we realized we didn't get it right the first time. And in Baltimore, the city council realized that realigned zoning could help neighborhoods get out of a postindustrial rut. To continually improve the way zoning affects place, administrators must be amenable to change. While zoning has built-in flexibility devices, like variances, these address specific sites and problems, not broader trends. Rewriting the code itself is sometimes necessary to ensure that zoning responds to changing times. Amid the array of uses a code can allow, communities would do well to accommodate small-scale makers. They and the magic they create help us keep in mind the ultimate goal of zoning: to encourage and enable the kind of development that facilitates enterprise and boosts a community's quality of life. Despite its reputation as the ultimate bureaucratic barrier, zoning at its best can support the most basic activities of human flourishing: to bake someone a cake, for instance, or to slake their thirst.

3

Cultivating Creativity

An internationally renowned sculptor and ceramicist who exhibits at the world's top galleries and museums, Theaster Gates is also a son of Chicago, one with an urban planning degree and deep commitment to placemaking, which he wields as part of his artistic practice to transform some of the city's most challenged neighborhoods. When I first met Gates at an event at the National Building Museum, he had just won the Vincent Scully Prize for his work in the neighborhoods of South Shore, along with Greater Grand Crossing, named for its location at the intersection of two major railroad company lines, as well as Washington Park and Woodlawn. Like Baltimore's Remington neighborhood, these areas were initially settled in the 1870s by railway and factory workers from Western European countries. Starting in the 1910s, in the aftermath of Reconstruction and amid the rise of Jim Crow laws, the Great Migration brought Black Southerners to Chicago, many of them finding housing on the South Side. As the Black population grew, race tensions mounted, culminating in thirteen days of violence in 1919—an ugly explosion ignited when a Black teenager who dared to swim at an informally segregated beach was murdered, triggering race riots that resulted in thirty-eight deaths, most of them Black Americans.

Looking for ways to enforce segregation, White property owners in Chicago turned to zoning. They were well aware that in 1917, the Supreme Court struck down an explicitly discriminatory zoning ordinance in Louisville, Kentucky. But they also knew that in other cities, leaders had figured out how to maintain racial and economic segregation through seemingly race-neutral provisions. In response to the Supreme Court decision, St. Louis, for example, jettisoned a 1916 ordinance preventing Black people from moving onto blocks where 75 percent of residents were White, and vice versa. That ordinance—supported by three-quarters of voters—reflected alarm about what local realtors called a "Negro invasion" of Black families into White neighborhoods. In 1919, the city adopted a new comprehensive zoning code that achieved the discriminatory intent of the 1916 ordinance but omitted mention of race. Instead, city leaders established districts restricted to single-family housing, ostensibly to protect real estate values. These districts, all the most desirable parts of the city, kept out apartment buildings, as well as two- and three-family homes, restrictions that effectively barred the door to many Black people—a discriminatory action hidden in technical, race-neutral provisions.

Chicago followed the St. Louis model of racial neutrality when it adopted a zoning code in 1923, two years after Illinois adopted the State Standard Zoning Enabling Act. In twenty-two pages of text, the code articulated rules for four districts: residence, apartment, commercial, and manufacturing. In many cases, the code mapped these districts according to land uses that already existed. But not always. Recently, researchers verified that the code assigned areas in and around the residences of African Americans and immigrants to manufacturing districts. They tied demographic and land use records to zoning classifications to expose the inequities, including lower property values, resulting from this treatment.

Compounding zoning's impact on settlement patterns, neighborhood demographics, and property values—at least for the first quarter-century of the code's existence—were racially restrictive covenants. Some parts of the neighborhoods in which Gates works today were developed to be middle- and upper-class White neighborhoods. In 1937, a Black family named Hansberry dared to purchase a house with a racially restrictive covenant in Woodlawn. They were harassed, threatened, and sued, but successfully argued—all the way to the U.S. Supreme Court—that the White property owners had not followed proper procedures to create a valid covenant. The invalidation of the Hansberry covenant, followed by the invalidation of all racially restrictive covenants by the Supreme Court in 1948, allowed Blacks to live anywhere in Chicago. Inexpensive apartments to accommodate them, some subsidized by the federal government, proliferated in the newly opened South Side. With these developments, the racial composition of the area rapidly changed, becoming overwhelmingly African American. One such resident was former First Lady Michelle Obama, who spent her first few years in Parkway Garden Homes, a complex of seven hundred units across thirty-five buildings, all now listed on the National Register of Historic Places.

Over subsequent decades, the demographics of these communities stagnated to a surprising degree. They remain racially homogeneous, with more than 95 percent of residents identifying as Black. Unemployment tops three times the regional average, and an exodus of residents seeking better opportunities has driven a drastic drop in population—a nearly 20 percent loss in the two decades between 2000 and 2020. Today, nearly a quarter of the area's residential units are vacant. Michelle Obama's childhood home now sits on Chicago's so-called "most dangerous block," a place notorious for gun violence, drugs, and building code violations. The segregation hoped for by long-ago drafters of zoning codes and covenants has come to fruition, albeit not exactly as they expected.

It was within this stark social and economic context that Theaster Gates built his real estate empire. In 2006 he purchased a home on Dorchester

Avenue, a north–south street at the border of South Shore and Greater
Grand Crossing. Unable at the time to afford significant improvements, he
started off by ceremonially sweeping the home with a broom, as an act
of performance art. With friends, he began to host exhibits, informal din-
ners, lectures, listening sessions, and small-scale gatherings. Soon he filled
the home with eight thousand LPs from the shuttered Dr. Wax Records
and nicknamed it the Listening House. In 2009 he bought the single-family
house next door for just $16,000, filling it with books and calling it the
Archive House. As these projects continued bringing artists and art-lovers
together, and attracted attention for their quirky novelty, Gates's ambition
grew. In 2012 he restored a handsome brick duplex across the street, reopening it as the Black Cinema House to feature films from the African diaspora.

Built in 1914, 1888, and 1893 respectively, the three homes Gates rehabilitated for nonresidential uses date to a time preceding zoning, and as
such were adapted by their occupants several times. The petite Listening
House, for example, once accommodated a candy store, next to an ice-cream
shop—one of the most delightful establishments to have next door. Today,
the houses' blocks have a mostly residential character, with not a candy store
in sight. Very likely as zoning became stricter, some of the more creative
adaptations were rendered nonconforming, or blocked before they could be
realized. However, the latest version of the code, dating to 2004, has a few
obscure provisions that gave Gates a narrow opening to do his work.

These provisions were included in an overhaul spurred by a zoning
reform commission convened by then-Mayor Richard Daley. The commission suggested rewriting the code to bring vitality to residential areas,
redevelop underutilized commercial corridors, create more predictable
review processes, and preserve the architectural character of the more historic neighborhoods, among other things. When the city council codified
these suggestions, they significantly trimmed and simplified the text. It
clocks in at just about three hundred pages—exceptionally short for a complex city encompassing 235 square miles. (By comparison, New York City's
code exceeds 2,700 pages, and Boston's 3,700—though those are outliers in
the other direction.)

At the same time, the council incorporated provisions that anticipated and legalized Theaster Gates's arts-centered interventions. Many large cities bar such uses—community gathering spaces, performance venues, cinemas, and archives—in residential neighborhoods. Instead, they put cultural institutions on large lots in important locations, including downtowns, arts districts, or other large public areas. The Field Museum, the Shedd Aquarium, and the Art Institute of Chicago, for example, boast prominent spots along the Lake Michigan waterfront. But Chicago does well to allow smaller cultural institutions to be embedded in neighborhoods. The Listening House, Archive House, and original Black Cinema House are in a primarily residential zone that allows "cultural exhibits and libraries" by right, eliminating the need for onerous public hearings or permitting processes. Why shouldn't these places be allowed to locate in this neighborhood—indeed, *especially* in this neighborhood? As Gates wryly noted in a 2015 lecture: "There are city policies that say, hey, a house that is residential needs to stay residential. But what do you do in neighborhoods when ain't nobody interested in living there?" Chicago's code answers this question by allowing artistic uses that bring in people—people who might eventually become homebuyers or home-renters, and whose presence and activities build energy.

The popularity of the Houses was such that they quickly outgrew their initial locations. After just two years, Gates relocated the cinema to a former beer distribution facility a few blocks away. Interestingly, the new cinema doesn't seem to fit so easily with the Chicago zoning code, as it sits in a zone intended to accommodate manufacturing and to "promote high-quality new development and reuse of older industrial buildings." It's possible that administrators gave the project a pass because it satisfied the district's goal of promoting rehabilitations, was less intense than manufacturing, and caused no harm to neighbors.

Gates also had to find a new location for the Listening and Archive Houses, which had functioned as community living rooms in a neighborhood with few similar options. In 2014, a company associated with Gates acquired a long-abandoned neoclassical bank building with a hole in the roof for $1 from the City of Chicago, saving it from imminent demolition. The three-story stone-clad structure was located on the neighborhood's busiest street, Stony Island Avenue, a wide, commercial avenue of retail chains and strip malls. A $6 million renovation followed, during which an elaborate sound system, galleries, performance space, and library shelving for a large collection of *Ebony* and *Jet* magazines were installed. Today, on any given evening at the Stony Island Arts Bank, while sipping on a craft cocktail, one might hear a jazz quartet, groove to a DJ's beats, or watch an African dance ensemble.

Here, too, Gates benefited from the 2004 zoning overhaul, especially code provisions enabling city planning staff to provide relief from some of the code's stricter terms, such as minimum parking requirements, which establish the number of parking spaces each residence, store, theater, or other place must build on the same lot. Normally, "cultural exhibits and libraries" require one parking space for every 1,000 square feet over 4,000 square feet—meaning that at 17,000 square feet, the Stony Island Arts Bank potentially triggered the requirement for at least thirteen spaces. But requiring the Bank to pave over property would have meant erasing one of the very few grassy areas on an avenue that is already overpaved with more lanes than necessary for regular traffic. Fortunately, as long as city planners give their blessing, commercial uses within 1,320 feet of Stony Island Avenue can be freed from all or part of their parking requirements. And so, instead of paving the site for parking, the Bank has created a memorial around the gazebo, relocated from Cleveland, where a police officer shot and killed twelve-year-old Tamir Rice.

The hallowed nature of this memorial did not eliminate the need for zoning review. Such installations are often permitted under the criteria for accessory structures, which in this case would require zoning administrators to judge whether the structure was "subordinate" to the Bank and "contribute[d] to the comfort, convenience or necessity of [the Bank's] occupants." Surely the gazebo contributes little to occupants' convenience or necessity. But perhaps it does contribute in some way to the residents' comfort, creating a place and opportunity for the neighborhood to remember and to express its collective grief. As a contemplative space on a busy street, this structure advances Gates's mission of fostering greater understanding of Black culture within a broader societal context. A zoning code that leaves ample discretion to administrators facilitated its erection. Once again, flexibility is all.

Meanwhile, Gates's projects proceed apace. In 2022 he broke ground on a transformation of the St. Laurence Elementary School, a few blocks away from the Stony Island Arts Bank, with plans to turn it into an arts incubator offering studios, coworking space, and classrooms for area artists. Throughout the years he has renovated bungalows and larger multi-family buildings alongside his arts projects, renting them to people, some artists, at below-market rents. The addition of these housing units has helped to stabilize the buildings and blocks on which they are located by adding "eyes on the street." Their successful construction also boosts the area's prospects of attracting more investment, along with residents to fill the vacant lots anew. Along these lines, a national organization and local funders announced the distribution of grants for capital improvements that enable religious buildings on the South Side to be used for performance space. Also bringing hope is a massive construction project in Jackson Park, slated to become the future home of Barack Obama's Presidential Library, with community amenities including a public library branch, parkland improvements, and homeowner improvement grants. City leaders and activists are doing their best to ensure these positive changes will come without displacing residents.

The through line connecting all these reinvigorations is the celebration of the creative spirit of a long-neglected neighborhood. This celebration draws on a past in which the area and its residents contributed to American arts and letters. Of many such residents, perhaps the most relevant to point out here is noted playwright Lorraine Hansberry, a child in elementary school when her parents fought the racially restrictive covenant back in the 1930s. Hansberry wrote her acclaimed work, *A Raisin in the Sun*, about her parents' experiences integrating a White neighborhood, depicting the violence and intimidation aimed at her family for doing so.

Today, the spirits of Hansberry and other artists live on in the neighborhood's filmmakers, vocalists, spoken-word artists, visual creators, sculp-
tors, painters, furniture makers, and other talented creators.

Like the potter he is, Gates has molded the shape and program of
existing buildings to create vessels that cultivate and showcase this talent. He has said in interviews that his complementary projects constitute
"redemptive architecture," elaborating a democratic and people-centered
vision of what powers successful development. "Projects like this require
belief more than they require funding," he said about Stony Island Arts
Bank. "If there's not a kind of belief, motivation, and critical aggregation
of people who believe with you in a project like this, it cannot happen."
But these projects require the right zoning, too. Gates's projects demonstrate the role that zoning can play as part of a multifaceted strategy to promote creative projects that generate economic momentum—even those
that start with modest budgets. City leaders would do well to continue
to make their code even more flexible, to facilitate dance, theater, comedy, painting, sculpture, and other forms of expression in more types of
places—warehouses and churches, factories and shopping centers. Each
change could bring long-lasting benefits to the spatial organization of the
city. According to economists who have studied Chicago's code, areas the
city zoned for manufacturing in 1923 tended to be more likely to remain
manufacturing, and undeveloped areas zoned for single-family housing
track that land use today. A little more mixing could draw on the creative
energy of Chicagoans and point the way forward to a development model
that cultivates creativity for decades to come.

———————

One of Dolly Parton's classic songs, "Down on Music Row," is an ode
to a well-known neighborhood a mile and a half southwest of downtown Nashville. Like the Windy City, Nashville is a city well-known for
its cultural scene—and in Nashville, that cultural scene revolves around
country music. Downtown has long been a mecca for fans eager to hear
a great musician playing live—sometimes someone famous, but mostly

lesser-knowns working the honky-tonk circuit and looking for their big break. But Dolly wasn't directing those who might follow in her footsteps to downtown. She was sending them to Music Row, the hub of the business side of the city's entertainment industry, home to recording studios, talent agencies, musicians' associations, publishing companies, radio stations, and music industry headquarters. When Parton talks about her path to superstardom, she often recounts how she pounded the pavement there, singing for executives to secure her record deal. It's fair to say that the entire country-music industry owes its existence to Music Row. And Music Row owes its existence to zoning.

In the early twentieth century, in the era preceding zoning, the blocks along Sixteenth and Seventeenth Avenues—which would later become Music Row—were developed as a "streetcar suburb" of Nashville's bustling downtown. At the time, downtown was bursting with banks, insurance companies, department stores, grand hotels, and the full constellation of institutions and businesses doing work at the State Capitol. Of course, it hosted the theaters and honky-tonks where musicians played too. Connected to downtown by convenient and frequent transit service, the neighborhood housed families in mostly modest one-story cottages and bungalows, with some two- and three-story homes in the northern part closest to downtown. In the post–World War II era, the neighborhood changed significantly, when the array of social dynamics that played out in cities like Baltimore and Chicago resulted in the move of Whites and the middle class to farther-away suburban areas. The cottages that once housed families dropped in value. As demand for single-family housing dropped, the homes were chopped up inside to serve as boardinghouses and rooming houses for a more transient and lower-income population. Disinvestment followed, property values plummeted, and eventually city leaders began to see the neighborhood as a nuisance—a problem to be solved.

In the 1950s the city decided to use zoning to change the dynamic. The key move was to rezone the homes along Sixteenth and Seventeenth Avenues from residential to mixed-use commercial. In making this change,

Nashville's leaders followed leaders in other cities engaged in rezonings at the same time—some comprehensive like Chicago's, others piecemeal—in order to achieve social goals. Rezoning, the idea went, would ensure these buildings turned over to new owners, getting rid of the occupants and raising property values.

Putting aside the classist views driving this zoning change, in retrospect it is clear that their belief that zoning could facilitate major shifts was correct. In less than fifteen years, the entire neighborhood changed. Drawn by low property prices, in 1954 bandleader Owen Bradley and his guitarist brother—according to popular lore, the first music industry professionals to arrive—purchased a duplex on Sixteenth Avenue. They blew out the first floor to make a basement studio, adding burlap sacks to the walls to soften the sound, and set up a Quonset hut in the backyard. The polished professional sound they produced there appealed to musicians who previously lacked a dedicated place in Nashville to make high-quality recordings for their music—and to the record label Decca, which struck a deal with the Bradleys to use the studio space. Momentum built in 1957, when RCA Studios became the first major company to build its own studio nearby, just in time to capitalize on Elvis Presley's arrival to the country music scene. Soon Decca, MCA Capitol Records, Columbia, and others opened offices nearby in the 1960s, attracting Willie Nelson, George Jones, Ray Charles, Johnny Cash, Roy Orbison, and Waylon Jennings, among other stars. As a whole ecosystem of songwriters, session musicians, singers, producers, and sound engineers sprang up, the area became known for intensive collaboration. Others wanted in. Demand for space in Music Row grew, many homes were demolished, and lots were consolidated for undistinguished but utilitarian small-scale office buildings. An eclectic and increasingly architecturally incongruous neighborhood began to emerge. By the time Dolly Parton arrived at Music Row in the 1960s, the neighborhood was approaching the height of its fame.

Over the next few decades, Music Row secured its position as the indisputable epicenter of country music in the United States. New recording techniques, different physical arrangements of musicians, innovative chord progressions, and distinctive vocalists helped to move country music from the more formulaic "Nashville Sound" into the modern era. Elvis, who over the course of his career recorded more than two hundred songs on Music Row, paved the way for country musicians to infiltrate both rock and gospel. Of course, debates about whether Nashville artists should remain pure country are as old as Music Row itself. In 1999, one of my favorites, George Strait, lamented country music's extension into other genres in a duet with fellow country singer Alan Jackson called "Murder on Music Row." But modern-day crossover artists like Taylor Swift, who have successfully bridged country and pop music, have solidified Nashville's dominance as the place for country musicians to shape their talents and then to launch.

Sometimes success creates its own problems, and today the essence of Music Row as a place-based incubator for arts and ideas has come under threat—not from modern-day Elvises like Taylor Swift, but from development pressures, spurred by the increased demand for urban living in downtowns and near-downtown neighborhoods around the country. People want to live where the action is, and this desire has ignited a seemingly insatiable demand for residential housing—especially apartments—in central Nashville. According to a 2019 report from the city's planning department, over 3,200 residential units were constructed in the neighborhood since 2010, a sizeable number for any neighborhood. During that period, property values increased by 176 percent, putting pressure on music industry stalwarts to sell to residential developers, and suggesting that supply is not keeping up with demand. Developers are undeterred by high land prices, because they know they can make even more money with high-rise apartments. So Music Row's bungalows and mid-century office buildings are being scooped up and demolished. And 2019 saw the shuttering of the last live music venue on Music Row, Bobby's Idle Hour, to make way for new apartments. Amidst blocks under threat, the only protected areas are a handful of properties that have been designated historic landmarks and a small part of the southern area of Music Row, which has one- and two-family bungalows and cottages clad with brick and stone. Covering these buildings is a conservation overlay district with design guidelines that discourage demolition and encourage "compatible" heights and massing.

The pace of demolition has startled industry insiders, city boosters, and preservationists alike. They might have had a premonition that such changes might come when, in 2001, the Country Music Hall of Fame moved downtown and the original building on Music Row came down for a parking lot. Since then, buildings associated with the music industry have disappeared at a rapid clip. The local nonprofit Historic Nashville reported that forty-three music-related buildings were demolished between 2013 and 2018 alone. Only about half of the remaining businesses are music-related. In 2019, the National Trust for Historic Preservation put Music Row on its list of eleven Most Endangered Places. That designation recognizes that even a neighborhood with lackluster architecture may have an identity worth preserving.

So while Music Row hasn't been murdered, it's in the crosshairs. Just as zoning helped to create Music Row in the 1950s, zoning is helping now to unravel it. It isn't so much that the zoning of Music Row has dramatically changed over the last seventy years: it has more or less maintained its mixed-use commercial nature, and the studios and offices continue to be allowed. However, the city's own planning department admits that zoning does not support, and, in fact, prohibits, "third places"—social spaces like coffee shops and bars—which helped to cultivate the artistic community that put Music Row on the international map in the first place. While existing coffee shops and bars can endure as legal, nonconforming uses, these third places have been naturally phased out, as business owners move on or get frustrated by the regulatory constraints. Indeed, under current zoning rules, Bobby's Idle Hour cannot be revived.

What's more, the city's planning commission frequently issues "plan exemptions" that enable buildings to exceed the height caps of the zoning code. Historic Nashville has requested that the planning commission stop this practice. The nonprofit argues that the more often the city issues permits for tall buildings, the more likely demolitions of historic places will occur. That's exactly what seems to be happening, especially in the northern portion of Music Row, closer to downtown. Why keep any cottage, when the value of the land underneath dwarfs the value of the building? The taller the proposed building, the greater the return on a developer's investment.

Planners in these situations can find themselves between a rock and a hard place: between satisfying an implacable market demand for new apartments and trying to preserve the history of a cherished and significant place. But if Nashville's leaders truly do want to protect such places, turning the city's zoning inside out can help. As a logical first step, the city could legalize the third places where creative people can gather and build community. That way, existing business owners who just want to keep serving coffee and beer can carry on without all the restrictions and uncertainty brought on by nonconforming status. And newcomers who believe in the perfection of their own dark roasts can serve one and all.

Going further than that, zoning can also make the preservation of businesses vital to Music Row financially attractive for their property owners. To this end, city leaders recently contemplated a unique zoning innovation that may hold the key to protecting what's left of Music Row and the creative economic engine it supports: "transferable development rights" (TDRs). A small number of American cities have used TDR programs to slow development in one area while intensifying it in another. In a nutshell, cities can reward the owners of highly regulated properties with TDRs, namely, the ability to sell off a right to build some amount of square footage or number of stories to a neighboring property owner. You might think of this right to build as a kind of density bonus. A property owner who buys TDRs can then use the bonus square footage or number of stories to build bigger buildings than the zoning code allows. In Nashville, the zoning code could offer TDRs to owners of buildings occupied by entertainment-industry offices and recording studios, as well as the third places that welcome their employees and clients.

If Nashville goes forward with its plans, TDRs could reshape market incentives to protect what's left of Music Row, allowing property owners in the core to sell TDRs to owners of parcels located along Music Row's edges. If prospective purchasers of TDRs know they can build higher if they purchase a TDR, they have an incentive to buy. Their purchases in turn would finance TDR sellers' preservation and rehabilitation expenses, allowing them to avoid demolition or conversion. As we saw with Music Row's early development, zoning has the power to influence property owners' economic decisions and to shape, sometimes rapidly, the way they use land. The cumulative effects of these decisions can transform a neighborhood, a city, an industry, and even, in the case of Music Row, an entire genre of music.

When we think of the arts, we tend to think of big cities like Nashville and Chicago. In these places, where arts have become an important economic driver, local policymakers have paid attention to zoning and its impact on artistic activity. Through flexibility and regulatory innovation, these policymakers can accommodate and encourage the creativity of their residents. But remember that the arts exist everywhere, not only in large cities—because people are everywhere. Local leaders should keep in mind that investment in the arts doesn't need to (and in the vast majority of instances won't) result in as massive a payoff as something like Music Row. Small towns and rural communities with zoning can also cultivate creativity, too, on their own scale—whether that means allowing dance halls, live music, live-work (artist-occupied) studios, galleries, or those third places that allow for serendipitous collaboration. Starting with a "main street" and the surrounding blocks and re-creating it as a locus for all types of artistic expression can diversify a small community's economic base and enrich its activities. It's another example of how a deliberate approach can add an additional layer to the way in which we are able to use and experience our places.

4

Rock Around the Clock

Fter dark, vibrant cities come alive with people gathering to catch a movie or theater performance, hear live music, go to a restaurant or bar or comedy club. The economic potential of nightlife is clear, and so is the civic boost it can provide—beginning with a sense of vitality, that active buzz that can attract new residents and retain younger populations, even as it offers businesses new clientele and maximizes building and infrastructure use around the clock.

Nightlife deserves our attention because it has unique considerations relevant to zoning. How and where people can enjoy themselves after sundown is almost always controlled by zoning. Movie theaters and traditional performing-arts facilities, even smaller-scale and low-impact cultural venues like Theaster Gates's recent projects in Chicago, tend to be the easy cases. While they have parking and loading needs that might cause intermittent grumbling, they generally operate in orderly fashion, conform with long-term community plans, and tend to be located in areas with infrastructure well suited to support them. Rigorous site plan reviews usually help them and their operators avoid most potential pitfalls.

But other facilities—late-night live music stages, bars, strip clubs, and other adult establishments—offer juicier land use stories. These stories reveal how badly conceived rules can generate chaos and how well-conceived rules can help prevent it, mediating conflicts between purveyors of these establishments and their neighbors. They also capture the way in which zoning can be deployed to mitigate the darker side of nightlife, keeping it on the safe side of the critical line where racy crosses over into seamy.

Zoning codes across the country have attempted to tackle all types of nightlife. Their successes and failures underscore the need for common-sense zoning rules that can balance competing concerns. Individuals rightly love nightlife, but cities should too. And love it they can, given deft use of the tools that zoning provides.

With a front man hailing from Austin, the rock band Old 97's often references the Texas city renowned as "the Live Music Capital of the World." The group's alt-country anthems have followed a long line of rock, blues, folk, and country tunes from more famous Austin-affiliated performers such as Willie Nelson, Janis Joplin, Lucinda Williams, and Stevie Ray Vaughn. Even among these greats, it's the Old 97's in their 2001 ballad about secret love, "Designs on You," who best evoke the earnest yearning of the city's center of nightlife: Sixth Street.

Designated "Pecan Street" in the original city grid of 1839, the street has always functioned as a prime east–west throughway. After the Civil War and the construction of the railroad a few blocks away, Pecan Street filled up with Austin's finest hotels, shops, and offices. Its success owed much to topography. "The street was far enough from the river to escape flooding," explains the National Register nomination for the Sixth Street Historic District, "and it was the last east-west street flat enough for wagons and pedestrians to travel comfortably." By the 1870s, gracious two- and three-story limestone Victorians lined the street. By the 1880s, the city had grown so much that it ran out of trees for its east-west naming conventions and had to number them instead. Soon after, on the newly christened Sixth Street, a cattle baron built the Driskill Hotel, a four-story Richardsonian Romanesque structure whose lavish appointments epitomized the vast wealth invested in Austin's downtown.

Until World War II, the area thrived as a commercial mecca typified by the diversity both of its businesses—barber shops, restaurant supply stores, banks, hotels, grocery stores, and many other establishments— and of their owners, which included Lebanese, Black, Jewish, Chinese, and Mexican families. Sadly, as elsewhere around the country, downtown business deteriorated in the postwar era. The streetcar lines were disassembled in the 1940s, and the rise of the automobile made suburban malls more appealing. In the 1960s the Driskill became derelict and was nearly demolished. As downtown's population and residents cleared out, Austin's central core suffered economically and culturally, and by the 1980s adult cabarets, adult theaters, pawn shops, and nightclubs proliferated.

In 1986, community leaders met to consider ways to reverse the decline. They landed on the idea of an annual, multiple-venue performing arts extravaganza that would showcase the talented musicians playing in downtown's seedy clubs. They called it South by Southwest—a play on the name of the Alfred Hitchcock film—and its 1987 opening far exceeded expectations. With fifteen stages featuring 177 artists, organizers expected a hundred and fifty people. Seven hundred showed, and the event immediately made national news. In just a year, the number of stages and artists doubled. Riding on the festival's success, bars incorporating live-music stages began to push out the adult uses on Sixth Street. As crowds grew, the city closed the street to cars on weekend nights so that people could mill about without having to contend with traffic. The charming low-rise limestone buildings, by then over a century old, provided a distinctive backdrop to the revelry. It was a scene, and a lively one.

I arrived in Austin to attend college in 1996. Back then, Austin still had a small-town feel. The vibe was casual, flip-flops and cowboy boots interspersed with sorority girls' heels, all people out for a good time and good music. My familiarity with that scene was limited because late nights more often found me working on drawings in the University of Texas's Goldsmith Hall than partying anywhere, much less on Sixth Street. But my interest in local music culture was piqued by a lecture given by the dean of the school of architecture, Larry Speck, about his design of the new Austin airport. While designing a structure to meet the logistical demands of moving millions of travelers, Speck had added an unusual flourish: a live-music stage, situated just after the security checkpoint. He explained that music should be the first thing people experience when they land in Austin, and the last thing they hear when they leave. In pushing for the stage, Speck may have also pushed some zoning boundaries, most likely stretching the meaning of "accessory use." In zoning, that term usually requires that a use be traditionally found with the principal use (in this case, an airport). A backyard swimming pool satisfies that standard because so many single-family houses have them but, as far as I know, Austin's airport has the country's first live music stage. For my part, I took the airport's opening in 1999, and the critical acclaim it garnered, as a cue to make my way down to Sixth Street, at least for architectural research purposes.

Even then, however, Sixth Street was evolving again, and in an unfortunate direction. South by Southwest organizers had recently added a film festival and an "interactive" component, drawing thousands more attendees than ever before. The commodify-it-all impulse, clearly designed to maximize attendance and profits, was so troubling that Lucinda Williams, the singer-songwriter and former Austinite who keynoted the festival in 1999, took the occasion to rail from the stage against the organizers and the music industry. "The whole music business has become corporate, and that's the problem," Williams said. "We're seeing the Wal-Mart consciousness taking over, and it's the dying of America." Her scathing speech presciently captured the shift that was underway. As commercial rents on Sixth Steet soared along with the city's international reputation, nightlife venues prioritized high-volume alcohol sales, the most efficient way to cover costs. Gradually, the already dwindling number of restaurants, beauty salons, and retail shops started to disappear altogether. Offering little to do during daytime hours, the area became less crowded and in turn less safe. The bars felt sketchier, too. On my twenty-first birthday, a friend took a black eye defending my honor in one of those bars. By 2007, when my husband and I stayed at the Driskill for our wedding, the Sixth Street vibe had deteriorated enough that guests gathered at the hotel bar rather than venture into the noisy, chaotic scene outside.

In the decade and a half since, the growth of the nightlife-industrial complex in Austin has only accelerated. Today's South By Southwest audiences number 50,000 people over the festival's nine or ten days. Organizers are quick to point to the economic benefits those audiences bring. According to their research, in 2022 the nine-day event generated 45,500 hotel-room night reservations and pumped over $280 million into the local economy. These numbers may be alluring. But more serious thought must be given to what happens to the city during the other 356 days of the year. Today, Sixth Street's busiest downtown stretch, between Congress Avenue and Interstate 35, is saturated with bars, and the clubs that were once laid-back launchpads for little-known bands function less as music incubators than high-volume alcohol dispensaries. All the predictable problems have resulted. Much like New Orleans's Bourbon Street, Sixth Street has become linear debauchery: open drunkenness, street brawls, and the occasional shooting. Not to mention the bachelorette parties.

A few years ago, an Austin-based *Texas Monthly* columnist noted that locals have nicknamed the street "Dirty Sixth," and confessed to feeling "embarrassed that so many out-of-towners form their impressions of Austin" there. The columnist and I must both have that Old 97's song running through our minds: we're all asking when all the crowds will go home.

It turns out that zoning is to blame, at least in part, for the "anything goes" turn of this storied street. The relevant blocks of Sixth Street sit in the central business district zone, where Austin's code allows property owners to freely erect multifamily apartments, offices, restaurants, shops, hotels, and medical offices. These uses are typical for downtown districts, and do not often have significant negative spillover effects. But the code also allows cocktail lounges, indoor entertainment, and liquor sales to operate, and in a relatively unconstrained manner. The few explicit constraints appear to be cosmetic, like a 45-foot height cap for most of the area. Only adult uses—bookstores, cabarets, lounges, and theaters offering products or performances involving activities of a sexual nature—have stricter regulations.

Poorly regulated nightlife can be a nuisance that spreads to the community at large. Austin's permissiveness is not typical of other American cities. More typical is Hartford, which requires bars to undergo a public hearing to obtain a zoning permit. Hartford bars must serve food if they are located near residences, the idea being that people who eat something will be less likely to get overly intoxicated. Prospective bar owners must submit plans not only for a kitchen but for a menu. If the bar will host musical acts, DJs, or other entertainment, the applicant must submit safety and noise-mitigation plans. The zoning commission can restrict opening hours as a condition of the special permit. Stores selling beer, wine, or liquor also require a public hearing. Together these measures give the city leverage—exerted by levying fines or withholding permit renewals—when things get out of hand.

Austin currently lacks the leverage it needs to get things under control. Fortunately, civic and political leaders have started a long-overdue public conversation about strategies to make Sixth Street safer. Changing policing, reintroducing modest vehicular traffic, and improving crowd dispersion techniques are all on the table. So are zoning changes, including consideration of provisions like Hartford's. Public hearings for new establishments and permit renewals for existing establishments could improve public oversight, ensuring applicants address the concerns of neighbors and others both initially and every time they request a renewal. Ramping up fines for code violations could improve the ability of zoning enforcement officers and police to rein in neglectful businesses. The city could mandate sidewalk and lighting improvements or require landscaping and security features to improve streetscape safety. To encourage a healthier mix of uses, the city could institute a modified dispersion requirement for new bars, as it already does for adult uses. It could even set a temporary moratorium on new bars.

The Downtown Austin Alliance, the area's business association, supports zoning changes in this vein. Such measures would slow the seemingly never-ending proliferation of bars and nightclubs, allowing daytime businesses some room to grow. Whether reining in the excesses of nightlife will restore Austin's rootsy vibe, or satisfy the "Keep Austin Weird" crowd, seems doubtful. But focusing on zoning might help recalibrate Sixth Street, ensuring that it becomes the primary driver of a more diversified and stronger local economy, one that works well for everyone year-round.

Deployed prudently, zoning can enhance a city's vibrancy and make it safer and more viable in the long term—whether in Austin or in Nashville. The story of Nashville's downtown is of course also inseparable from music. Dolly Parton started her career there, at just thirteen, when she first performed onstage at the Grand Ole Opry. Introduced as "a little girl here from up in East Tennessee" by none other than the Man in Black, Johnny Cash himself, the teenaged Dolly sang during the show's weekly broadcast from Ryman Auditorium, a former church with perfect acoustics located five blocks south of the State Capitol building. Even back then, she received three encores. Dolly would not forget how elated she felt, and, five years later, one day after graduating high school, she left her tiny town of Little Pigeon River and headed back to Nashville to pursue her dream of becoming a songwriter and singer.

Downtown's musical die had been cast decades earlier, during World War II, when the Ryman started hosting the Grand Ole Opry musical review. Radio stations across the country carried the performances, and soon people were flocking to Nashville to try to grab a seat. The fast-growing music action at the Ryman supported honky-tonks and saloons that clustered in the area and showcased less-known acts. These entertainment venues coexisted with furniture and hardware shops, grain stores, offices, and hotels already located nearby; they didn't concentrate on a linear stretch of blocks, as on Austin's Sixth Street, but instead spread across a thirteen-block area encompassing the Ryman along with the historic neighborhoods of Printer's Alley, Broadway, and the area between First and Fifth Avenues, together known as the District. The dispersion of venues across the District turned out to be beneficial; it meant that nighttime revelry, although focused in one neighborhood, could "breathe" a little.

Nashville's story in the postwar era parallels that of Austin, both cities suffering the downtown disinvestment and suburban flight seen all over the country. By the late 1960s, the neighborhood around the Grand Ole Opry House hosted a seedy array of adult bookshops and peep shows, and in 1974 the show moved to the suburbs, leaving the Ryman Auditorium empty in an increasingly sketchy downtown. Also left for dead were dozens of historic buildings, attractive masonry structures between three and six stories in height, built between the 1890s and 1920s. Over the next decade, most were listed on the National Register of Historic Places, and their nomination forms document dire conditions. The nomination for the Printer's Alley blocks, for example, noted that eleven of the fifteen structures under consideration had "vacant upper stories that have been allowed to deteriorate," while those for the Fifth Avenue and Broadway corridors noted a large number of vacant buildings and vacant upper stories, lamenting widespread "physical decay, unsightly signs, and unsympathetic modifications."

Despite these degradations, the nominations articulated reasons to stave off potential demolition. In time, the buildings' successful listings on the National Register would become key in rallying community support for reinvestment. Nashville began its revival in the late 1980s, around the same time as Austin. At first, just a few individual buildings were rehabilitated. Then the Ryman Auditorium itself was renovated, reopening in 1994, spurring hope among local businesses that the heyday of downtown might return. Yet momentum stalled, and many of the historic buildings that had endured so much already remained vacant on their upper stories through the 2000s. I visited Nashville in 2008, hopping around to a few places with a friend who lived there, and eventually landing at Robert's Western World, a historic warehouse converted into a western-wear store with a bar and performance stage. I can't remember the singers we heard, but I do remember that we lingered too late, and the walk to the car felt pretty desolate.

City leaders eventually attributed downtown's persistent vacancies to zoning. One can see why. The city's zoning code was so restrictive that every new business or activity downtown required either rezoning—that is, entirely new rules—or a variance permitting legal deviation from existing rules. Both the cost of the applications for these procedures and the chronic uncertainty about their resolution deterred investment. The code also imposed high minimum parking requirements, impossible to satisfy on lots that were already fully built out. As a result, even while the neighborhoods and suburbs of Nashville experienced some of the most rapid growth in the country, developers would not invest in downtown.

In 2010 Nashville leaders addressed this issue through the adoption of an ambitious new "Downtown Code," which aims to "[e]nsure that Downtown remains the civic, cultural, and entertainment center for Nashville, Middle Tennessee, and the Southeast." The overhaul permits a huge range of uses by right, including multifamily apartments, hospitals, concert halls, banks, microbreweries, fraternity houses, and even monasteries. Bars, nightclubs, and liquor stores are also permitted by right, though after-hours establishments open between 3:00 and 6:00 a.m. are subject to conditions.

Coupled with the new use-based rules are "form-based" rules covering specific aspects of a building's design (including its façade, bulk, and orientation) and providing both guidance and flexibility. The code requires multistory buildings because they are more likely to house a variety of uses than single-story buildings—and diversifying uses makes it more likely that the city will achieve its goal of creating a 24/7 neighborhood, with something to do at all times. The code also eliminates minimum parking requirements in downtown altogether, freeing up land for development. Finally, it gives staff and the commission more discretion in approving projects that previously would have been required to undergo several costly reviews, creating the flexibility that we have seen prove crucial elsewhere.

These changes have virtually eliminated the need for downtown projects to apply for variances. They have also expanded infill development, which makes use of the space occupied by surface parking or vacant lots, and rehabilitation. So a downtown that had 134 surface parking lots in 2003 now has only about a dozen. The emphasis on attracting residential and daytime uses to activate the neighborhood at all times of day seems to be working. Over a twenty-year period, the city has nearly septupled its downtown housing stock.

As a result of these efforts, Nashville's downtown streets are no longer daytime ghost towns. Nightlife has surged, and with few of the extreme problems Austin has seen (other than the bachelorette parties). Though bars don't have a dispersion requirement—which means they can locate side by side—the number of blocks where they are permitted ensures nightlife is spread across many blocks, its venues dispersed among other businesses and overseen by a strong merchants' association that keeps things tidy. All these factors have helped make Nashville one of the fastest-growing cities in the United States, with a high-octane start-up scene and a roaring tourist trade, whose after-dark essence was captured in a recent national news headline: "Music City Tourist Boom Led by Thriving Nightlife."

All this discussion about nightlife and its role in a city's vibrancy points toward one last, delicate question: what to do about what zoning codes euphemistically categorize as "adult uses"?

Baltimore has taken a unique approach to this perpetually troublesome question—an approach that is historically intertwined, strangely enough, with apocalyptic incidents of flooding and fire. The story traces to the late nineteenth century, a time when Jones Falls, the waterway running alongside the Remington neighborhood and through much of the city, had become diverted, dammed, and filled with debris. New construction, meanwhile, had encroached on the natural floodplain, which meant that during intense rain events, water had nowhere to drain. As Jones Falls got narrower and the amount of built- and paved-over land increased, the city experienced intermittent flooding. The deadliest and costliest flood occurred in 1868, when a storm and high winds drew rising waters from the tidal Patapsco River into Jones Falls. This "Black Friday" flood claimed fifty lives, damaged more than two thousand homes, and caused millions of dollars in economic losses. Later that year, a special committee convened by the city council recommended that Jones Falls either be channelized underground or reshaped above ground.

The city ignored that recommendation. Worse, every time the water receded, the city permitted more and more development. Over the next thirty-five years, Baltimore's population doubled. An influx of people, some new to the United States, sought work at the harbor, in downtown businesses, or in the factories. Speculators sought to satisfy newcomers' demand for housing with shoddily built tenements. To serve the ever-growing population, virtually every neighborhood included saloons, gambling joints, and brothels. Then came the 1904 fire. Like the Black Friday flood before it, the Great Fire devastated the city—taking five lives and obliterating over 1,500 buildings, including offices, retail stores, banks, civic institutions, and harbor infrastructure. The city quickly moved to rebuild, but only after adopting new building codes (and purchasing state-of-the-art fire equipment).

The reconstruction process—long and difficult as it was—provided an opportunity to reexamine Baltimore's relationship with the Falls, which in 1914 was finally diverted to an underground conduit and rerouted to empty into the Inner Harbor. At the same time, the city took the occasion to reconsider its treatment of the vice-oriented businesses that had proliferated in neighborhoods all over the city. Officials decided to compel the brothels in the area to cluster in a four-block area on East Baltimore Street—an area just a short walk from the harbor that was being rebuilt virtually from scratch. Though brothels became illegal a decade later, "the Block" enjoyed a catlike multiplicity of lives, muddling through Prohibition and emerging after World War II as a strip of cabarets and adult clubs. Neither raids, nor prostitution stings, nor the many politicians' crying shame succeeded in cleaning up the Block, its persistence a tribute to the inexpungeable nature of human desire. Today, just a short walk from the Inner Harbor, sit Larry Flynt's Hustler Club, the Bottoms Up Club, the Red Room Cabaret, Indulge Gentlemen's Club, and several similar establishments. Though prime time at these emporiums occurs at night, several are open during the day and even round the clock. But it should be noted that someone in city government had a sense of humor: the police headquarters and the federal district court keep a watchful eye from one block away.

Between the Block's establishment a century ago and its current incarnation, the adjacent Inner Harbor underwent fundamental changes. Even with Jones Falls out of sight, Baltimoreans did not forget their connection with the water. In the 1950s, city leaders developed a plan to replace decaying shipping infrastructure with a six-block waterfront promenade. Today, what they created remains one of the quintessential urban tourist meccas in the country: the Baltimore Waterfront Promenade, a destination attraction complete with a science center, planetarium, children's museum, aquarium, and historic ships, all drawing over a million visitors annually. Hotels and restaurants abound in the waterfront area. Sightseers take walking tours. Venues put on wholesome events like "Let's Science Happy Hour" and the "Urban Pirates Nighttime Cruise." And the adjacent downtown blocks offer the usual array of family-friendly entertainment options for visitors and Baltimoreans alike.

Some might consider the juxtaposition of a family-centered fun zone with a two-block erotica market, well, awkward. If you are one who does, or if you ever wonder why the adult-use businesses show up in your town even when no one seems to want them (or at least will say so publicly), blame the Constitution and the U.S. Supreme Court, which has ruled that banning them altogether infringes on First Amendment protected "speech." American cities have to put these businesses somewhere.

But where? In Baltimore, zoning officials assigned adult uses, defined as "sexually explicit materials or entertainment that, applying contemporary standards, the average individual would find . . . appeals to the prurient interest," to the adult use overlay district. The base district beneath that overlay, typical of a mixed-use high-density downtown district, imposes some extra requirements, like design review for all types of construction and additions, and offers some freebies, like exemption from the code's parking mandates. To establish an adult use within the overlay, an applicant must apply for a conditional use permit and prove that the new use will not infringe on the public health, safety, and welfare, increase traffic congestion, or add public expense for fire or police protection. The applicant must also pledge to screen any "material that depicts, describes, or relates to specified sexual activities or specified anatomical areas" from view by passersby. While large storefront windows may not reveal the ecdysiasts inside, the glass dance floor above patron seating in Larry Flynt's club is perfectly legal.

In these definitions and regulations of adult uses, Baltimore's code generally follows hundreds of zoning ordinances across the country. Yet in concentrating these businesses in just two blocks of its 92-square-mile expanse—and in close proximity to the heart of its tourism trade—the city has taken an approach different from most. Austin, for example, allows "adult-oriented businesses" downtown and in a few other zones so long as they make their case successfully at a public hearing and are 1,000 feet away from other such businesses, schools, churches, public parks or playgrounds, daycare centers, museums, or libraries. Hartford's code stipulates they may be anywhere within an industrial zone encompassing about 10 percent of the city, so long as they keep 1,000 feet from a variety of uses, including hospitals and residences. New Jersey, meanwhile, establishes a statewide thousand-foot-radius dispersion requirement between "sexually oriented businesses," and also between such businesses and religious institutions, parks and playgrounds, hospitals, child care centers, or places zoned for housing.

The concept of a thousand-foot *cordon sanitaire* traces to a 1976 decision by the U.S. Supreme Court that articulated communities' obligation to allow—and their ability to regulate—adult uses. The case involved a Detroit ordinance that prohibited adult theaters, bookstores, and cabarets from locating within 1,000 feet of each other or 500 feet of any residential neighborhood. The Court upheld this ordinance, ruling that the code's definitions were clear, and that the dispersion requirement merely functioned as a "time, place, and manner" rule targeting the "secondary effects" of the adult uses. A decade later, another Supreme Court case upheld a Renton, Washington, dispersion requirement prohibiting adult theaters from locating within 1,000 feet of any residential zone, home, church, or park, or within one mile of any school. The Court pointed to the ordinance's stated purposes of preventing crime, stimulating retail activity, maintaining property values, and protecting quality of life—all goals that could be undermined by the secondary effects of adult theaters. It also noted that the ordinance was narrowly tailored and allowed for adult theaters to locate in various places within the city, thus providing them with reasonable alternative avenues of communication for the aspects of expression protected by the First Amendment.

These two cases effectively required cities to justify their regulation of adult uses through studies highlighting negative secondary effects. One of the most widely cited of such reports was a 1991 study done in Garden Grove, California, by two University of California-Irvine researchers who examined the effects of adult businesses on crime, property values, and quality-of-life nuisances such as noise and litter. Analyzing over 34,000 reported crimes, the researchers found that crime rises in a statistically significant manner any time an adult business opens or expands, and rises even more when the adult business is within 1,000 feet of a bar. It also surveyed households and real estate professionals, finding that both groups shared a perception that adult businesses decreased property values and quality of life while increasing crime. The report recommended that adult businesses not be operated within 1,000 feet of a residence, tavern, or other adult business. Garden Grove eventually adopted regulations dispersing "adult entertainment businesses" by 1,000 feet for these uses, adding requirements of 700-foot distances from "any church" and 200-foot distances from any residential zone or from any public building. Similar studies have been conducted elsewhere. Austin chose its dispersion strategy after a 1986 study of adult-oriented businesses showed that crime increased 66 percent in areas with two or more adult uses and that 88 percent of real estate brokers and appraisers believed that the presence of an adult business would decrease residential property values. That study reinforced others showing that while these businesses generate economic activity within their walls, they often deter it outside.

Cities have attempted to regulate adult uses in other ways, testing the limits of criteria established by numerous court cases. Imposing reasonable restraints on the operating hours of these establishments, for instance, usually survives legal challenge. Giving neighbors a veto, or the power to approve an adult use, however, has usually ended up being struck down—as have onerous licensing requirements. One strategy with mixed results is amortizing, or phasing out, adult uses. This happened successfully in New York City in the 1990s, when the city amortized the seedy peep shows and bookstores in Times Square as part of a long-range transformation of the area. Amortization has often been struck down elsewhere, however, especially when the places such businesses are allowed to relocate are deemed undesirable or too limited, or when adult uses claim protected status as a nonconforming use. For most cities, simply replicating regulations already approved by the Supreme Court causes the least headaches. It's worth noting that the court cases mentioned earlier made clear that, from a constitutional perspective, either a dispersal or a concentration approach to adult businesses can pass muster. Austin chose a dispersion strategy. Baltimore went the other way.

Every community must make choices, weighing economic and social costs, about where nightlife can safely flourish. It's hard to point to any place that gets it perfect, and even a zoning code that on paper looks great is only as good as its enforcement. Fines have to be significant enough to deter bad behavior and to hold owners of nightlife establishments accountable for the representations they made in their zoning applications. The police and zoning enforcement officials must be adequately staffed, and trained to deal with and persuade recalcitrant owners. And, as obvious as it may sound, some of the people charged with enforcing zoning codes actually have to keep their working hours at night.

This last concept is slowly catching on in the United States, inspired, at least in part, by the city of Amsterdam. About a decade ago, Amsterdam hired the world's first "night mayor," Mirik Milan, and charged him with managing all aspects of the city's nighttime activities. His responsibilities have included taming the city's red-light district and its out-of-control cannabis-related tourism. He also conducts more mundane tasks, like liaising with local hotels, restaurants, and entertainment venues and overseeing tourism strategy. In 2016, Milan came to Austin to sit on a panel at—you guessed it—South by Southwest, called "Why Every City Should Have a Night Mayor." Drawing from this example, Nashville hired a nightlife director in 2022 to work with local musicians, nightlife operators, government agencies, neighborhood associations, and residents to address behaviors and practices that raise safety or quality-of-life concerns. New York City, New Orleans, Washington, D.C., and a few other American cities have created similar positions. In virtually every case, the people in these positions have leaned on zoning as one of the tools they use to coordinate the nighttime economy and culture.

Ultimately, anyone seeking to promote a healthy nightlife understands the need for balance. Zoning and other policies must balance the interests of the performers, service workers, business owners, neighbors, and police. They must provide order and be ready to impose discipline—without squashing fun. They must shield the vulnerable from immorality, while protecting the free speech of the purveyors of "adult" experiences. Adroit zoning, designed with legal requirements in mind and focused on finding ways to mix nightlife with other uses, can help capture the benefits of a robust nightlife while curbing its potential excesses. Or, at least, it can try.

Part II

THE
ESSENTIALS

(5)

Making It Home

Just about every summer during elementary and middle school, my parents would haul my sister Kathleen and me into central Houston from Crosby, a drive that took an hour door to door. Our mission consisted of preparing a rental property that our family owned in West University Place—an eighty-year-old wood-frame bungalow—for new tenants. Making frequent trips to the nearby home-improvement store for tools and supplies, we would paint walls, caulk, wash windows, weed the lawn, make repairs, and assess whether carpets and window treatments needed to be replaced. The amount (and misery level) of the work each year depended on how the last tenants had left the place. We often returned to Crosby late at night, dirty and tired. But our family bonded through this shared experience, and my sister and I learned some important lessons—first and foremost, that we never wanted to be landlords.

My parents had bought that lot—just three miles from my childhood home in Gulfton—in 1981, after Hurricane Alicia tore through Houston.

In the hurricane's aftermath, my dad worked overtime at Southwestern Bell, repairing and installing cable, earning a sizeable boost above his normal engineer's pay. My mom felt they should use the money to make their first investment, so she perused the *Greensheet*'s real estate section. She found an advertisement for a for-sale-by-owner property in West University Place. On paper, it boasted an excellent location, inside the I-610 Loop ringing central Houston, close to the medical center and museums, and two blocks from a grocery store, pharmacy, ice-cream shop, and other necessaries. When my parents toured it, however, they found it sat just twenty feet from a busy railroad track running east-west across the city. Every couple of hours, when a train passed, the little house shook. Worse, the Texas heat warped the tracks every summer—one especially hot year, a train derailed into a neighbor's property. Nonetheless, my parents decided that the underpriced lot had value, and so they gambled their savings on the down payment.

Their investment paid off. Year after year, they managed to find renters, often medical residents and young couples, willing to tolerate the trains. After eleven years, they had amassed enough money to demolish the house and place a deposit for a two-story custom build—not for a rental, but for our own home. To boost the deposit, they sold our house in Crosby, and we all temporarily moved back in with my grandparents. Construction on the place started just in time: I had gotten a scholarship to an all-girls' Catholic high school in central Houston, and the long drive from Crosby had become taxing for everyone. In 1993, during my sophomore year, we moved in. With a two-car garage taking up a quarter of the façade, the new house lacked the old bungalow's charm. But with its brick cladding and double-insulated windows, at least it shook less.

West U, with its tidy, tree-lined sidewalks abutting neatly landscaped single-family homes, is an anomaly within Houston. It's a separate municipality that has adopted zoning. An island bordered on all sides by unzoned Houston, it looks and feels different from the rest of the city. A little history reveals this feeling to be intentional. Over a century ago, West U was conceived as a suburb of country homes for the affluent, near what was then the Rice Institute, now Rice University. Residents incorporated it as an independent municipality in 1924 in order to pool their resources to pay for better flood infrastructure than the City of Houston offered. A look at a map reveals that, as if in homage to the single-family home, West U's founders shaped the neighborhood to resemble a house. My parents' home, at the very edge of the map, is located in the "chimney."

Early West U officials had a law-and-order streak when it came to land development. Their first land use ordinance prohibited disorderly or bawdy houses (brothels and other places of illicit activity), followed two years later by an ordinance prohibiting keeping fowl. In 1937 the city adopted a zoning code, dividing land into "single-family dwelling districts" and "retail business districts." In part because of its attractive location, West U soon became one of the fastest-growing cities in the nation, its population peaking in the 1950s. Abiding by the zoning code, developers purchased, subdivided, and developed virtually all remaining open tracts of land for freestanding, single-family housing. By 1970, West U had 5,200 homes, having doubled its housing stock in just thirty years. The City of Houston surrounding it was growing, too.

But in the early 1980s, the paths of Houston and West U diverged. In unzoned Houston, growth continued, slowed only temporarily by that oil bust that laid the backdrop for my family to decamp from Gulfton to Crosby. In the decades since, Houston has counted itself among the fastest-growing cities in the country—primarily because it simply builds more housing than other places. Its light-on-regulation approach means more people who want homes can get them, and they can get them at lower prices, when they need them.

I emphasize "light-on-regulation" because while Houston is unzoned, it is not totally unregulated. Indeed, as others have pointed out, some of Houston's land development rules are also found in zoning. The subdivision ordinance, for example, establishes building lines (front setbacks), parking requirements, and minimum lot sizes, all commonly found in zoning codes. The historic preservation ordinance, another example, requires some properties to undergo design review, a process sometimes required by zoning procedures. Technically, these ordinances are not zoning—a fact recently confirmed by the Texas Supreme Court. But they do deploy several zoning-like mechanisms.

Take, for instance, the city's minimum lot-size requirements, which dictate how much land each unit of proposed housing will sit on. While Houston has implemented these requirements through the city subdivision ordinance, most other cities implement them through zoning. Zoning codes almost universally impose lot-size requirements on single-family neighborhoods, typically measuring the required size in acres, and in most cases on multifamily housing as well. Because they necessarily limit the amount of housing that can be placed in any given area, minimum lot sizes reduce supply and increase competition for housing. In the process, they raise prices—a frustrating obstacle to some, but a benefit to others. For those who own homes already, higher prices increase the value of a home as an asset, and simultaneously enable the exclusion of "undesirable" neighbors. So it should be no surprise that wealthier homeowners who historically have controlled land use policy, shaping it to promote their own interests, embrace minimum lot sizes.

Given this political dynamic, many communities don't just impose minimum lot sizes—they impose huge minimum lot sizes. However unsurprising a reality, the numbers can nonetheless be startling. In a study of Connecticut towns, I found that zoning codes require 80 percent of the state's residential land to have a minimum of one acre per home. That's almost the size of a football field. And it's worse in New Hampshire. Using the same methods I used, researchers found that only 15 percent of the state's buildable land allows housing on plots less than an acre.

A one-acre lot requirement begs the question of what else might be done with a football field, other than host a game. One researcher found that if Connecticut's lot sizes were reduced by half, the number of smaller and less expensive homes would increase, and more racial minorities would be able to afford housing. Such a code change would also help existing homeowners by giving them the option either to subdivide and build more housing, or preserve the land for those people who demand an acre and are willing to pay for it. How many such people are there, anyway? Having a yard—often a spacious one—is one of those homeowner aspirations so prevalent in American life during the last century, it's almost taken for granted. But there's plenty of evidence suggesting that the incidence of large lots is at odds with true demand. Not everyone wants to live on huge tracts of land. A study of four growing suburbs in Texas found that even moderate lot-size mandates resulted in underproduction of the smaller lots where more people actually want to live. Similarly, a study of eighty-three New Jersey suburbs found that there is more demand for small lots, but the suburbs primarily offered large lots.

Within the broader spectrum of big-city U.S. zoning, unzoned Houston's approach is about as hands-off as you can get. Houston's lot-size requirements have always been modest in comparison with places with zoning. For decades, the city required a minimum size of 5,000 square feet—less than one-tenth the size of a football field—for lots connected to the city's sewer system and 7,000 square feet for septic-based lots. Twice in recent years, the city has reduced those mandates even further, to a requirement of just 1,400 square feet of land for homes within the I-610 Loop (subject to some open-space requirements) in 1998, expanding that change citywide in 2013. This reduction has enabled property owners to build housing on much smaller lots than previously allowed—thereby tripling the housing capacity in any given neighborhood. The overall effect of liberalized lot-size policies is impressive. Today, at least nine Houston lots can be created out of one typical Connecticut lot.

Houston's lot-size reductions have resulted in not only more housing being built, but more kinds of housing, and cheaper housing. Researcher Nolan Gray has documented how the minimum lot-size change alone significantly increased density in previously underbuilt neighborhoods in central Houston. "Infill" housing on vacant or underbuilt lots, including attached townhomes, diversifies the housing stock by ensuring Houston builds more than just detached single-family homes. U.S. Department of Housing and Urban Development figures confirm that Houston has issued more permits for multifamily housing than single-family housing—over the last decade permitting 63 percent more multifamily than single-family units, and more units per year (now up to about 15,000). Where single-family lots were converted to townhomes, the resulting units were affordable to people who earned about the average area median income. These results are consistent with broader research. A study of greater Boston, for example, revealed that for every additional acre in average lot-size mandates, the number of permits declined by 40 percent over a twenty-year period. The inverse has proven true in Houston. Following the *Field of Dreams* "if you build it, they will come" model, Houston issues permits for almost three times the number of housing units per capita as New York City. One beneficial aspect of such prolific construction is that over the last decade, the city was able to house 25,000 previously unhoused people, cutting the homeless population by 63 percent. According to the *New York Times*, Houston is doing "more than twice as well as the rest of the country at reducing homelessness." The supply of housing also has an impact on prices. When I visit my parents, I've stopped being surprised at the new townhouses and small-scale residential infill within the Loop.

West U, meanwhile, has maintained its restrictive zoning, including minimum lot-size requirements of 8,250 square feet—far smaller than Connecticut's football field but almost six times as large as Houston's. This minimum drives up the cost of housing and simultaneously limits the number of homes that can be built within city borders, especially since all of West U has been developed already, and the only way to increase the amount of housing would be to subdivide existing lots into smaller ones. (West U cannot change its boundaries to annex more land, because the City of Houston surrounds it.) In addition to its minimum lot-size requirements, West U prohibits multifamily housing. It also constrains the size, height, and width of homes, mandates strict setbacks, and requires parking spaces for each home.

As a result of this combination of restrictions, the number of housing units in West U has stagnated, barely increasing in the past half-century. This is consistent with economists' finding that restrictive zoning and other land use constraints dampen production. And because people want to live in new homes in West U but lack land on which to build, the neighborhood has seen the demolition of perfectly usable historic homes, as property owners like my parents replace smaller bungalows with larger, custom-built single-family homes. With smaller household sizes today than in the 1970s, the population of West U has declined to just under 15,000 residents.

It's fair to say that West U conveys the dual valence of the term "exclusive"—a desirable term for some (and a staple of upscale real estate advertising), but not for those who are excluded. Its zoning-driven exclusivity has benefited people like my parents, financially anyway. Zoning's limits on the supply of housing help existing homeowners maintain the value of their investments. Indeed, West U takes the official position in its comprehensive plan that zoning is the means by which single-family property values will be "protected." By making it harder to build new housing and to subdivide lots, and by prohibiting more than one dwelling per lot, the city has achieved this narrow goal, and in spectacular fashion. The lot my parents purchased for $65,000 in 1981 would probably sell for nearly a million dollars today. Even accounting for the costs of the house they built, these numbers wildly outperform Houston real estate values over the same period. The Census documents the median value of owner-occupied housing in West U as of 2019 as $1,113,500—seventeen times the value of Gulfton's. By contrast, condos in the complex where my parents purchased our first home for $48,000 in 1978 are on the market today for just $60,000.

The comparison between West U and Gulfton illustrates a kind of pick-your-poison aspect to zoning and its outcomes: exclusivity, promising quality to the few but yielding nothing to the many; or inclusivity, providing access, but reducing or eliminating the "protection" of stringent regulation. In comparison with a place like West U, Houston offers many price points for entry-level buyers; as American cities go, it is affordable.

But that good news on the affordability front obscures the fact that not all homeowners benefit from the Bayou City's lax approach to land use. The best way to understand the negative consequences of deregulation is to dig deeper into the links between affordability, zoning, ethnicity, class, and race, in Houston and elsewhere.

The most affordable areas in Houston are the low-income and minority neighborhoods in the parts of the city that are the least regulated, either by the city or by private covenants. Some of the resulting conditions are anything but pretty. The scrapyards, adult theaters, and open-air auto repair shops allowed in these neighborhoods drag down property values. Toxic fumes from industrial plants threaten residents' health. Flooding in low-lying areas—where unscrupulous developers build, because the city lets them—leads to mold and mildew in living quarters. A founding figure of the environmental justice movement, Robert Bullard, has extensively chronicled the problematic aspects of Houston's anarchic siting procedures in a series of books and articles. Bullard argues that the city's lack of regulations fails communities of color, who suffer both the direct impact of pollution and health hazards, and the indirect costs of depressed land values.

Houston's problems may be more egregious than most because the city lacks even the simplest rules segregating uses from each other. On the other hand, places with zoning don't always get things right. In Hartford, for example, before we changed the zoning code in 2016, the most noxious uses—including a sewage treatment facility, trash incinerator, and landfill—were permitted to locate in the industrial zones adjacent to or upwind from the city's poorest communities, who suffered the long-term effects of polluted air and filthy runoff. The same was true in Chicago, where, as noted in Chapter 3, zoners put industrial uses in minority neighborhoods. Extensive documentation about zoning's racially motivated origins—with race-based exclusion written explicitly into early codes—suggests less-than-noble motivation behind the long-ago decisions to zone these areas for industrial uses. Many cities' decisions to perpetuate industrial zoning for so long hurt nearby residents across generations.

Unfortunately, the impact of toxic industrial uses on predominantly minority and poor communities is only one discriminatory consequence of too many American zoning codes.

Still more insidious than the influence of industrial zoning is how zoning treats residential uses themselves. Today's seemingly race-neutral zoning in fact has disparate impacts. Because income, race, and ethnicity are interrelated, exclusionary zoning—defined as any provision or combination of provisions, including single-family-only zoning and large lot-size minimums, that make it harder to build housing—tends to keep poor and minority people out of a community by driving up prices. One scholar has determined that 25 percent of racial segregation in the United States results from zoning policies that require low residential densities.

Comparing Houston and West University Place once again illustrates the point. West U practices exclusionary zoning in all the ways described above. Perhaps as a result, its residents are not very diverse—just 7 percent Black or Hispanic, and 17 percent foreign-born—when compared to Houston as a whole (67 percent Black or Hispanic, and 28.9 percent foreign-born). Hartford, which is 85 percent Black, Hispanic, and other people of color, and is one of the poorest cities in the country, is surrounded by wealthy suburbs that are upward of 95 percent White. My research with the Urban Institute found that Connecticut suburbs and towns had more zoning constraints on multifamily housing than the state's larger cities, and that areas with less restrictive zoning had higher concentrations of low-income, Black, Hispanic, and other residents of color. Segregation is not just an urban-suburban issue; it is an issue within cities, too.

Exacerbating income inequality and limiting social mobility, segregation has serious, tangible, and negative effects on individuals and households. Studying five million tax records of families that moved from one county to another between 1996 and 2012, Harvard researchers have found that for every year a low-income child spends in a county with high levels of segregation, he or she earns measurably less income years later as an adult. Such "childhood exposure" effects stem from the fact that minority-dominated segregated communities tend to have more concentrated poverty, more income inequality, and higher crime. At a larger societal level, urban and regional economic conditions are negatively influenced by segregation. The Chicago region, for example, is recognized as one of the most segregated in the country, especially when it comes to Black isolation and Hispanic segregation. This segregation costs an estimated $8 billion in gross domestic product, $4.4 billion in lost income, and 229 lives lost to homicide annually. Across the country, segregation is only getting worse. University of California at Berkeley researchers have showed that residential segregation in the 209 largest cities in the United States has increased over the last thirty years.

The takeaway from all of this is that zoning policies that condemn people to segregated neighborhoods are locking in generational poverty. That is why, in some situations—and especially in neighborhoods with high vacancies—zoning policy changes that may bring a gradual increase in higher-income or White residents should not necessarily be rejected out of hand. Remember Theaster Gates's pointed question: "What do you do in neighborhoods when ain't nobody interested in living there?" Bringing new residents in, including residents of a different race, ethnicity, or economic status, can be healthy for a place that has suffered as a result of long-entrenched racial segregation.

Better-designed land use controls could reduce disparate impacts on racial and ethnic minorities—and keep housing affordable. One place to start is the provision virtually ubiquitous in American zoning codes: the single-family-only zone. A close look at recent changes in Minneapolis illustrates both the promise and limitations of changing single-family zoning.

Segregation in the Twin Cities dates back to 1910, when tens of thousands of White homeowners rushed to record racially restrictive and single-family-only covenants on their properties after Black families began to legally purchase homes in White neighborhoods. The first Minneapolis zoning code, adopted in 1924, reinforced development patterns established by racially restrictive covenants, zoning land for single-family purposes in exactly the same places that these covenants existed, and limiting most multifamily zoning to specific neighborhoods in Minneapolis and St. Paul. Ever since, Blacks, Latinos, and other people of color have lived primarily in these neighborhoods. Perhaps because these neighborhoods have so much rental housing, minority renter households cannot seem to access the path to homeownership. As a result, the Twin Cities region has the highest Black-White homeownership gap in the country, at 51 percentage points. A variety of factors, including financial system practices, have contributed to this reality, but just as in West U, zoning in the Twin Cities has reinforced patterns of exclusion.

Despite a legislative mandate that requires the city to review its comprehensive plan every ten years and then to adopt zoning ordinances implementing the plan, Minneapolis leaders chose to maintain single-family zoning for close to a century. That changed in 2016, when the city launched its most recent decennial comprehensive planning process, "Minneapolis 2040." Local political leaders, planning staff, and advocates engaged with one another to audit and plan for the future of the city. Led by Lisa Bender, a city council member and chair of the council's planning and zoning committee, they floated many different ideas in public forums, soliciting input from a wide range of stakeholders. Janne Flisrand, landlord of a four-unit building (a "fourplex"), became a leading voice for Minneapolis residents. In 2017 she founded a group called Neighbors for More Neighbors (N4MN), aiming to boost public participation in the planning process and to ensure that the resulting plan proved equitable. To encourage participation, N4MN provided babysitting and food, as well as training for people on how to write testimony and how to address the city council. Members deluged the council with hundreds of comments requesting more diverse housing types. They recommended that the city rezone all its single-family neighborhoods to allow duplexes, triplexes, and fourplexes—types of housing they insisted could comfortably sit alongside single-family housing. Members also asked that the zoning code more freely allow accessory dwelling units, which are small apartments on the same lot as a single-family home. Accessory housing can tuck into existing structures and can help homeowners earn a little rental income, making ownership more affordable.

These "middle housing" or "gentle density" proposals were hotly debated, with N4MN mobilizing a chorus of voices urging their adoption. Becoming president of the city council in 2018, Lisa Bender made adoption her top priority. With her leadership, the final plan, which mostly reflected pro-housing advocates' views, was adopted in 2019. By 2021 the city implemented the plan's suggestions in its zoning ordinance. It was said to eliminate single-family zoning because it allowed triplexes—three units, housing a total of three families—across all single-family districts, and fourplexes in some residential districts. It also loosened accessory dwelling unit limitations, legalized single-room occupancy, and eliminated minimum parking requirements.

This type of zoning makes Minneapolis a wild outlier within the Twin Cities metro region as a whole, where nearly three-quarters of all land subject to zoning is restricted to single-family detached homes, more than two-thirds has a minimum lot size of a quarter-acre or more, and less than 10 percent allows duplexes, townhouses, or mobile homes. Given this split, the politics that took shape around these issues deserves mention. As in many zoning battles, a clear division separated the "not-in-my-backyard" (NIMBY) opponents of change from the pro-housing, "yes-in-my-backyard" (YIMBY) proponents. The NIMBY-YIMBY debate is a national one, but it plays out in hundreds of local zoning decisions on specific projects and on proposed amendments to the zoning code. As Flisrand told a U.S. Senate subcommittee in 2023, YIMBY-style change requires three groups: community groups like N4MN, city staff that encourage public participation in zoning policymaking, and elected officials with the courage to enact reforms. Minneapolis had all three, adopting reforms that reflected the collective desires of a more diverse coalition of constituents.

The phrase "eliminate single-family zoning" gained traction in Minneapolis and has become a rallying cry for YIMBY zoning reformers nationally. Yet early returns on the actual production of diverse housing in the city have so far fallen short of expectations: a mere seventy-six units in two- to four-unit buildings were permitted in 2021. The truth is that it was not enough for Minneapolis simply to legalize these new uses. Zoning provisions still continued on the one hand to cap the square footage of these buildings through what is called a "floor-to-area ratio," and to require a minimum floor area of 500 square feet for most housing units. For accessory apartments, the code not only has a minimum of 300 square feet (larger than required by the building code), but a maximum square footage of 1,000 for detached units and 800 square feet for attached units. In other words, you can build, as long as it isn't too big . . . or too small. The code also sets design standards covering materials, entrances, and height—and, more stringent still, requires owner occupancy of the main domicile as a condition of the owner renting out any attached accessory dwelling unit. So unless the owner anticipates a long tenure, he or she may be unlikely to invest in all that is required to create an additional unit. With so many conditions still placed on accessory dwellings and middle housing, it is unlikely that the new code alone will lessen existing segregation or dramatically increase regional housing affordability.

In a recent research paper, I called these under-the-radar restrictions on housing development "zoning by a thousand cuts." If reformers don't heal the thousand cuts—eliminating minimum and maximum unit sizes, floor-to-area ratios, parking mandates, minimum lot sizes, and so much more—multifamily housing is unlikely to get built, no matter what the code theoretically allows. In Connecticut, for example, my research team found that while duplexes were nominally allowed as of right on over a quarter of residential land in the state, they were subject to so many hidden requirements that few duplexes (just 8 percent of the total housing stock) have been built. As for three-or-more-family buildings, we found that 94 percent of Connecticut districts that allow such buildings require a public hearing to obtain a permit. This seemingly innocuous procedural requirement not only adds delays and uncertainty to a project, but may also introduce bias into decision-making. Perhaps worse, it puts the public participation at the wrong time: at the tail end of an application, when an owner has expended sums on planning and design, instead of on the front end, when the rules are being drafted. Planning scholars Michael Lens and Paavo Monkkonen use the thought-provoking phrase "segregation of the affluent" to describe the ways in which these types of substantive and procedural regulatory burdens can effectively maintain the housing status quo, even when zoning has been changed in the hope of creating more diverse and affordable housing. Those seeking to make zoning more equitable will need to possess the kind of bird's-eye view that enables them to go granular on all aspects of a code.

As reformers in Minneapolis and elsewhere work to gather the data and political momentum needed to truly change their code, it's important to emphasize that their efforts must also go beyond merely liberalizing zoning. Property owners need to be educated about their new rights, and banks need to be willing to lend to property owners seeking to build middle housing. To get more voices to the table while decisions are being made, community members should fundraise for food, babysitting, testimony-writing workshops, and other support, as N4MN did in Minneapolis. Market conditions and demand for housing might also require patience, especially where the physical costs of construction exceed the payoff. Changing zoning is a long game, and promoting integration and a more equitable future will not be quick or easy.

Alongside the issue of small-scale housing, which Minneapolis and other places are tackling, comes the question of what to do about larger apartment buildings. After the Supreme Court declared that such buildings are "mere parasite[s]" on single-family neighborhoods, it was pretty clear how things were going to go. Many communities continue to espouse that view, adopting codes that either preclude apartment buildings altogether or relegate them to undesirable areas on the outskirts of town. When multifamily is allowed, it is rarely permitted freely, or "as of right," subject only to a staff review of compliance with the stated requirements in the code. Instead, it is often subject to public hearings and onerous area and bulk requirements. In Connecticut, just 2 percent of land in the state is zoned for as-of-right construction of larger apartment buildings, while 91 percent of land allows for as-of-right single-family housing. Even in locations where apartments make sense—like the many empty office buildings in our post-pandemic era—zoning can throw up substantive and procedural barriers for residential conversions.

In some cases, well-intended zoning policies can go awry. Among the more hotly contested rules being debated in zoning circles today is the requirement that apartment developers create affordable units via "inclusionary zoning" mandates. An inclusionary zoning ordinance requires a developer to reserve a percentage of the proposed housing units in any new apartment development for people with modest incomes or in certain lower-paying occupations. Inclusionary housing policies first sprang up in the 1970s in mid-Atlantic communities around Washington, D.C., and today, roughly nine hundred local governments have inclusionary zoning rules.

Among the latest to adopt them is Pittsburgh, a declining Rust Belt city whose population peaked at 650,000 in 1950 and stands at less than half that today. Last year it gained one new resident in my sister Kathleen, who moved there to spend more time with her boyfriend, Josh, a real estate attorney and developer. Josh brought the city's inclusionary zoning change to my attention—calling it shortsighted and describing how residential project developers stalled projects because of it.

Curious to confirm his anecdotal reports, I dug further into the particulars. Pittsburgh is one of the five poorest large cities in the country, with one-fifth of its residents living below the poverty line. As the city considered the inclusionary housing ordinance—seemingly a welcome measure to address the reality of poverty among its residents—two camps emerged. Proponents argue that integrating affordable and market-rate housing produces better health, economic, and educational outcomes for disadvantaged residents. They also argue that inclusionary zoning could help address the rising rents that had pushed longtime residents from the city. However, no research has shown that inclusionary programs actually create new housing. On the contrary, existing research suggests that inclusionary zoning actually increases overall prices, because developers recoup the costs of building their units by charging more for market-rate units. One study found that in California jurisdictions, supply was reduced by 7 percent and prices increased by 20 percent during a ten-year period in which inclusionary zoning was adopted. Opponents believe that for these reasons, inclusionary zoning constitutes a hidden tax on real estate development.

A Pittsburgh city council committee nonetheless recommended that the city pilot an inclusionary zoning program geared at providing rental housing to households earning no more than 50 percent of area median household income, or homeownership for households earning no more than 80 percent. In 2019, it did so by rezoning select parcels in Lawrenceville, a largely historic and moderately gentrifying neighborhood. Two years later, the pilot program was made permanent, and then the inclusionary housing overlay district expanded into neighboring Bloomfield and Polish Hill. Pittsburgh's inclusionary housing provisions apply to developments with twenty or more units, requiring at least 10 percent of units to be designated affordable. Unlike many jurisdictions with such ordinances, the city does not offer developers the option of tendering a payment in lieu of actually constructing on-site housing. The Pittsburgh zoning code requires a developer to record a deed restriction that maintains the affordability for the rental and ownership units for thirty-five years, with the added provision that the thirty-five-year period begins all over again any time the ownership units are sold. Such restrictions are typical of programs around the country, with 90 percent requiring affordability periods lasting thirty years or longer.

That all sounds promising, and yet Pittsburgh's experiment with inclusionary zoning presents a puzzle. Prior to the adoption of the new rules, the city did not appear to have a very active housing development scene. Between 2017 and 2021, the city issued building permits for an annual average of just 644 units of housing, about four in five in multifamily buildings. These figures suggest that market-rate development was already difficult. Adding an inclusionary zoning requirement makes it more expensive for residents who fall outside of the affordable housing criteria. Developers have railed against the new rules, saying that they will make new housing construction financially infeasible. The Builders Association of Metropolitan Pittsburgh filed a federal lawsuit alleging violation of its members' property rights and seeking an injunction to stop the city from enforcing the ordinance. It claimed that developers would suffer economic losses because the ordinance requires them to offer units at prices below market rates, to make amenities like gyms and pools available to occupants of the affordable units, and to suffer unreasonable constraints on rental and sale of the units.

While the success of this suit strikes me as doubtful, the filing itself speaks to the anger about and concern over the zoning change, and research suggests that those opposing Pittsburgh's adoption of this ordinance may be right. Fifty years after their inception, inclusionary zoning ordinances remain an unproven mechanism for creating new housing except in areas where strong demand for housing and the likelihood of profits keeps developers in the game. Especially in low-growth, struggling cities like Pittsburgh, the better path toward creating housing is likely loosening zoning barriers, not creating new ones.

———

It's easy to get the gloomy impression that no place correctly zones for optimal housing outcomes: Houston is too loose, while West U is too rigid; Minneapolis tried with its middle housing and other proposals but didn't quite get it right; Pittsburgh legislated for expanded affordability, and possibly ended up shooting itself in the foot. I don't want anyone to get the wrong idea. Such outcomes testify not to the impossibility of good zoning, but merely to its difficulty. In addition to the obstacles that persist in systems still structured by long-outdated land use regulations is the uncomfortable fact that sometimes even policies that seem conducive to making housing more equitable may not, in the end, actually accomplish the goal. Such outcomes demand that planners remain ever alert to the sometimes unexpected ways that policies play out. So along with flexibility goes a necessary humility.

Meanwhile, local authorities across the United States are experimenting with many other specific zoning techniques intended to enable more affordable housing, more diverse housing, and simply more housing. Communities like Jackson, Wyoming, and Aspen, Colorado, are trying to figure out how to house the workers who sustain their tourist economies. Large cities, including New York and San Francisco, are crafting policies to reduce the price-hiking impact of overseas investors and Airbnb-type short-term renters on their rental and homebuyers' markets. Others, like the college town of Ames, Iowa, have wrestled with their definition of "family," often restricted to relatives by blood or marriage, to balance their need to house students against the need to keep frat parties out of the quieter neighborhoods.

For our part in Hartford—a low-growth, low-income city, where 40 percent of the city's housing stock is deed-restricted affordable—we took some unusual steps to generate new possibilities. For one thing, we eliminated public hearings for all housing applications, a rare and possibly unique move for a city of Hartford's size. As a result, almost 50 percent of land in the city allows multifamily housing as of right (and 60 percent allows duplexes as of right). That means that city staff only review an application's compliance with specific requirements of the code. Property owners do not have to undergo a full public hearing, saving time and expense. The code also allows accessory dwelling units with any single-family home, and there are no inclusionary zoning mandates. While Houston's success suggests that communities should reduce lot-size mandates, in Hartford we went further and eliminated them altogether. We're seeing the fruits of these streamlining measures in hundreds of multifamily housing units, and if Hartford sees more demand for residential living, maybe we'll see more property owners taking advantage of the new rules to add more units.

Abundant, inexpensive housing benefits renters and first-time home buyers, and particularly facilitates access for young families, older singles, and people of color, who frequently experience housing insecurity in more expensive or more homogeneous markets. While it is easy for planners to get lost in the myriad details of any zoning initiative or controversy, it's important to keep the big picture in sight. Different localities face their own problems, and solutions perforce must be tailored to address those particulars, but zoning should always make it as easy as possible to build more housing—and thus for the people who live there to make it *home*.

A Bigger Menu for Movement

"A wonderful welcome to you who are worshipping in the drive-in congregation this morning," pronounced a beaming Robert Schuller on February 8, 1970. "Don't toot your horn, but just smile at me through the windshield." So began the very first *Hour of Power*, a church-service broadcast that's still running on television today—and one that owes its early success in part to zoning rules that prioritize cars and car travel above every other way of getting around.

Schuller was a vehicular kind of preacher from the get-go. Fifteen years earlier, he held his first drive-in church service at the Orange Drive-In Theater in Anaheim—renting it and its massive parking lot on Sunday mornings, when it was not being used for movies, and delivering his homily from the tarpaper roof of the snack bar. His congregation grew apace with the sprawling southeastern suburbs of Los Angeles. Just four months after Schuller's initial rooftop sermon, Disneyland opened its doors, putting Anaheim on a global stage and attracting hordes of tourists. Riding this wave, Schuller quickly raised money to buy twenty-two acres of land for a permanent worship facility just a mile down the road from Disneyland, in the city of Garden Grove. In 1959 he audaciously hired the internationally renowned Austrian-American modernist architect Richard Neutra, tasking him with building a facility that would allow Schuller to preach simultaneously to crowds seated both indoors and in their cars. The new building, surrounded by 1,700 parking spaces where drivers sat in what Neutra called "pews from Detroit," held its first service in 1961. A multi-story glass wall opened to reveal an indoor-outdoor balcony from which Schuller launched his sermons.

Abetted by these impressive digs, the soaring popularity of *Hour of Power* translated into financial contributions to the church, which enabled Schuller to commission yet another world-renowned architect, Philip Johnson, to design a larger hall on the now thirty-four-acre campus. In 1981 the Crystal Cathedral, seating about 3,000 people, opened for worship. Said to be the largest glass building in the world, at 78,000 square feet, it included two movable ninety-foot glass walls that opened to the parking lots. A 2003 visitor center by architect Richard Meier rounded out a remarkable trifecta of works by three of the world's greatest twentieth-century architects. Yet there is one incongruity in the arrangement: All these buildings are depressingly encircled by acres of parking lots, their unique architecture stranded in a sea of asphalt.

The Crystal Cathedral complex is emblematic of the car-centric developments that sprang up virtually everywhere in the United States after World War II. Such developments were part and parcel of a shift in the organization of American society, one based on an ever more widespread devotion, for which Schuller's church provided both a locus and a metaphor: the worship of the automobile. While the advent of our car-based, suburban way of life can seem inevitable in retrospect, it's important to point out that its foundational structural realities were not driven by the popular demands of the market. Rather, they were spurred by federal policy, and especially the government's response to the needs of returning World War II veterans for housing.

To meet this need, the Federal Housing Administration heavily sub-sidized the construction of new suburbs, residential neighborhoods that were accessible only by car—and only to certain types of people. The location of this investment was premised on the notion that White veter-ans deserved better than to live in central cities, which increasingly were deemed unsafe and decaying. As historian Richard Rothstein has chron-icled, while these suburbs were theoretically available to all, only White veterans ended up living in them. The Federal Housing Administration gave preferable terms to developers building White-only subdivisions, such as the massive Levittown development in Long Island. The agency also developed underwriting guidelines for mortgages that "redlined" majority-Black neighborhoods, deeming them too high risk for loans. Blacks were further prevented from moving into newly created neighbor-hoods by banks that refused to lend to them, by racially restrictive cove-nants, and sometimes by blatant intimidation.

To ensure that the new subdivisions endured as they were originally built, the Federal Housing Administration called on local governments to adopt zoning laws restricting them to large-lot, single-family housing. The development of the interstate highway system after the Federal Aid High-way Act of 1956 accelerated the construction of the infrastructure that would help more people move between urban cores and their suburban homes, leading to more residential subdivisions in farther-flung areas. A massive amount of new development centered around cars and was locked into place through zoning, which established sprawl as the primary mode of development ever after.

Having the ability to move around is as essential to our lives and our well-being as having food and a roof over our head. But too many commu-nities are zoned in ways that prevent this and instead facilitate car-centric environments. As in suburban Houston and Connecticut, exclusively single-family neighborhoods and excessively large minimum lot sizes have proven to be two provisions that work together to condemn people to drive virtually everywhere. They result in sparsely developed neighbor-hoods that put residents far from the goods and services they need. Among the condemned were me and my sister, doing homework in the back seat of our parents' aptly named Suburban.

As for those who might have preferred to travel by bus or train, the new suburbs stymied any such hopes. They were not dense enough to support government investment in public transit, like buses or commuter trains. The result was a closed loop of car-based daily routines, with no alternatives. By now, decades later, American sprawl has dramatically increased the number of "vehicle miles traveled"—the total number of miles we travel in cars—to over three trillion annually. This has, in turn, increased our reliance on fossil fuels and driven up greenhouse gas emissions. Transportation now accounts for 28 percent of such emissions, the most of any economic sector. Indeed, my team in Connecticut found that towns that zone most of their single-family-zoned land to require minimum lot sizes of two or more acres per home have 35 percent higher vehicle miles traveled and 36 percent higher transportation-related emissions, on average, than other towns.

In addition to the long-range environmental costs that will be borne collectively, all that driving becomes very expensive for households. In Connecticut, for instance, it costs upward of $10,000 more per year to own a vehicle than to subsist on public transit, and on average 20 percent of the household incomes of Connecticut residents is spent on transportation—a figure well above the 15 percent cost threshold that experts consider affordable. Unsurprisingly, this affordability gap primarily burdens Connecticut's poor, who spend more of their incomes on transportation than they should, which makes it harder for them to afford the other things they need. Many Connecticut residents—14 percent overall and about a quarter of urban residents—are also transportation insecure, lacking the resources needed to move from one place to another in a safe or efficient manner. That makes it harder for them to get to work and school, to the grocery store or to doctor's appointments. Nationally, the problem is even worse, with nearly a quarter of all adults, and more than half of those living below the poverty line, experiencing transportation insecurity. Again, as might be expected, those affected are disproportionately people of color who live in urban areas.

We don't have to view this situation as inevitable. Changing zoning can open up a broader menu of choices and foster a stronger and more resilient transportation system—one that will promote transportation security, and provide people with multiple, affordable ways of getting around. Rezoning residential neighborhoods to have a broader mix of uses and to be denser are the two most effective ways to do that. But both these changes will take a mindset shift among elected officials and other policymakers, and most likely require a lengthy time horizon. Once again we must play the long game: it's vitally important to undertake ambitious strategies and stick by them. Meanwhile, though, there's one zoning provision that can be changed easily in the short term, with significant benefits.

The simplest and most direct way that zoning furthers car-centric infrastructure is by requiring developers to build it. I'm not talking about highways, but something far more quotidian: parking. Zoning codes almost always mandate a certain number of parking spaces for different uses that can be built in a particular place—housing, offices, hotels, movie theaters, hardware stores, and so on. Properties affected must include that specified number of "off-street" parking spaces on the same lot as the building itself. When there are multiple uses in the same lot, say shops downstairs and apartments above, the requirements for each use are often added together, rather than shared. Ubiquitous in zoning codes since the 1950s, these parking requirements have created decentralized, privately funded infrastructure that facilitates driving. At first glance, this might seem logical: if people drive, why not ensure they can easily park their cars? And yet anyone surveying the ills of conventional zoning would be hard-pressed to find another technical provision that causes as much harm.

To grasp the nature of that harm, consider the story of a bank in the small downtown of Sandpoint, Idaho, population 8,300. When applying for a zoning permit to expand in 2009, the bank's owners were told they needed to build 118 more parking spaces to satisfy the town's zoning code, which required a parking space for every few hundred square feet of the bank. To meet this obligation, the bank purchased adjacent properties, demolished historic buildings, and evicted numerous small businesses. This is no anomalous case. All over the country, parking requirements, especially those imposed in urban locations or small-town "main streets," have resulted in the teardown of historic buildings. Sandpoint not only saw beloved buildings and businesses destroyed but also its municipal coffers depleted, because property owners pay far less in property taxes for parking lots than for buildings. In Hartford, for instance, parking lots that should be buildings cost the city a badly needed $50 million a year in uncollected revenue.

Now consider a housing development subject to the typical American zoning requirement of two parking spaces per apartment. Multiplying the number of required spaces by the number of apartments proposed, the typical developer often ends up building as much or more parking than housing. Two spaces occupy about 700 square feet—as big as or bigger than many apartment units. This is significant not only as a comparison, but as an actual building constraint, since space devoted to parking cannot simultaneously be used for housing. If there are other uses (like a retail shop or hair salon) on the lot, the developer follows the code-required formula, then adds the residential parking requirement, rounding up to the next whole parking space. In this way, the required parking for a unit that has been built renders another unit impossible to build. Beside making housing scarcer, parking mandates also make it more expensive, disproportionately hurting people with lower incomes—including those without access to cars to begin with. Lest you think that an empty space must at least be cheap to develop, a 2014 study by UCLA professor Donald Shoup found that it costs a jaw-dropping $34,000 to build a single underground parking space and $24,000 to build one in a parking structure, price tags that have surely risen since. Parking requirements add to maintenance costs, too, since lots must be repaved, lighting replaced, and striping repainted. Developers pass these costs on to tenants or buyers by raising monthly rents or increasing sales prices, a practice extensively documented for the housing sector, where estimates have ranged from a 10 percent parking premium to an average per-unit increase of about $86,000. Moreover, these requirements reduce the developer's incentive to build smaller, more affordable units, because rents from larger units are more likely to subsidize the extra costs of parking.

All these parking spaces also have serious ramifications for the environment. Pavement contributes to polluted stormwater runoff that ultimately ends up in our watersheds. Pavement traps heat, adding to the urban heat-island effect, which is the increase in temperature caused by hardscapes and buildings in urbanized areas. And parking minimums actually lead to more driving, and in turn more greenhouse gas emissions. Obviously, people with cars drive more than people without cars, and research has shown that when the cost of parking is "bundled" with the price of housing, and its cost thus hidden, people are 60 to 80 percent less likely to be vehicle-free. According to one study, an increase in parking from 0.1 to 0.5 spaces per resident led to a 30-percentage-point increase in commuters who chose to drive.

Finally, there's the aesthetic dimension. No one ever said they wanted to take a pleasant stroll through a parking lot. Parking lots that bump up to sidewalks or streets, parking lots that replace buildings, parking lots without landscaping, parking lots stretching as far as the eye can see. You don't need to be Joni Mitchell, singing about paving paradise, to see how these all detract from the quality of our daily experience.

Given the costs imposed by parking mandates, you might think that they were developed through well-established studies showing a clear need. But no. Shoup refutes that misconception. "Where do minimum parking requirements come from?" he asks, and answers: "No one knows." Shoup notes that planning directors generally establish parking standards either by surveying nearby cities or by consulting *Parking Generation*, a manual published by the Institute of Transportation Engineers (ITE) and purporting to identify peak parking space use through surveys of ITE members. Shoup criticizes both methods as flawed. Regarding the first, he mentions the "serious problem" of replicating past mistakes: if a zoning administrator from one jurisdiction picked numbers out of the sky, then others who follow suit simply repeat the error. As for the second, he points out that the ITE bases 22 percent of its parking generation rates on a single survey, and half on four or fewer surveys, none of them current. He also charges that the surveys fail to gather responses relevant to urban locations, locations near public transportation, and off-peak times, likely overstating parking demand.

The city of Garden Grove, home to the Crystal Cathedral, epitomized the postwar boom, the influx of returning GIs transforming it from a rural farming community with a few hundred residents to a suburb of 4,000 people by 1950. In 1956, these new residents voted to incorporate Garden Grove as a city. As tract housing overtook agricultural land, Garden Grove for a while became the fastest-growing city in America, burgeoning to 84,000 residents by 1960—sixteen-fold growth in a single decade. No sooner had it incorporated as a city and adopted a zoning code than it was sued by a disgruntled property owner—a religious congregation denied a permit to erect a church in a residential district. According to the city, the congregation had submitted an application with inadequate parking spaces and poorly designed driveways. Upholding the city's decision, the court said that the city had appropriately considered parking needs in rejecting the permit. So Garden Grove, like so many cities before and after it, regulated the heck out of parking.

Today, as then, most of Garden Grove (population 170,000) belongs to a residential district devoted to single-family detached housing. For ordinary single-family housing, the zoning code requires four parking spaces, two in garages and two outside. Given that families consisting of one or two adults and one or two children occupy most of these homes, a four-parking-space minimum seems a little much. It is especially excessive considering that lots in this district need only be a third of an acre large. On the smaller lots in the city, in other words, easily a tenth of a lot might have to be paved to meet the city's parking mandates.

The requirements differ for multifamily housing, which is mostly clustered around the city's primary commercial thoroughfare, Garden Grove Boulevard. For these developments, the zoning code requires 2.75 parking spaces for studio and one- and two-bedroom apartments, and 3.5 parking spaces for three-bedroom apartments. Common sense would dictate that even in car-happy Los Angeles someone living in a studio apartment is unlikely to have three cars to park. On the flip side of excess supply of parking is the problem of excess supply constraints on housing: Garden Grove's parking mandates effectively limit the number of housing units that can be built on any given lot. Doing the math, someone seeking to build ten one-bedroom units would need to provide twenty-eight parking spaces on the same lot as the housing. Using a rule of thumb of requiring 350 square feet of land for each parking space, plus circulation, the parking would occupy 10,000 square feet, or about a quarter of an acre. That is a significant limitation on the footprint of any proposed building.

The curious might ask how much parking the Crystal Cathedral, consecrated as a Catholic cathedral in 2019, would legally be required to provide. For "religious assembly" uses, Garden Grove requires one parking space for every three fixed seats, plus one space for every 250 square feet of gross floor area not used for assembly purposes. With new pews expanding seating capacity to 3,000, the code would require 1,000 parking spaces for the worship-hall seating. Estimating that 15,000 gross square feet of the building serve auxiliary functions, an additional sixty spaces would be required, making a total of 1,060. The current lot, accommodating 1,700 cars, means the cathedral is 600 spaces overparked, 60 percent beyond the excessive standards of the Garden Grove zoning code. This oversupply reflects the ethos of a place whose very existence derives from catering to drivers' spiritual needs, a congregation on wheels, with a vast parking lot as its asphalt sanctuary.

I wish I could say that the ska punk band Sublime's song "Garden Grove," about driving around the suburb in a smelly van, depicts an atypically dystopian scene. Or that Garden Grove's requirements are particularly onerous, owing to the fact that Los Angelenos depends so heavily on cars. Unfortunately, it's all sadly typical.

To loosen the car's chokehold on our communities, a few jurisdictions have combined parking reforms with a multifaceted approach to the many transportation issues that can be addressed by zoning. Buffalo has received the most attention, so let's spend a little time in the City of Good Neighbors, which could hardly be more different from Garden Grove.

Once an industrial boomtown, Buffalo at the turn of the twentieth century was reputed to have more millionaires per capita than any other American city. Today, one can catch a glimpse of the city's former wealth in the presence of restored masterpieces from such architectural luminaries as Frank Lloyd Wright and Henry Hobson Richardson, and landscapes created by Frederick Law Olmsted. But Buffalo has fallen on hard times, a poor city struggling like many postindustrial American cities searching for a new identity. In fall 2017 I visited the city with two of my kids, setting an itinerary focused on the historic places toward which we gravitate when traveling. Louis Sullivan's Guaranty Building topped my list. Built near Buffalo City Hall in 1896 by some of those millionaires, this thirteen-story skyscraper combined an innovative steel structure with a terra-cotta curtain wall, all arranged in a simple classical style. Even on a cloudy day, the exquisitely detailed tile exuded warmth and beauty. A triumph! But as we walked around, seeing few other people on that Saturday afternoon, it was clear that while Sullivan's building had been preserved, something awful had happened to the places around it. Then it hit me: downtown had been swallowed up by parking.

To understand zoning's shameful role in creating these parking craters, we should look not at Buffalo's original 1926 code, adopted during the first wave of American zoning code enactments, but to its second, adopted in 1953, just as the automobile roared into American households and the urban-suburban exodus began nationwide. Many provisions in the second code—from single-use zoning to minimum lot-size mandates to parking requirements—squarely aimed to reorient a dense, vibrant, and walkable city around cars. Around the same time that code took effect, the city

doubled down on highway construction and road expansions and disman-
tled a streetcar system that had successfully ferried passengers for about
seventy years. Maybe Buffalo's leaders thought that doing everything they
could to promote cars was good for residents working in factories manufacturing steel and automobile parts. Perhaps, as Hartford's leaders did
at around the same time, they thought the city should ensure that those
who fled to the suburbs still found it comfortable and convenient to zip
into their downtown offices. Whatever the rationale, the city's approach
proved fateful, as fully half of downtown buildings ultimately fell to parking, and over-wide roads plowed through thriving neighborhoods. As the
years went by, the city lost both industry and people—with less than half
of the roughly 580,000 people it had when the 1953 code took effect. And
downtown gained that desolate feeling we registered that bleak Saturday
we visited.

There are only so many things that a half-full city like Buffalo can do to
attract the population, wealth, and vibrancy it enjoyed in its heyday. Bringing the streetcars back would be amazing, but few public entities would
spend the billions necessary to hear that clang again. Tearing down highways costs money too, though Buffalonians have long agitated federal officials for just that. One of the things a city can control, though, is the way
it uses its power to regulate the activities taking place within its bounds.
When it comes to the rules of the real estate game, there's no better place
to start than zoning.

In 2016, Buffalo took as much as it could into its own hands, adopting
an entirely new land development ordinance and dubbing it the "Green
Code." Among its positive changes are the small one I mentioned in Chapter 1: re-legalization of small-scale commercial uses in historic residential
areas. But the code is also chock-full of bigger changes on housing and sustainable design. Interestingly, the Green Code is best known for making
Buffalo one of the first major cities to undertake citywide parking reform.
Upon first read of the code, one provision gave me pause about its effect:
the requirement that developers of new construction over 5,000 square
feet, substantial renovations over 40,000 square feet, or changes in the use

of an existing building submit a transportation demand management plan describing how they will reduce the number of solo car rides and the number of vehicle miles traveled by site users, and promote alternative forms of transportation (walking, biking, and public transit). Such plans can be expensive and time-consuming, though the problem is less their cost than the fact that the city planning board can require off-street parking after reviewing them. When I first read the code, it seemed to me that Buffalo did not really put the final nail in the parking-requirement coffin.

As I read on, though, I noticed other aspects of the Green Code that deserve praise. As part of the transportation-demand management plan requirement, the code suggests several strategies that developers might include, such as free or subsidized transit passes and carpooling programs or benefits. Not every developer of a large building would naturally think of these types of programs for the eventual occupants. In addition, the city has instituted changes that will result in new infrastructure for "active transportation," a term that includes walking, biking, and public transportation. The Green Code specifically spells out how property owners must site their buildings to ensure safer pedestrian access to parking lots and public transit. In addition, multifamily residences, hotels, shops, and offices must provide long-term and short-term bicycle parking. The number of spaces required is determined on a per bed or per dwelling unit basis for residential uses (for example one for every five apartments), or a per square foot of gross area basis for most other uses. Instead of requiring infrastructure for cars, the city requires infrastructure for walkers and bikers—in other words, for actual people.

The national attention Buffalo received after passing the code attracted development. When we visited, less than a year after the Green Code was passed, it was too early to see the impacts of the change. But you certainly see it today—and, as it turns out, I shouldn't have worried so much about the transportation-demand management provision. In 2020, the Census revealed that Buffalo's decennial population increased for the first time in seventy years. Since the Green Code was adopted, over ten thousand units of multifamily housing have been built. When my kids and I were there, we enjoyed visiting Canalside, a development at the historic terminus of the Erie Canal, which now includes a boardwalk, beer garden, paddleboats, and a roller rink. A study of fourteen mixed-use projects built in the three years after the Green Code was adopted showed that about half of major developments included fewer parking spaces than were previously required, and four provided no parking at all. All in all, Buffalo paved the way for other cities to build on its work. Perhaps in time, Sullivan's lonely masterpiece will have new neighbors.

In the years since Buffalo's reforms, other major cities have enacted similar reforms or expanded suites of changes. San Diego, Nashville, and Chicago have eliminated minimum parking requirements around transit, in and around the downtown, and near certain commercial corridors, respectively. The thinking behind these changes has been that people taking light rail or bus rapid transit, or people living or working in more densely populated mixed-use areas probably don't need a car to get around. The rural Idaho town of Sandpoint—the one that required a bank to build 118 parking spaces—also repealed parking minimums for its downtown. That repeal allowed a local taqueria to add new seating, while a growing tech startup remained in town, both impossible before, because they could not pack the additional parking required onto their lots. Moreover, the town allowed nearby properties with different functions, like offices and residential buildings, to apply for approval to share parking facilities, rather than each providing their own.

More recent efforts have promoted citywide reform, rather than reforms targeting just one area of town. We have already mentioned how during comprehensive planning and zoning reviews, Hartford—which I maintain is the first major city to completely eliminate minimum parking requirements—and Minneapolis eliminated minimum parking requirements. It is worth noting that Hartford's code also imposed maximum parking caps for every use, which are intended to prohibit overexpansive lots like those at the Crystal Cathedral. Our parking design requirements, too, require the inclusion of trees, landscaping, and decorative details to improve the aesthetics of lots. Like Buffalo, Hartford requires individual property owners to provide minimum bicycle parking spaces for nearly every use beyond small-scale housing. New offices, hospitals, and college buildings must include a shower and changing facility for 0.5 percent of full-time occupants—facilities often pushed by bike advocates to enable riders to commute to their workplaces. In Minneapolis, Janne Flisrand has hinted that vocal public debates around middle housing likely distracted the NIMBYs from focusing on the parking changes—thus smoothing the way to their passage. But the politics of parking minimums are rapidly shifting, with broader coalitions supporting repeals.

A couple more examples from the West Coast can round out the discussion—if only to illuminate how different cities have addressed the same issue. In 2018, San Francisco repealed virtually all minimum parking requirements while, like Hartford, establishing the maximum number of spaces allowed on each lot. For housing around the commercial areas of Pacific Avenue, for example, the code provides a cap of 0.5 parking spaces for an apartment, or up to one space only if the property owner successfully navigates an extra round of reviews. These are tight maximums, worth duplicating elsewhere. To address the possibility that property owners might apply for a variance, or a legal right to deviate from these requirements, the code identifies fifteen districts for which no variances for parking requirements will be granted under any circumstances. While this may seem draconian, city leaders thought it necessary to clamp down on a persistent urban ill. Sometimes, reversing the status quo means turning inside-out the old, car-centric priorities and the codes that promoted them.

As San Francisco was repealing its minimums, Sacramento—an arguably more car-centric city a hundred miles away—was experimenting with a broad range of smaller-scale reforms. Sacramento slashed parking minimums by half for affordable and senior housing, eliminated them for locations within a quarter mile of an existing or proposed light rail station, and reduced them by half for locations about a ten-minute walk from such stations. The city also fully exempted small residential lots of 6,400 square feet or less; the nonresidential uses in mixed-use buildings that were mostly residential; and historic buildings converted to residential use. Finally, the zoning code divided the city up into four parking districts, including a central business district that had no parking minimums and a maximum of one space per 400 square feet for commercial uses, as well as bike parking requirements. The other three districts reduced parking mandates from the prior version of the code as well. After incrementally testing the waters, Sacramento, too, eliminated minimum parking mandates in 2021. Its decision is especially interesting given that the same proportion of people drive in Sacramento as in Los Angeles County. It gives some hope for Garden Grove. As the Sandpoint, Idaho, planning director pointed out, just "one line of your zoning code can make a world of difference."

Zoning, like many other arts of governance, is a matter of carrots and sticks, deploying regulations to encourage some kinds of development and to discourage others. Once cities erase parking minimums and their attendant terrible consequences, and zone for active transportation, they can round out their reforms by enabling dense development around transit lines and stations. Called "transit-oriented development," this strategy creates mixed-use, medium-to-high-density development around nodes of transit, which tend to thrive in densely developed areas. Buses can successfully operate along many commercial and residential thoroughfares, in busy cities and suburban areas, and even through and between smaller towns. Light rail and trams, which depend on fixed tracks, require more clustered development to ensure ridership, though some car-dependent places like Dallas, Atlanta, and Seattle have laid light rail tracks first, with density coming after. Subways and monorails, colossally expensive, have only worked in our very densest cities, including Washington, D.C., New York, and Boston.

Cities interested in transit-oriented development can pull several different zoning levers. Focusing on fixed stations (rather than, say, ordinary bus stops, which move as routes change), they can identify the areas around the station to be rezoned; a half-mile radius from the station, about a ten-minute walk, is a good place to start. Then they can identify the best mix of uses—the more, the better—and make these uses as-of-right to fast-track their permitting. They can also strip away minimum lot sizes, which force buildings farther apart and make density impossible. And they can focus on the building itself: removing or increasing caps on height, which often unreasonably limit the number of stories for our buildings; eliminating or increasing lot coverage caps, or the amount of a lot that can be covered by buildings; and eliminating floor-to-area ratios that establish a formula tying the amount of buildable area to the size of the lot.

In pushing for these changes, cities shouldn't lose sight of the need to provide housing for all. San Diego's elimination of parking requirements around transit has been combined with another zoning provision—its density bonus program, which gives developers permission to build more square footage in exchange for the developer providing affordable housing units. Incentives to build affordable housing in high-growth areas may well work better than mandates in slow-growth areas, like the inclusionary zoning ordinance that has flopped in Pittsburgh. But, once again, it's critical to take a comprehensive look at removing barriers and building the right incentives. The density bonus program in San Diego produced just 145 units (15 affordable) in 2016, before the elimination of parking minimums. But in 2020, the year after parking mandates were lifted, the program produced 3,283 homes (over 1,500 affordable), many in the transit areas and many in 100 percent–affordable buildings made more financially viable when they did not have to provide parking.

States, too, can get in the transit-oriented zoning game. After all, when it comes to zoning, states hold all the cards. They're also more likely to see the big picture. That was true in Massachusetts, where through the 2010s state leaders observed an increasingly acute housing shortage driving some of the highest housing prices in the country. At some point, they realized that much of the land near the state's extensive public transportation network, concentrated in Boston and its suburbs but serving half of the state's cities and towns, was underutilized, devoted to low-density, single-family development. In 2021, the governor and legislature responded by enacting a law requiring 177 cities and towns in the state to allow more as-of-right multifamily housing near subway and commuter rail stations. The law directed these cities and towns to rezone to create least one district "of reasonable size" within walking distance of a station that allows at least fifteen units per acre, as of right. (That's fifteen times denser than most lots in the neighboring states of Connecticut and New Hampshire.) Boston, far denser overall, is exempt from these requirements. Local governments that fail to comply will be ineligible for certain state grants for housing and capital improvements. In this case, the "stick" of funding loss demonstrates seriousness. But the proof will be in the pudding, as my dad says: namely, in how these individual zoning codes are written and administered. It's possible that the exclusionary suburbs near Boston will dream up novel means of subverting the law's intent. One can imagine a clever local zoning official trying to limit apartments to elderly-only units or studios and one-bedrooms—apartments less likely to bring children (and in turn, theoretical costs to the town). State legislators already thought of that move, mandating in the 2021 law that multifamily housing "shall be without age restrictions and shall be suitable for families with children." I predict state legislators will have to play a bit of Whac-A-Mole, tweaking the law to curb creative bad actors.

Part of what I have tried to illuminate in this chapter is the way in which outcomes are predetermined by infrastructure, which in turn is determined in significant part by zoning. The task of changing how we organize our living and working environments requires, perhaps above all, an effort of imagination—and not only by planners and civic leaders, but by regular citizens accustomed to the way things are. The facts around us demand that we question the status quo and revise our assumptions. But we often default to skepticism about alternatives, even to an unexamined and fatalistic belief that this status quo reflects a "natural" state of things. It doesn't. Any given arrangement of social reality is in fact the result of hundreds of decisions made in the past.

Anyone interested in working for change is helped enormously by existing examples of where we might like to get to. Sometimes we find these examples in unexpected places. For those skeptical about market demand for transit-oriented development, I recommend a visit to Disney—not the one near Crystal Cathedral, but the campus on the East Coast. An all-American kingdom of forty-three square miles, Florida's Disney World is about the same size as San Francisco and bigger than Hartford and Garden Grove combined. It moves over a million people a week with a sophisticated, multimodal transportation fleet. Upon arriving there, visitors must park in one of the vast lots accommodating thousands of cars each, all located on the periphery of the theme parks. Once they abandon their cars, Disney Transport whisks them to their various destinations. The Disney system boasts 350 buses (the third largest fleet in Florida), a gondola, 750 boats (making it the world's fifth largest navy), a monorail with twelve trains (among the most used in the world, with 150,000 daily riders), and small-capacity vans (called "Minnie Vans"). Surveys show that riders do not complain about leaving their cars behind. Far from it. Instead, most revel in a feeling of freedom. For a few fleeting days, Disney World charms them, as one of the only self-contained communities in America to ban personal cars. Though Disney World itself lacks typical zoning authority, its enduring popularity suggests that people might actually be willing to use, and might even enjoy using, modes of transportation beyond the car. In an America that's still all too dependent on cars, making it possible to experience life without cars is part of the magic of the Magic Kingdom. Through zoning, we can make that magic more viable in more places.

———

Over half a century ago, just up the road from the site of what would soon become the other Disney, the very first *Hour of Power* service ended with an exhortation that Robert Schuller later made the title of a bestselling book: "Remember: You can become the person you want to be." As it stands now, most of us are Reverend Schullers, called by higher forces to practice an automobile ministry, surrounded by our asphalt sanctuaries. But is that who we want to be?

Change never stops, and in figuring out how best to transport ourselves we will need to continue to adapt as new ways of moving emerge. Among

current trends, car-share and ride-hailing services have changed our patterns of traffic, requiring more loading areas and diverting both riders and
revenue from public transportation. Self-driving autonomous vehicles are
laying claim to our streets. And massive subsidies of personal electric vehicles and charging stations reinforce the car as the primary way of getting
around. I've laid out how we can start to reverse the ways in which zoning
has perpetuated a reliance on cars via an infrastructure that forces us to
use them. The creation of this reality, as we have seen, was a multifaceted
project. Our strategies must be similarly multifaceted if we want to curb
cars' strong hold on our communities and move toward a richer mix of
transportation options, one that makes our lives better.

You Reap What You Zone

J ust north of Hartford's downtown sits an indoor-outdoor concert venue which, in 2018, hosted Farm Aid, the annual benefit concert created by music legends Willie Nelson, Neil Young, and John Mellencamp. Farm Aid first convened musicians and fans in 1985 to promote family farms, bring young people and veterans into farming, and curb the influence and spread of industrial agricultural operations. Centering its mission in its operations, the organization invites local producers and regional farms to sell their goods, offers farming demonstrations in its "Homegrown Village," and composts on a truly epic scale. In the days before the actual concert, Farm Aid also hosts local events, including the community panel where they asked me to discuss the role of zoning in promoting sustainable food production. I'll never forget hearing the incredible Chris Stapleton for the first time a couple days later—and seeing Willie Nelson perform live once again.

As someone who grew up working in family restaurants, I've always had a strong interest in food. And next to housing and transportation, it's among the most basic of human needs. Yet, while serving on Hartford's planning and zoning commission, I realized how little I knew about the economic and social policy dimensions of our food system. Fortunately, members of the city's Food Policy Commission had the patience to help me and my fellow zoning commissioners understand the urgency of food insecurity, defined by the USDA as the lack of consistent access to enough food for each member of the household to lead an active, healthy life. About one in ten Americans, and a third of those living below the poverty line, suffer from food insecurity. In Connecticut, high housing and transportation costs (driven in large part by zoning policies) take a disproportionate chunk of household income, and the state's food insecurity is worse than the national average, afflicting one in six residents—and 28 percent of those living in Hartford and the state's other cities.

Many food-insecure households live in "food deserts," or areas with limited access to healthy and affordable foods, such as fruits, vegetables, grains, and dairy products. The U.S. Department of Agriculture reports more than 6,500 Census tracts qualify as food deserts, noting that the incidence of food deserts is higher in Census tracts where residents have high poverty rates, lower income and education levels, and higher unemployment rates. Cities are, by definition, crowded places, and we tend to think of them as having correspondingly numerous basic amenities. A lot of people, a lot of groceries, right? Too many parts of Hartford, including the Albany Avenue area that I toured that hot summer day with Denise Best, lack conventional grocery stores with full produce sections, reliable farmers' markets, or other equivalent fresh-food outlets. Instead, they have only convenience stores selling canned or processed foods—and fast-food restaurants selling worse.

The issue of food production taken up by Farm Aid and the issue of food security addressed by the Hartford Food Policy Commission are intricately linked. The public sector has a huge influence on how farmers farm, and how much they produce, through a variety of means: production and insurance subsidies, guaranteed contracts, conservation incentives, land trusts, and international trade deals. But zoning can play a large role, too. It can promote sustainable food production by specifying the location and the scale at which farming and ranching are allowed, from community gardeners to industrial farms, and can also dictate where and how fresh food may be sold. One way of combating food insecurity is to make it easier for people to produce food near where it's needed most.

In colonial days, life in Boston revolved around residents' ability to produce food. The early city was rich with common grazing and farming lands, including the Boston Common, used as a pasture for the city's wealthiest families starting in the 1630s and continuing for two hundred years. During that time, virtually every Boston household used vegetable gardens or raised chickens, goats, or other animals, which together provided easy access to fresh, healthy food and allowed families to be self-sufficient. No doubt some nuisances arose: roosters crowing early in the morning, animals roaming the streets, and rats feasting on gardens. But people recognized agriculture as a critical part of urban life.

Things started to change in the mid-nineteenth century. As Boston's residential density increased, so did complaints about farm animals by residents living in closer quarters. Local leaders acted to mitigate their concerns. Boston was among many cities that passed laws prohibiting the keeping of swine, which had previously roamed streets eating waste. In 1830, the mayor banned cows from the Common, and in 1836 removed its pasture fencing. By the turn of the twentieth century, the city had instituted dispersion requirements for dairies, keeping them 300 yards from marshes and other farm animals. In cities across the country, animal husbandry was waning, and zoning's arrival in the 1920s sounded the death knell. In Boston, a 1924 ordinance banned horses, cows, goats, rabbits, bees, pigeons, and chickens. Two city-planning scholars have explained that these agriculture bans "redefined the economic geography and opportunities of the city, especially for the poor," who relied on their access to livestock for survival. For the low-income families living in Boston's tenements, this meant losing the food security that they had previously, if tenuously, enjoyed.

For almost ninety years, the zoning code and other ordinances made it difficult—often impossible—to grow or raise your own food within Boston city limits. These regulatory barriers, hindering both food production and food security, resulted in a city that sourced its food from beyond its borders. And often far beyond. Across New England, food-producing land has diminished to just 5 percent of total land, and 90 percent of the food residents eat comes from beyond the region. The current dynamic is wholly incongruent with the region's agricultural, fishing, and hunting past.

This reality has proved displeasing to many Bostonians, including a local agricultural entrepreneur named Glynn Lloyd. He had founded several commercial and nonprofit enterprises, making him one of the most prominent leaders of the region's food industry, and in the late 2000s he was beginning to feel that the city needed to get back to its food roots. His personal tipping point occurred when he set out to convert some vacant city lots to food gardens, only to find himself thwarted by zoning rules. Lloyd bent the ear of then-Mayor Thomas Menino, and in 2012 the mayor convened farmers, neighborhood leaders, and advocates in a working group to consider whether and how Boston could facilitate agricultural activities. Two city agencies—the Redevelopment Authority (which handles zoning issues) and the Office of Food Initiatives—participated, giving the discussion broad institutional backing. These groups also held several dozen public meetings to work through their ideas. Lloyd later recounted how at 8:45 a.m. on each public-hearing day, "agricultural activists, farmers, beekeepers, rooftop growers, and compost specialists" gathered in the overflow section of city hall.

In 2013 the group emerged with what became Article 89, a comprehensive law promoting urban farming. The law allows a broad range of agricultural uses, from farming (including aquaponics and hydroponics) and farmers' markets to composting, hen keeping, and beekeeping, regulating each of these activities to capture the benefits of food production while mitigating potentially negative impacts. As of right, the code allows "urban farms" both on the ground and on rooftops, permitting them in most places, after a review conducted by the city's zoning staff. This review focuses on design issues, with specific provisions for "compatible" structures, perimeter fencing, landscape buffers, lighting, and vehicular circulation. Providing clear standards for size, bulk, materials, and design, the code ensures that prospective farmers understand exactly what they need to do to obtain a permit. Regarding size, the code allows ground-level farms up to an acre in all types of zoning districts and farms over an acre in all industrial districts; larger farms must undergo commission review. It also allows roof-level farms of any size as of right, except in residential and small-scale commercial districts, where farms 5,000 square feet or more must undergo commission review.

As for selling what you grow, where the prior code forbid farm-stand commerce, Boston's farmers can now retail their produce on-site. Alternatively, they can sell at farmers' markets, and Article 89 allows farmers' markets as of right anywhere the zoning code allows retail stores, and in all other zones with a conditional permit (and extra review). Boston's code also now allows composting, hen keeping, and beekeeping as accessory uses, if these activities follow some specific, common-sense requirements. Compost bins must be set back five feet from property lines when on the ground and must be enclosed when on a roof. Hen keepers must house hens in coops or runs made of "washable and sanitizable material such as fiberglass reinforced plastic," subject to reasonable minimum and maximum sizes. (The code forbids roosters and on-site slaughtering.) Beekeepers must keep honeybees in a maximum of two hives, set back ten feet from the public sidewalk, and facing away from windows and doors. For each of these activities, other rules—such as public health codes and state regulatory requirements—apply. By articulating these uses and providing clear conditions for allowing them, Boston's revamped code eliminates some of the barriers zoning had presented for food security.

Article 89 has changed life in Boston. A few years ago, I sat on a panel with Marie Mercurio, a planner from Boston who helped craft and implement it. Proud that the city had empowered those seeking to grow their own food, she noted the creativity with which Bostonians approached this new opportunity. And she talked animatedly about the law's success in facilitating an entire ecosystem of small- and large-scale producers who are now growing food for profit. There is something special about buying produce from a neighbor, as opposed to a big-box chain. Instead of outsourcing the economic benefits of growing to rural and suburban areas, the zoning changes restored city residents' ability to benefit economically from urban land. Word of these transformations spread widely. In 2017, the British newspaper *The Guardian* heralded "Boston's rapidly growing reputation as a haven for organic food and urban farming initiatives," citing the expansion of a container-farm company that, among other things, brings leafy greens to area farmers' markets, and singled out Fenway Farms, a rooftop hydroponic facility that sits atop the famous baseball stadium.

Glynn Lloyd remains hard at work too, expanding beyond directly selling vegetables to area restaurants to leading a community development financial institution to capitalize and support Black and Latino entrepreneurs, including agricultural entrepreneurs. Meanwhile, nonprofits have been teaching community members more about the business of the food industry, helping them to become self-sufficient growers, and more food-secure themselves. They have also offered training in the variety of jobs needed to participate in the agricultural economy. In 2023, Boston Mayor Michelle Wu announced the creation of a new cabinet-level office named "GrowBoston," which will focus on food production and work in partnership with the Office of Food Justice to address the inequities in access to the food system.

I first learned about Boston's permissive approach to agriculture when the Hartford planning and zoning commission began researching ideas for our own code. Hartford, like Boston before Article 89, had long banned virtually all agricultural activities, though it allowed community gardens to operate on a few city-owned lots and informally sanctioned farmers' markets run by reputable nonprofits. But Hartford remained a resource-poor city full of food deserts, and local advocates and the city's Food

Policy Commission urged us to modify the zoning code to find new ways of bringing fresh produce to residents. In 2015, we followed Boston's lead, duplicating many of its provisions and allowing community gardens to operate virtually anywhere. When we completely overhauled the zoning code in 2016, we authorized many types of commercial agricultural growing, including aquaculture and medical marijuana production facilities, in the definition of "craftsman industrial" uses. We wanted to be sure that zoning erected no barrier to these creative pursuits. Of course, we placed a few reasonable conditions on these uses, just as Boston did.

The zoning changes quickly ignited small bursts of agricultural activity within city limits: community gardens with improved fencing and water supplies, some new beekeepers, and a dozen or so regular farmers' markets. But no beneficiary of our code has made me happier than the Keney Park Sustainability Project, which should be a national poster child for urban-agriculture strategies that work. I first got to know the project's visionary founder, Herb Virgo, in 2014, when I solicited a walk with him during my first few months as a zoning commissioner. He took me, my husband, and our three kids to the historic horse trails of Hartford's Keney Park ("Keney," to locals), a 693-acre tract of land gifted to the city by wealthy grocer Henry Keney. The city hired the firm founded by native son Frederick Law Olmsted to design the park as a sylvan landscape, filled with meadows, forests, and trails, and the newly designed park was opened to the public in 1924. Ninety years later, the park was showing its age, and Virgo had been hired to clear out the horse trails brush, invasive species, and trash. On the walk, he showed us his progress—but then started talking about an idea he had about finding a place in or near Keney to start agricultural activities in a serious way.

Henry Keney might have smiled on the idea. Within a year, Virgo had inspired sufficient excitement and confidence that the city leased him an underutilized plot of land at the edge of Keney. He turned it into a productive urban farm with two large, enclosed greenhouses, an aquaponics facility, a woodworking shed, and a composting station, along with goats, chickens, and bees. As the farm grew, the new zoning code easily accommodated everything Virgo wanted to do—and he's done a lot. On this campus, the Sustainability Project produces bountiful harvests of vegetables, fruits, and flowers, which are sold at farmers' markets and to Hartford Public Schools or given away free to the community. From other parts of Keney, the Sustainability Project taps maple trees for syrup, which it bottles and sells along with honey, and the project salvages tree debris to make furniture and decorative items, which Virgo trains local youths to create.

Nearly everyone who works on the farm is a young person living in the surrounding Northeast neighborhood, whose residents, almost all Black, are coping with some of the toughest economic conditions and worst health outcomes anywhere in the country. As Virgo has told me, for many of those who come to work, the farm is a place of nourishment for both body and soul, and he works with them to appreciate the benefits of healthy eating and living. Along with direct employment opportunities, the Sustainability Project has distributed hundreds of home garden kits annually to neighbors, given away hundreds of rain barrels through a partnership with the local water utility, held gardening classes on-site, and held cooking classes on a mobile bus. It has also partnered with four public schools to build food gardens the students can enjoy. All these interventions promote a stronger and more resilient food system, and greater access to healthy food for residents in the heart of a neighborhood who need that access most.

People like Herb Virgo—with a green thumb and a heart of gold—have more important things to do than deal with zoning bureaucracy. I relish that Hartford laid out clear rules that supported every phase of his work on-site—and all of his off-site activities too. There are others like him, in many cities around the country. Zoning has to get out of their way.

———

While Boston and Hartford have reimagined their zoning codes to spur small-scale food production, most cities continue to make it difficult for residents and businesses to grow their own food. Rural communities, which tend to revolve around farming and raising livestock, have the opposite problem: many decline to use zoning to regulate agricultural activities at all, or do so only minimally, allowing them to take place nearly everywhere. An increasingly lively debate questions the extent to which zoning should regulate one particular activity: concentrated animal feeding operations, or CAFOs. A bulwark of industrial agriculture, these facilities have proliferated across rural America and currently produce 50 percent of the animals our nation uses for food. CAFOs pack large numbers of animals into cramped and often unsanitary quarters, preparing them for slaughter or for milking at an industrial scale. In regulations relevant to CAFO's environmental impacts, the U.S. Environmental Protection Agency defines a CAFO to include, at a minimum, 1,000 head of beef cattle, 700 dairy cattle, 10,000 sheep, 2,500 large swine or 10,000 smaller swine, 125,000 chickens used for food ("broiler chickens") or 82,000 egg-laying hens, or 55,000 turkeys. Family farms these are not.

From both a land use and an environmental perspective, the most significant challenge presented by CAFOs is handling the waste from so many densely confined animals. Operators often allow waste to fall through floor slats into an underground storage area, to be washed into lagoons, or even to accumulate on the ground outdoors. This manure contains not only phosphorous and nitrogen naturally common in manure, but also hormones, *E. coli*, salmonella, and antibiotic-resistant bacteria. It can leach into soils and run off into waterways, contaminating the drinking supply and hurting plant and animal life. CAFO manure has polluted waterways including the Chesapeake Bay, the Gulf of Mexico, Lake Erie, and the Hudson River, among other waterways, causing toxic algal blooms and killing fish and shellfish, sometimes in mass quantities.

CAFOs also release odors and particulate matter, and do so through various means. Industrial blowers intended to circulate air within barns end up spewing feathers and feces into the open air. Breezes carry smells and particles from the top of open manure pits and lagoons. Farms that spread large quantities of thick, fermented manure on neighboring fields distribute fecal matter across wider tracts of land. These releases cause an array of health problems for employees and neighbors, including headaches, respiratory ailments, and heart disease.

Despite these negative impacts, all fifty state legislatures have adopted "right-to-farm" laws that shield most CAFO activities from lawsuits based on claims that they effect a nuisance. This lax treatment may be no surprise given the amount of money CAFOs generate, and the powerful and well-funded lobbying groups working for them at the state level. Indeed, some states have changed their zoning rules to support further proliferation of CAFOs. In the most extreme example, Iowa modified its zoning statute in the late 1990s to prevent county governments from adopting zoning laws that would limit CAFOs—and CAFOs there have grown fivefold from 789 in 1990 to 4,200 in 2022. Wisconsin's legislature in 2004 empowered a new state board to create and administer uniform rules for livestock facility siting and expansion. The resulting law prohibits local governments from disapproving livestock facilities, including CAFOs, in areas zoned for agricultural uses. For a few years, some local governments still tried to use zoning to limit the impact of CAFOs. When the small town of Magnolia approved a large CAFO called Larson Acres, the operator objected to conditions the town imposed (reasonable ones, like crop rotation and soil testing), and six years of litigation ensued. The Wisconsin Supreme Court ruled in favor of the CAFO, confirming that the state's siting law preempted local decision-making and authorizing the state board to reverse conditions imposed by local zoning officials. Today, Larson Acres has expanded to 2,800 milking cows—four for every person living in Magnolia—and Wisconsin, which in 1995 had just six CAFOs, now has 337.

In the great majority of states, local governments can still use zoning to tame CAFOs. They can limit the number of animals kept on a property, ban the practice of spreading manure, or require odor management technology. Zoning can impose a dispersion requirement that prohibits CAFOs from clustering or from locating near rivers and lakes, and can require structures to be more suitably (and humanely) constructed. The zoning permit process can be amended to slow down reviews to ensure that a community can fully understand the consequences of a CAFO. Public hearings, for example, could require applicants to answer questions about their proposals. Requiring applicants to submit an environmental impact statement could help a community identify and mitigate a proposal's worst externalities. Finally, zoning boards can also review and incorporate scientific studies that show the effects of CAFOs on health, air, groundwater, rivers and streams, and property values. These studies can help justify the board's denial or conditional approval—useful if a disgruntled applicant challenges its decision.

Despite the potential that zoning codes have to help, few rural communities explicitly address CAFOs in their codes and thus end up treating them the same, permissive way they treat traditional family farms. So the number of CAFOs continues to grow—topping 21,500 as of 2022—swallowing up smaller and more sustainably managed farms in the process. Their combined and increasing impact makes them one of the biggest land use problems facing rural America.

———

That night in 2018 as I attended the Farm Aid concert in Hartford, Chris Stapleton closed his set with what may be his most food-related song, his R&B-influenced cover of "Tennessee Whiskey." (The reference to strawberry wine definitely counts as agricultural.) Turns out musicians George Jones and David Allan Coe sang the same song at the very first Farm Aid in 1985. Point is, Farm Aid has gone on so long that the setlists are being recycled—with Willie Nelson still on stage, in his nineties.

However enjoyable the music, it's unfortunate that the concert—as an environmental fundraising and consciousness-raising vehicle—remains as necessary as it was almost forty years ago. That's partly because the goalposts keep moving on federal and state action, given the strong hold of CAFO proponents over Congress and our statehouses. Farm Aid's efforts would be boosted if we could seed small growers through zoning's fertile ground. In our cities, loosening zoning rules à la Boston and Hartford can promote the local food production that's best for the environment, for growers, and for members of the community. Across our countryside, tightening zoning rules, including instituting procedural requirements and outright bans, can help us suppress toxic, large-scale animal farms and industrial growing practices that hurt our land, our animals, and us. Zoning is a constant push and pull between the urban and rural, the small-scale and large, the humane and the abusive, the sustaining and the toxic. Getting it right can improve the equity, access, sustainability, and security of our food system—which, along with housing and transportation, is key to our survival.

The issue of zoning and food production raises again the question adapted from Robert Schuller at the end of the last chapter: who do we want to be? It's a crucial question not only for us as individuals—humans in bodies that need to live and eat healthily—but collectively, as a nation situated in a living, breathing ecosystem of soil and water, plants and animals. Zoning requires the constant weighing of costs and benefits, and nowhere more than vis-à-vis a food production system that has evolved to maximize efficiency and drive down costs by every last penny—and that has done so by hiding the real environmental, medical, and economic costs. We may go down in history as the generation that kicked these ever-more-colossal costs down the road for future generations to deal with. That can't be who we really want to be.

Part III

DESIGNING FOR DELIGHT

The Force of Nature

At noon on August 22, 1856, not far from the State Capitol in Hartford, the Colt Armory Band played a woeful dirge before a large crowd that included "Chief Justices and Reverend Doctors intermixed with sturdy laborers," according to the *Hartford Daily Courant*. Hours later, at sundown, the bells of the city tolled a requiem, and in the following days, newspapers from New York to London covered the fateful loss—not of a great man, but of a monarch: the Charter Oak, thirty-three feet around and perhaps eight hundred years old, felled during a violent storm.

The Charter Oak holds an exalted place in Connecticut's history. Its name refers to a royal deed that King Charles II granted to the colony in 1662, acknowledging the rights to self-governance established in a constitution written twenty-three years earlier. Connecticut, the Constitution State, claims this constitution as the first in history ever to be written by "the people" themselves. Legend holds that in 1687, a prominent Connecticut resident hid the royal charter in the cavity of the Charter Oak, shielding it from the soldiers of the new king, William III, who demanded that it be relinquished. The tree went on to become a cherished symbol of Connecticut, the subject of books, museum exhibits, a monument, poems, songs, and paintings—including one that I frequently visit at the Wadsworth Atheneum (the country's oldest art museum, located in downtown Hartford) and another, by Frederic Church, that I traveled to the Hudson Valley to see. Carved from the felled tree itself were intricate pieces of furniture, including a cradle made for the Colts—also exhibited at the Wadsworth—and a chair on display at Church's Hudson Valley estate. In 1935, the adoration became official, as the U.S. Mint issued a half-dollar commemorating Connecticut's three hundredth anniversary with the Charter Oak on the back, followed by a state quarter of similar design in 1999.

My desk in Hartford overlooks the Scion of the Charter Oak, a first-generation descendant that occupies a prominent place in Bushnell Park, the country's oldest publicly funded park. "My" oak was planted over a hundred and fifty years ago. Since then, significant investments have gone toward pruning, fertilizing, and protecting it from disease. It's a virtually perfect specimen, full and beautifully formed, and it has brought me great joy and calm as the seasons change around it while I work and write. My vista owes its preservation to the tree's historic significance, its association with patriotism and self-determination. The Scion must endure.

From a zoning perspective, Hartford uses many tools to ensure that its trees do, in fact, endure. The city needs all the healthy trees it can get, as like many urbanized areas, it has lost much of its canopy to development, neglect, disease, and pests—and over the years, hasn't planted enough trees to replace that canopy. To restore some of the look and feel of a city shaded by trees, the zoning code starts by trying to prevent the loss of the city's largest and most significant trees—those with a diameter of thirteen inches or more. To achieve this goal, it prohibits the removal of those trees unless they are dying or pose a danger to human safety, health, and welfare. It also tries to prevent damage to all trees, regardless of size. Construction crews, for example, must protect trees and not build trenches through, or even expose, root systems. To grow the next grove of Charter

Oaks, our code requires tree planting on each residential and commercial lot, and continuous canopy coverage along downtown streets. These planting requirements are flexible, allowing applicants who cannot plant enough trees on-site to work with the city forester to plant trees elsewhere. We developed these provisions with the city's Tree Commission, a body that—much like the Food Policy Commission—brought its expertise to bear during our zoning overhaul, ensuring that nature got its due. The commissioners made an important point, one I hadn't quite grasped: that romanticizing trees, as countless poets and painters have done—or even as we've done with the Charter Oak—risks focusing too much on their beauty, while overlooking their brawn.

The unromantic view allows us to think in terms of their function. Trees flex their muscle in contributing what ecologists call "ecosystem services," or benefits provided to us through natural phenomena by nature itself. As one ecosystem service, trees clean our air through natural processes that capture carbon and convert it to oxygen. They also cool the city, reducing the urban heat-island effect, as well as the energy costs of alleviating it, by providing shade during hot summers. They soak up stormwater and reduce erosion through their roots and branches. While it's impossible to assign a precise dollar amount, our city forester posited that Hartford's trees annually generate nearly $5.5 million in benefits, including the capture of nearly 600 billion gallons of stormwater and savings of nearly 5 million kilowatt-hours in energy. Oh, and trees also improve property values by up to 20 percent and drive up retail sales when they're planted in commercial areas.

In short, trees are the gift that keeps on giving, and the bigger and older the tree, the greater its gifts. Similarly, meadows, coastal ecosystems, and wetlands offer a visual respite from our overbuilt environment while providing ecosystem services in the form of habitat creation, flood management, biodiversity, and cross-pollination. Rainforests recharge underground aquifers and yield wood, material for clothing and household tools, and medicines. Deserts add to biodiversity; provide fuel, minerals, medicine, and even (through sand) building materials; and preserve archaeological artifacts and sites. So while nature is a landscape—one that Frederic Church and the other nineteenth-century Hudson River School painters exhibited at the Wadsworth so luminously celebrated—it is also a habitat regulator, not only our delighter, but our provider.

For all its wonky technicalities, a zoning code can be a powerful tool to protect this natural environment that does so much for us—culturally, spiritually, and physically. Unfortunately, most zoning codes have often done the opposite, enabling and even requiring us to build our cities in unattractive and environmentally destructive ways. Codes push development outward into forests, farmland, and other wildlife habitat. They facilitate the overuse of water, to the detriment of ecosystems we need to thrive. And they have codified all sorts of backward ideas about the landscaping (including trees) that we must incorporate into new development. For too long, we have let this problem slide, but that has to change. We must rewrite our codes to build more beautiful and more resilient places. Zoning can reposition nature as a vital form of infrastructure necessary to our health, well-being, and survival.

In 1932, the American architect Frank Lloyd Wright first wrote about his vision of Broadacre City, a suburban utopia where every home would sit on an acre of land and highways would connect residents to their jobs. In many ways, Wright's vision was the antithesis of good urbanism, separating uses and forcing occupants to rely on cars. But it fell within the intellectual tradition of the "garden city," an idealized suburb surrounded by farms and fields, far from industrialized areas. Wright spent the rest of his life advancing this idea, articulating every detail of Broadacre City, from proposed school enrollments to bans on roadside billboards. While his exact vision never materialized, it captured, or perhaps reflected, the American imagination: homes as little islands in green-lawn seas.

Zoning codes requiring minimum lot sizes for residential development made this imagined America real, reserving the vast majority of zoned land in the United States for freestanding, single-family homes with large yards in low-density subdivisions—creating sprawl and driving up costs, while entrenching racism and classism. But they also wreak havoc on our environment. They prevent us from clustering development to reduce the amount of land we consume—in the process pushing stores, workplaces, and amenities even farther apart. Large-lot neighborhoods impede walkability and condemn residents to drive their own cars to do almost anything. What's worse, lot-size mandates gobble up undeveloped land for housing, since existing neighborhoods do not have enough land to provide the required lot size for each new house. Forests. Farmland. Ecosystems previously undisturbed. Most zoning codes push us to destroy more and more of them. Indeed, minimum lot-size mandates have become zoning's most devastating strike against the natural infrastructure that sustains us.

That's certainly true in the Charter Oak state, where half of Connecticut's residential neighborhoods must have lots the size of at least one and a half football fields. The state even has large-lot zoning requiring at least half-acre lots within walking distance of most train stations, where you would think that towns would want more walkable neighborhoods. Put another way, most towns require lots so large that residents need a car to live near the train station. Plenty of evidence suggests that there's a growing demand for neighborhoods where you can live independent of the car. But even as demand for more compact living grows, zoning codes lock in an antiquated model that prevents that demand from being met.

Not only antiquated, but damaging. Researchers have found that large-lot residential subdivisions have resulted in 4.5 percent of the state being converted, between 1985 and 2010, from natural landscapes to roads, rooftops, and parking lots or covered by turf or grass. That figure might not sound like all that much, but 4.5 percent of Connecticut adds up to almost 300,000 acres. Most of the converted land had previously been forest land, farmland, and watersheds that contributed valuable ecosystem services to Connecticut's human residents. Over that same twenty-five-year period, Connecticut lost 6.5 percent of its forest land and 5.3 percent of its core forest. These losses have in turn diminished watershed health, reduced carbon storage, and obliterated wildlife habitat, most problematically in core forest areas previously insulated from development by surrounding forest. Connecticut also lost 15 percent of its agricultural field land and 22 percent of its highest-quality agricultural land. These losses force us to source food from out of state, expanding the carbon footprint of the food system. Finally, Connecticut has lost significant riparian (riverside) lands, leaving a quarter of the state's watersheds in poor health. Riparian losses include forty square miles of natural vegetation in streamside corridors, a loss that worsens water quality, since vegetation removes pollutants and stabilizes riparian banks.

Zoning largely has escaped blame for these negative changes in land cover. One reason that few people link zoning to environmental degradation is that zoning's environmental consequences do not manifest all at once. Rather, they appear gradually, over time, as new projects are permitted. It's both the trees and the forest: environmental degradation results from thousands of individual decisions to build a house, pave a driveway, extend a road, or seed a lawn. Towns whose zoning enabled these decisions may not have realized their codes' effects. But they must reckon with the uncomfortable truth that large-lot zoning, which makes it difficult to build anything but sprawl, destroys the ecosystems we need to survive. This is true across our great country. By embracing minimum lot sizes, we have built versions of Broadacre City everywhere, realizing the worst idea of an otherwise brilliant architect.

———

From an environmental point of view, Frank Lloyd Wright had better instincts for architecture than planning. Taliesin West, his 1937 home and studio nestled into the foothills of Arizona's McDowell Mountains, is a testament to his unique design ethos. Built low and close to the terrain, Taliesin West consists of a series of buildings clad in stones sourced on-site, with rooflines that mimic the surrounding mountains. Terraces and a central vine-shaded walk create outdoor rooms that take advantage of both breeze and sun. From inside these buildings, windows at eye level and high windows by the ceiling, called clerestories, frame views to the landscapes and skies beyond. Gardens with vegetation native to the Sonoran Desert surround the buildings, along with shallow reflecting pools and a few patches of grass. When I first visited the site over a decade ago, I was struck by its sensitive siting and construction, and finally understood how deftly—and gorgeously—Taliesin West realizes Wright's belief that buildings must interact with and draw from their environments.

The Sonoran Desert, which stretches from Nevada to Baja California, possesses the greatest species diversity of any desert on earth. The ecosystem services it provides include grazing, mining, and timber production, as well as plants used for fuel, drink, and medicine. The fruits and stored water of the mighty saguaro cactus, for example, nourish animals, birds, and bats, as well as Indigenous people. The desert also regulates air quality and atmosphere composition. Just as important, the desert offers recreational benefits from trails to rock climbing, and spiritual benefits, especially to tribes historically rooted in the area. Tribal nations, like those memorialized at the Gila Cliff Dwellings National Monument, survived by maximizing their use of the desert's gifts.

For non-Indigenous people, the dry and drought-prone Sonoran Desert might seem an improbable place to settle. Yet hundreds of thousands of homes have sprung up right in the middle of it, in fast-growing cities like Phoenix, within whose sprawl Taliesin West now sits. Spurred on by large-lot zoning and car culture, this sprawl has damaged the desert that attracted people in the first place. In converting desert land to housing and asphalt, new residents have obliterated and fragmented the habitat of countless species. Human settlement has blocked pollination pathways and animal migration, including that of the endangered and threatened Sonoran pronghorn, desert tortoise, and cactus ferruginous pygmy-owl. Humans compete against desert animals and plants for the resource that all need to live: water. Over the last fifty years, precipitation has dropped 40 percent, and droughts occur frequently, making water access singularly important.

Once again, zoning doesn't just enable development patterns that increase residents' water consumption; it often requires them. Scottsdale, the Phoenix suburb that grew up around Taliesin West, has embraced the Broadacre City aesthetic—and has enshrined rules promoting that aesthetic in its zoning code. Driving to Taliesin West, you pass through two lush, green golf courses and single-family residential neighborhoods with minimum lot sizes of about an acre. (Other Scottsdale neighborhoods require more than four acres.) Green lawns abound, part of the twentieth century trend that made lawns one of America's leading "crops," now covering more than 31 million acres. Scottsdale's code has contributed to this result, mandating that landscaped areas be finished with "turf, ground-cover, planting, organic mulch, or at least two (2) inches deep decomposed granite or expanded shale" and be served by an automatic irrigation system. The inclusion of turf among the required landscape treatments gives Scottsdale homeowners legal comfort in planting grasses that are water-intensive and often pesticide-dependent, too. The irrigation-system mandate assumes that property owners will plant non-native vegetation that requires irrigation. The code also has a provision that the landscaping be well-maintained in a "healthy" condition, with no provision for home-owners to cut back in times of drought.

Satellite images of Taliesin West's neighborhood show that virtually every house has its own private pool, and in fact 70 percent of the water consumed by Scottsdale households goes toward outdoor uses like land-scaping and pool maintenance. The well-watered yards tend to be cooler than the desert beyond, and the greenery and water features give occupants the feeling of an oasis. But these individual benefits come at a huge societal cost, diverting a scarce resource to thirsty Bermuda grass and private pools. Scottsdale's zoning requirements are at odds with the ecosystem around it, not just physically, but also visually. The residential areas, with that sea-of-green lushness, look strange within the desert context, which has its own mysterious beauty.

The zoning of Tucson, just two hours away, has produced very different results. One major difference, obvious from a windshield survey, is that Tucson is laid out in a more compact way than Scottsdale, with homes on smaller lots taking up less land. That's a product of zoning: Scottsdale's highest minimum lot requirements are nearly thirty times as large as Tucson's, which clocks in at 7,000 square feet. Many Scottsdale homes sit on acres of land, while Tucson homes neatly tuck side by side. A second major difference is the appearance of the man-made landscapes. In Tucson, the typical yard contains agave, prickly pear, and golden barrel cacti, among other desert plants, all set in a sea of sand-colored gravel and decorative rocks and boulders. This aesthetic aligns better with its natural surroundings than Scottsdale's—and it, too, is a product of the zoning code, which says that most property owners seeking zoning permits must plant native vegetation or drought-tolerant plants. It's worth noting that Tucson's code would not condone planting the oaks and maples of Hartford. Connecticut's ecology differs significantly from that of the Arizona desert, and while I've extolled the virtues of New England's trees, they would be wholly out of place in the Sonoran Desert. To produce ethical outcomes, a zoning code must respond to its context.

To achieve the sensitive landscaping that harmonizes human habitation with the environment, Tucson deploys many different zoning provisions working in concert with each other. The code mandates that landscape plans protect existing native plants and incorporate water-conserving designs and reclaimed water. Property owners can fulfill this mandate by using rain barrels or digging natural landscaped basins that collect scarce rainwater. For multifamily housing, the zoning code caps the amount of the site that can be covered by non-drought-tolerant landscaping, such as turf grass, to 5 percent in most instances. For commercial sites, property owners must submit a rainwater harvesting plan that ensures sites can use rainwater to meet half of landscape water demand. Owners must also plant one tree for every four new parking spaces, which promotes stormwater absorption and reduces the heat-island effect.

Together, these and other provisions—in place for around three decades—have helped Tucson's development harmonize better with the natural environment than Scottsdale's. The results are telling. Geographically, Tucson is slightly larger than Scottsdale, but its population density—the number of people per square mile—is twice Scottsdale's, which means that Tucson takes up less of the desert per person. Its zoning provisions have contributed to a dramatic water reduction—down 32 percent between 1996 and 2020—so that today Tucson households use a mere 40 percent of the water used by Scottsdale households. When drought-prone jurisdictions in our era of rising global temperatures need a model of how zoning can influence water demand and promote sensible use of scarce water resources, they should look to Tucson.

From arid Arizona to soggy Seattle, zoning can be used as a tool to manage all types of water issues including, in Seattle, the problem of too much water. Precipitation has increased 30 percent over the last century in Seattle, and stands to increase even more in the future. Without careful planning, water could inundate the city's streets, homes, and critical infrastructure. The city's zoning code has become a key part of this planning. It begins by ensuring that new development sites are designed to handle stormwater on the lot. Each new multifamily or commercial building must choose from a menu of stormwater management strategies to achieve enough points to satisfy a "Green Factor" score. Property owners receive points for planting new trees or preserving old ones and installing permeable paving that allows stormwater to soak into the soil below. They can also earn points by installing new systems, such as bioretention facilities (shallow depressions engineered to manage and treat runoff), green roofs (roofs partly or totally covered by plants), vegetated walls, and harvested rainwater irrigation. To make sure its measures last beyond the issuance of a permit, the city's code requires property owners to maintain any landscaping approved during the zoning process. Scofflaws may see fines, mandatory fixes, or even the revocation of their certificate of occupancy, meaning no one may legally occupy the building.

Of the strategies receiving Green Factor points, green roofs deserve some special attention. Green roofs have been used by Indigenous peoples for millennia. In modern American architecture, none other than Frank Lloyd Wright wrote about installing a green roof in a house for his son back in 1954. Today, these roofs deploy vegetation—usually low-maintenance native plants, or sometimes food gardens, like those sprouting up in Boston—planted over engineered systems complete with waterproofing, root barrier, drainage, and irrigation. Green roofs are cool to look at, either from atop or from a nearby building, in part because they are unexpected, and in part because their colors are more pleasing to the eye than the typically black, white, or brown roofing. But green roofs are also useful. They can reduce stormwater runoff by 60 percent, which especially helps in those areas with increasingly intense and frequent storms. They also absorb heat, and studies show that green roofs are 30–40 percent cooler than black-surfaced roofs, which in turn cools the occupied spaces below.

Despite these benefits, the only major city to require green roofs is Denver, whose building code mandates that developers planning new construction and additions over 25,000 square feet either include green roofs (along with solar panels) or pay into a "green building fund" if they cannot satisfy requirements on-site. Other jurisdictions—including Chicago and Portland, Oregon—offer incentives for installing green roofs. Austin, whose location in central Texas makes it vulnerable to both intense storms and extreme heat, offers property owners density bonuses, allowing them to build higher than the code otherwise allows in exchange for installing green roofs. To qualify for the bonus, the green roof must meet certain performance standards at least six months of the year. In addition, at least half of the water must derive from nonpotable sources (like HVAC condensate and rainwater), 90 percent of plantings must be native or adapted, and no fast-release fertilizer may be used. Leading by example, when the City of Austin built a new City Hall in 2005, it installed a 13,000-square-foot green roof over its parking garage and occupied spaces. Topped with three feet of soil, the City Hall roof includes both trees and shrubs, and uses HVAC condensate for watering. By 2018, fifty-eight green roofs had been installed in the city. The up-front expense is significant, but smart builders know a green roof can cool the building in summers and trap heat in the winter, saving energy costs down the road.

In general, when people think of zoning, they think about buildings, but zoning need not just regulate the man-made. From the trees of Hartford to the green roofs of Austin, zoning has a crucial role to play in maintaining and optimizing the natural infrastructure that we need to survive and thrive. If we allow it to, nature can perform all sorts of self-regulating and human-protecting functions, cleaning our environment, reducing energy consumption, buffering wetlands and environmentally sensitive habitats, and shielding us from hazards like floods and extreme heat. What's more, nature can soothe our spirits and delight and inspire us. Would you rather be on a tree-shaded street or a denuded one? These are not frivolous concerns, just as trees are not merely decorative. Studies have shown that people who spend time in nature both have better health outcomes—and feel like they do, too.

That's why it is so important for zoning to harness the benefits nature provides—its brawn, and not just its beauty. Zoning codes can be written to protect trees, promote plantings, and manage water. They can curb sprawl by reducing or eliminating minimum lot sizes that, unchecked, currently accelerate our consumption impulses. They can promote landscapes that are regionally appropriate and biologically diverse. They can repopulate the tree canopy needed to cool our cities and re-create the habitat we have uprooted. They can manage water, through on-site interventions that add up to big savings. And they can buffer the most sensitive lands, including wetlands and endangered species habitat, from development altogether.

Carefully conceived and properly executed, zoning can help us continue to build where we want, to integrate ourselves into deserts, swamps, and forests. But that truth comes with a caution. Even if we can develop the tools we need to live in environments not necessarily well-suited for human settlement, should we? At some point, even with careful management, water resources will run dry for Tucson and Scottsdale residents. As a canary in the coal mine, consider the unprecedented heat wave in the summer of 2023, when Phoenix sweltered in temperatures of a hundred degrees or more for a month straight. In other places, sea level rise, storm-related flooding, high winds, wildfires, and erosion will increasingly disrupt more and more lives. Yet we continue to build in vulnerable places—even as we're increasingly aware that what we build, nature may well destroy. We must think more carefully about how zoning can be used to curb misguided development, or even manage our retreats from existing settlement.

Taking nature's cues and harnessing its benefits can transform our daily experience and safeguard our very existence, even as it helps us decelerate the rate at which we destroy the ecosystems we need to survive. Beneath these strategies lies an ominous and irrevocable truth: if zoning continues to disregard nature, the long-term consequence is more than inconvenience. It is an existential threat.

Completing the Street

Returning to Connecticut from a road trip in Canada in the summer of 2018, my family did what city lovers do and got off the highway to explore downtown Burlington, Vermont, a place we hadn't been to before. We started at City Hall, a three-story red brick, marble, slate, and granite building topped with a clock tower, erected in 1928 and designed by the well-regarded architecture firm McKim, Mead, & White. The nomination for the National Register of Historic Places describes key elements in detail to thrill the design nerd: "Bays are defined by fluted pilasters with Corinthian caps, and twelve-over-twelve sash with gauged brick flat arches. . . . The round-arched central entrances have panelled doors with tracery fanlights and surrounds of fluted Ionic pilasters supporting swan-neck pediments. Cupola enrichment includes clocks, balustrades with urns, columns and arches in a Palladian motif, and a gilded dome embellished with swag." The long façades of City Hall, virtually identical, front a large park with a fine assortment of maples, London planes, white oaks, and honey locusts to the west, and Church Street, which the city closed to cars in the 1970s, to the east.

When we rounded the building to view its eastern façade, we were surprised to find ourselves at the mouth of an outdoor pedestrian mall with about a hundred restaurants and retail stores. Conceived as one of the many federally funded "urban renewal" projects that used federal funding to carry out a big idea in the 1960s and 1970s, the Church Street Marketplace extends four blocks northward, allowing east–west vehicle traffic to intersect it. Although urban renewal has become something of a taboo, associated with dysfunctional public-housing developments and massive highways that obliterated neighborhoods, the Marketplace has endured as a rare success story. That late Sunday afternoon of our visit, the outdoor cafés were filled with people of all ages, a local guitarist and a vocalist filled the air with tunes, and art and oddities—from the controversial "Everybody Loves a Parade" mural (painted over in 2020 for its failure to reflect diverse histories) to granite boulders strewn about— added visual interest. Trees provided the kind of soothing canopy that graces our best public spaces. We wandered past the shops, charmed by the artsy vibe and eclectic architecture, mostly three- and four-story buildings of brick and stone. It's a great place to hang out, and to meet a city for the first time.

When the Marketplace ended at Pearl Street, we kept walking, eager to see more of Burlington's center. But what followed was a disappointment after the vitality that came before. Pearl Street spans about forty feet, an inhospitably wide combination of two travel lanes of fast-moving traffic and one parking lane on either side. Along Pearl, several blocks host large surface parking lots, their empty gaps making a sharp contrast to the cheek-to-jowl historic buildings lining the pedestrianized Marketplace. As we continued through downtown, we saw more and more concrete and asphalt, fewer and fewer trees, and less and less street life. It was a hot day, and all that pavement made it hotter. We felt relief when we finally reached the crêpe place next to the Waterfront Park for dinner. Burlington so far had given us a compact study of a city's ups and downs in two streets.

Where Church Street made for joyousness, streets like Pearl did anything but glimmer.

The contrast reminds us that streets—defined as a type of road lined with buildings, as opposed to rural roads or highways—are more than arteries for traffic. In fact, they are incredibly important public spaces. They provide the stage for our buildings, they facilitate movement, and they connect us to each other. They take up an enormous amount of our public space. As with so much else, the way they do this—and the way we experience them as a result—is at least partly determined by zoning codes.

Like all streets, Burlington's comprise several components. The most obvious one is the roadway itself, the public right-of-way used primarily by cars and sometimes by bikes. The roadway includes at least one travel lane for cars, but usually more, and might include lanes for bikes, buses, parking, and in some cities light rail or streetcar tracks. Beyond the roadway's curb is often a buffer area, a dedicated space for lights, benches, newsstands, bus stops, and bike racks, as well as landscaping and trees. Then comes the pedestrian realm, which includes both a clear right-of-way for people walking or using assistive devices such as wheelchairs, and finally a frontage area that includes the few feet in front of a building, where people can window-shop or sit at outdoor cafés. The pedestrian realm runs along the buildings, which are the boundaries and outer walls of any street. Our experience of a street is really the combined experience of all these parts, from the façade of one building all the way to the façade across the street. More precisely, it is the experience of the way all these parts relate to each other.

At the time, the crisscrossing street grid of Burlington, population 42,000, had a design fairly typical of downtowns of similarly sized and larger American cities—one that makes for a lousy experience for anyone other than drivers. That's because no one person or entity is really thinking of, or responsible for, the overall way all the parts work together. Instead, the approach is piecemeal. City engineers and public-works departments make design and funding decisions for the publicly owned portions of the street, including roadways, often the buffer area, and sometimes all or part of the pedestrian realm. Meanwhile, planning and zoning authorities typically establish guidelines for the privately owned portions of the street: at a minimum the buildings, sometimes all or part of the pedestrian realm, and less often the buffer area.

The division of responsibility between the engineers and the planners depends on the location of property lines: zoning generally begins where public property ends. This means that even where zoning requires low-scale housing, a city engineer focused on functionality can erect a thirty-foot cobra-head streetlight. It means that the elimination or shrinking of a sidewalk might occur during a road widening, even in a commercially zoned area where shops depend on foot traffic. And it means that it's no one's responsibility to plant a tree, if neither the zoning code nor the engineering design manuals call for one. In other words, the parts don't mesh, because the contributors are often working at cross-purposes.

If we want better streets, we need to plan for them—holistically, not haphazardly. If we do, everyone, from the asphalt contractor to the lane striper, will be able to see how attention to each part can help create a larger and more cohesive whole. Zoning can help create that holistic approach. But that involves expanding zoning's traditional scope beyond the lot line to the entire cross-section of the street.

Little did we know, as we took in Pearl Street and its disappointing surroundings that summer Sunday, that the city of Burlington was already moving toward a more holistic regulatory approach to its streets. The roots of that shift dated back to 2011, when the state legislature authorized Act 34, creating Vermont's first "complete streets" policy, which governed new transportation infrastructure including the highways, rural roads, and arterials built and maintained by the state, as well as local governments' streets. The statute dictated that streets must comfortably and safely accommodate people of all abilities, whether they are taking transit, walking, biking, driving, or using assistive devices—everyone from the mom pushing a stroller to the elderly person pushing a walker. According to Smart Growth America, a national nonprofit that tracks such reforms, Vermont is now one of thirty-seven states, plus Puerto Rico and D.C., that have formally embraced complete-streets policies, along with about 1,600 local governments. These policies can come in many forms, but they all set forth a vision for streets designed for all users, while creating new decision-making protocols for projects and establishing standards for how streets will perform over time.

In 2012 Vermont issued further guidance for local governments, identifying six different types of neighborhoods, from undeveloped to village to suburban to urban core, and enumerating likely potential users for each neighborhood type. Burlington's downtown exemplifies the urban core. According to the guide, its streets must accommodate pedestrians of all kinds, whether dawdling people-watchers or purposeful walk-to-workers; bicyclists, as well as city buses, school buses, and paratransit vans and delivery trucks and emergency trucks. To do so, the guide suggests sidewalks at least eight feet wide, plus tree wells for shade, curbing, on-street parking, well-marked crosswalks, and provisions for bikes to share the roadway with cars, among other measures. Importantly, the guide also recommended revising zoning regulations, suggesting that communities adopt "form-based" zoning codes, which, unlike traditional zoning codes, set forth explicit aesthetic rules for building designs and siting. Through a form-based code, local jurisdictions can develop their own menus of allowable designs, which can guide a building's height, rooflines, entrance sequence, and windows, helping a community shape the exact type of development that can occur.

Act 34 and its related guidance jump-started conversations about complete streets across the state. In Burlington, leaders felt added pressure to rethink streets because of a seemingly unrelated issue: the pollution of Lake Champlain. After my family and I polished off some delicious crêpes that day six years ago, we walked across the street to the lake's verdant Waterfront Park. With the cool evening air and beautiful sunset, we did not realize that this freshwater lake—which straddles Vermont, New York, and Canada, and is over a hundred miles long—has been dirty for decades. I subsequently learned that in the 1990s the Environmental Protection Agency required the State of Vermont to develop a pollution management plan. In 2011, federal officials decided the plan no longer passed muster and asked the state to revise it. The EPA reported that one major source of the pollution was the rainwater that accumulated along the streets and sidewalks, all hard and impenetrable surfaces like asphalt and concrete, picking up oil, grease, rubber, bacteria, and other pollutants along the way. All that contamination flowed into open drains, which led straight into Lake Champlain. In addition to chemicals, dirt and sediment contaminated the runoff and accumulated in the lake, blocking sunlight from reaching aquatic plant life and suffocating fish. In a very real way, the city's decisions about street design were strangling its lake.

Burlington Mayor Miro Weinberger, who trained as an environmentalist, inherited this problem when he came to office in 2012, one year after the request from the EPA. Pressure from the feds, local constituents, and the state's Act 34 built up for a few years. Then, in 2015, the mayor launched Great Streets BTV, a planning collaboration with business owners, neighborhood groups, environmentalists, and other stakeholders to establish goals and vet ideas relevant to the issues that had been raised. Great Streets identified four priorities: walkability and bikeability, sustainability, vibrancy, and functionality for all users. The group aimed to achieve these priorities through a building-to-building approach to the city's streets.

In 2018 the city began laying out new rules for the design of the public portion of the streets, codifying a complete-streets approach in a design and construction manual. The manual calls for roadways to be narrowed, reducing the amount of pavement devoted to cars and slowing drivers. It also requires the roadway to be lined with "rain gardens"—plant beds that absorb stormwater and prevent it from running into sewers that run out to the lake. The rain gardens will flank bicycle paths, helping protect bikers from cars. A "tree belt," including benches and lighting, will sit between the bicycle paths and the buildings. Directly next to the buildings, pedestrians will find wide sidewalks with space to window-shop and sit at cafés.

Two years after publishing the downtown streets manual, the city tack-
led the buildings that line the streets, establishing complementary form-
based zoning code provisions that followed the state's recommendations.
The new provisions ensure that incremental improvements made by each
individual property owner result in a consistent look and feel for the block.
The value of this coherence is manifest in the Church Street Marketplace,
which feels welcoming in part because the building façades create a consistent and connected experience within the public realm, framing the
vibrant activities happening in the outdoor area between them. Extending this consistency to other blocks in Burlington's downtown depends on
the zoning code clearly delineating relationships between the buildings,
streets, and lots.

To define how buildings and structures relate to their lots, the zoning code regulates how far away from a property line a building must be
located. A traditional zoning code would normally specify a setback for
all four sides of the lot, outlining the general area within which someone may build. Suburban lots have very large setbacks, which means that
buildings are surrounded by lawn or landscaping, while urban lots tend to
have small setbacks, allowing more of the lot to be covered by a building.
In either setting, a traditional code allows a property owner to construct
a building of any size anywhere within the setbacks—right up to the setback line, in other words, or couched far back from it. A form-based code
flips this idea and instead identifies a "build-to" line to which the property owner must build. The owner cannot build an undersized building
far back from the build-to line but must build a suitably sized building
within a set range near the line. In Burlington's downtown, that range is
now between zero and six feet of the front property line. The result will,
over time, be a relatively uniform building line, with a modest, six-foot
variation adding some visual interest.

Consistency also depends on frontage requirements and height limits that define how buildings and structures relate to other buildings and
structures around them. A building's frontage, as we first discussed in the
context of San Diego's new mixed-use zoning provisions, is essentially the

width of a building at the front lot line. Traditional zoning codes do not usually have frontage requirements, which means that property owners can generally build narrow buildings that leave space, or even parking, right next to the sidewalk. This changed for Burlington with the new downtown code. It requires a 100 percent frontage requirement for "primary" streets, which are streets with many restaurants and shops, and an 80 percent frontage requirement for secondary streets and streets in the outer areas of downtown. The requirement means that buildings will either touch each other or come close, strengthening their visual and functional relationship. Similarly, buildings must be between three and fourteen stories, which is consistent with, and even denser than, existing architecture. The code also requires buildings to step back every few stories as the building gets taller, a wedding-cake effect that allows street trees, rain gardens, and other landscaping to have sunlight—boosting plant life and alleviating sidewalk gloom. The previous code set no height minimums, meaning that one-story buildings could be built, and they were; and it set no stepbacks, meaning that downtown's tallest buildings could maximize their height along the sidewalk, creating dark canyons. Together, the new frontage and height standards prevent the disjointed aesthetic of undersized and overly tall buildings with gaps in between them.

Finally, the Burlington zoning code shapes how downtown buildings and structures relate to sidewalks. Entrances must now front the street, a requirement that makes the buildings feel welcoming and accessible, and must be designed to accommodate wheelchair users, who are too often relegated to side doors and alley entrances. Smaller buildings may have porches, whose elevation protects occupant privacy while allowing occupants to engage safely with passersby. Medium-sized buildings may have stoops or terraces, which mediate between the public sidewalk and the private building as people enter. For shops, the code requires a substantial amount of glass at the ground level and requires that the pavement match the public portions of the sidewalk. Awnings and canopies that offer shade and refuge from rain and snow can legally encroach on the public right-of-way if they are ten feet above the sidewalk. The overall effect of these requirements and allowances is to create an experience that centers around people and generates movement and activity on the street itself.

Burlington's new zoning code intentionally blurs the delineation between what happens in buildings and what happens in the publicly owned portions of the streets, and it does so by reaching beyond the buildings. It allows outdoor dining both on private lots and within the public right-of-way, promotes public amenities that will add to streets' vibrancy and functionality, and encourages pocket parks and other green spaces between buildings. A property owner who provides access to a public restroom on the ground floor earns a height bonus allowing taller construction than the code would otherwise allow. And to fill out the tree canopy to achieve necessary stormwater and heat-island management priorities, the zoning code requires two trees to be planted for every ten parking spaces, stormwater runoff to be retained on the lot wherever feasible, and rain gardens and channels to collect or redirect runoff from impermeable surfaces. In all of these ways, the code attempts to extend to private lots what the design manual requires on publicly owned land.

Burlington overhauled its zoning code to codify a vision for downtown streets. As Great Streets BTV plans are realized, Burlington will become a more inviting place, by intention and design. It's already happening. The city has already begun piecemeal street improvements, and it has issued bonds for millions in large-scale stormwater infrastructure. City Hall Park has been regraded and landscaped for rain gardens. Hundreds of shrubs now slow and filter stormwater. Public art in the park designed in the Japanese kintsugi style includes stone disks named for tributaries of the Champlain watershed, beckoning parkgoers toward the rain gardens. There is much more to do, but if the city continues to follow the path it has set for itself, the over-paved, under-treed status quo will inevitably change via the proliferation of refreshed streets that are compatible with their natural context and that set the stage for the full range of human activities. Before too long, a much bigger part of Burlington will offer residents and visitors alike the delightful experience previously limited to a few blocks.

When Burlington deployed zoning to reshape its streets, it required property owners to adhere to a consistent design when making any changes. Combining the code and the downtown streets manual, the city created a holistic approach using both zoning and nonzoning tools. A more unitary approach would conceive of zoning's scope as including street design itself, at least for local roads (as opposed to federal highways or state thoroughfares). This entails going slightly beyond Burlington and fully upending, rather than merely blurring, the notion that zoning ends at the property line—a notion that unnecessarily constrains what zoning is, and what it was set up to achieve.

There are clear historical justifications for doing this. Zoning's founding fathers (they were virtually all men) almost certainly conceived of zoning as a means of improving the quality and function of our streets, as evidenced by the Standard State Zoning Enabling Act of 1926, the model act that ignited zoning's proliferation nationally. The act articulated the specific aims of "lessen[ing] congestion in the streets" and "facilitat[ing] the adequate provision of transportation" among them. Twenty-seven states still maintain the exact phrase "to lessen congestion in the streets" in state law, while others over the years have substituted different language meaning the same thing. So why do most local governments decline to regulate streets through zoning?

One reason may be the longstanding practice of exempting public land from zoning, a practice derived from long-ago judicial decisions that held that government officials and decisions should be "immune" from certain types of regulation. These decisions extended exemptions to all kinds of properties owned by local governments, including schools, libraries, fire and police stations, offices, parks, and community centers, and, by extension, streets. State and federal governments—which own the same types of resources, in addition to highways, post offices, intercity roads, military bases, and other larger-scale infrastructure—have also historically enjoyed immunity.

Modern judicial decisions take a different approach. When a Boston homeowner sued the city's zoning commission for approving a federal post office right next to her home, the court dismissed her lawsuit after the U.S. Postal Service submitted a copy of a land contract asserting immunity from state and local zoning laws. When reviewing a suit challenging local authority to zone public land, a court looks at a range of factors, including whether a federal or state law specifically exempts public owners or the particular use from zoning, and whether a public entity is acting in a governmental capacity. In the absence of such a law, the court will consider other evidence to determine whether the federal or state government intended to exempt such uses from local zoning. Where courts can identify some stated or implied intent to exempt a public use, they will find that local zoning has been preempted. Few judicial decisions these days focus specifically on streets, but a 2018 decision from the New Jersey supreme court found a state university immune from zoning in the town of Passaic, ruling that the university acted within its governmental authority to further its educational mission when it planned to modify its campus streets to manage traffic concerns.

The New Jersey case speaks to the continuing ability of the state and state-government entities to circumvent the application of zoning, but most roads within incorporated areas are local roads, owned and maintained by local governments. When it comes to locally owned public lands, cities and towns have plenty of leeway to govern their own activities. The fact that the officials doing the zoning are themselves part of local government helps, placing them on the same level with public-works departments, fire officials, park and library heads, and school boards. Accordingly, many local governments have swept municipal lands into zoning, either by expressly writing them into zoning codes or by applying ownership-neutral rules to projects. Except, that is, for streets. Despite the fact that most roads within incorporated areas are local roads, owned and maintained by local governments, cities around the country have enacted rules that exempt streets from zoning's purview. Denver, for example, limits zoning's scope to "zone lots," which are constrained by private property lines, and which do not include the public portions of streets. Even in its "campus" zone, which allows a single zone lot to have multiple buildings and to cross streets, streets remain unregulated.

This approach is misguided. Beyond any legal technicalities, there's a simple but important substantive justification for zoning to extend to the entire cross-section of the street, from one building to the opposite building. That is the simple fact that our streets are, for the most part, dangerous and dismal.

Despite the guidance provided by hundreds of complete-streets policies that have been adopted across the country, most American roads continue to give cars and their drivers priority. This priority has not happened by chance. Rather, it is embedded in two technical manuals governing road design with far-reaching consequences: the Association of State Highway and Transportation Officials' *A Policy on Geometric Design of Highways and Streets* (known as the "Green Book") and the Federal Highway Administration's *Manual on Uniform Traffic Control Devices* (the "MUTCD"). Both are written and regularly updated, without wide engagement or public debate, by exclusive professional associations dominated by traffic engineers. Together they govern every aspect of the roadways you use every day: lane width, median design, intersections, crosswalks, and signage. Beyond physical design rules, the MUTCD also establishes a process for setting speed limits.

The manuals share one overarching priority: to facilitate the smooth movement of cars. To that end, both the Green Book and the MUTCD measure a road's success exclusively by its "level of service": the extent to which cars may travel freely without having to slow down or queue. Another reflection of this priority, primarily enshrined in the Green Book, are requirements for overly wide lanes, which in turn promote speeding. And then there's the MUTCD's speed limit protocol, which allows speed limits to be raised to the 85th percentile speed of traffic, even if drivers are exceeding the existing speed limit. In other words, it's a speed limit set by those who are breaking the speed limit.

These two manuals directly conflict with complete-streets principles. In prioritizing the speed of cars, they raise both the incidence and the impact of crashes, making our streets more deadly. They support the ever-increasing expansion of pavement, which environmental journalist Ben Goldfarb has argued disrupts animal habitat and contributes to a negative, global shift in ecological conditions. The manuals are also wholly insensitive to neighborhood context and make no accommodations for different zoning or different uses. Neither manual offers a vision for streets that complement the buildings that line them, or how a street's cross-section might be arranged to balance utility and beauty.

Yet they continue to dominate road design. Local engineers who control the public portions of streets rely on these manuals and apply them rigidly, with little or no consideration given to the specific context of a particular setting. Institutional inertia plays a role: people tend to do what is easiest and most familiar, and a busy city official simply does not have time to rewrite a road-design manual. In an ironic twist, the legal doctrine of immunity also contributes to the persistence of these misguided guidebooks. State legislatures and courts have generally granted immunity to governments who use the Green Book and the MUTCD from litigants claiming an injury resulting from inadequate road design, reasoning that the ubiquity of these manuals, and their wide acceptance as industry standard, pardons local governments who build manual-compliant roads. For instance, a Georgia statute says the state is not liable for losses resulting from road design "where such plan or design is prepared in substantial compliance with generally accepted engineering or design standards." Citing this statute, the Georgia court of appeals partly dismissed a lawsuit by the widow of a man who died in a fatal car crash on a state route, convinced by the state department of transportation's expert witness, who asserted that the state route was designed to comply with sight distance principles of the Green Book. In that court, the anonymous engineer-authors of the Green Book all but wrote the legal decision.

The Green Book and the MUTCD aren't the only guides upon which cities can rely when designing better streets. The most well-known alternative manual is the National Association of City Transportation Officials' *Urban Street Design Guide*. Reflecting complete-streets principles and rejecting the underlying pro-car ideology of the Green Book and MUTCD, the guide shows how existing streets can be retrofitted to promote the kind of multimodal use we saw implemented in Burlington's new code—and shows how new streets should get it right from the start.

Bowles Park, a 61-acre parcel in Hartford's North End, saw Hartford's first streets designed with NACTO principles in mind to serve all users. The site had long been occupied by decrepit apartment buildings operated by the local housing authority. In 2016, the housing authority solicited proposals for redevelopment, awarding the project to a team that proposed replacing the existing buildings with a mix of ownership and rental homes, and replacing the wide, meandering streets with an entirely new street grid. I was nervous and proud to chair the commission when it reviewed and approved a master plan for the whole project, including the particular aspects of its street design. The first phase resulted in a series of small two- to four-unit buildings resembling single-family homes, set along "neighborhood streets." Built from scratch, the streets have a generous buffer area with trees every ten feet, ample sidewalks, bike lanes, and on-street parking tucked between bulb-outs (curb extensions). The streets complement the new homes, each unique in architectural design while sharing similarly sized front yards, as well as porches. The first 135 units have been completed, nearly all reserved for low-income households; the second and third phases are well underway. The new neighborhood is lovely in a welcoming way that reflects a comfortable and coherent sense of place—that feeling one gets when the pieces of an environment just somehow fit together. Hartford residents who recall its prior dismal condition can marvel at what's there now.

The success of that project owes perhaps to the bold step of our commission taking for granted that we had the power to influence the entire building-to-building cross-section. Thus, during our 2016 code overhaul we included a street-design chapter in the zoning code itself. We took a hard look at Hartford's existing streets: relatively narrow streets in some neighborhoods, wide one-way streets downtown (like Burlington's), and a few grand boulevards. We also heard from residents and business owners about the kinds of qualities a great street should have. Shop owners told us that they needed street parking, but that they also needed wider sidewalks with more trees. Residents told us that some residential streets were too wide, causing people to speed. We attended seminars on the design of the public realm, which revealed that pleasant streets that were comfortable for pedestrians helped to reduce crime—especially when they were lined with trees, slowed cars, and had appropriately scaled lighting.

Based on their feedback, the street-design chapter of the Hartford code delineates basic parameters for a modest menu of five ideal street types. Neighborhood streets, with two unmarked lanes of eight or nine feet wide, a landscape buffer of at least eight feet, and a sidewalk of at least five feet, serve areas with rowhouses and single-family housing. Residential connectors, with two marked lanes ten or eleven feet wide and a land-scape buffer of at least two feet plus sidewalks, function as neighborhood main streets and serve residential areas with minimal businesses. Commercial connectors, with more businesses and connecting neighborhoods across town, must be equipped with bike lanes, landscape buffers of at least three feet and sidewalks of at least six feet, and may include parking lanes. Avenues, which resemble commercial connectors but serve denser areas, can have a center turning lane and greater overall width. Finally, faster-moving boulevards have up to two lanes in each direction, each eleven or twelve feet wide, with pedestrian protections like sidewalk bulb-outs to reduce the width of intersections. For each of these street types, we identified appropriate building types and established overall standards for trees and street furniture. After setting out these particulars, we included a catchall reference to the NACTO guide, saying it governed anything the zoning code does not address.

Certainly, creating new streets as the developers did in Bowles Park is easier than retrofitting existing streets. But the same principles apply when streets are reworked. Extending zoning's reach to publicly owned portions of streets can improve the way all the pieces fit together. It can help communities manage everything from street furniture upgrades on a single block to enormous redevelopments covering many areas.

Chicago's Theaster Gates characterized his vision for Stony Island Avenue, the big and busy thoroughfare, nine lanes wide, just outside the front door of his community arts center, as "a beautiful green belt" in the French tradition, connecting handsome buildings designed for South Side residents, who deserve beautiful things. It's easy to imagine what that would look and feel like. A well-designed street is invigorating. It's fun. And it's for everyone. Streets set the stage of our experience, wherever we are—and whether in Burlington or Hartford, San Francisco or Chicago, we should push zoning to do more to set those stages. This kind of boundary-pushing has strong legal grounding and gives us a new way of delivering streets that fix the failures of the past. Streets, so foundational to our places, have for too long been ignored by zoning, but it's time for zoners to pay attention.

A Curatorial Approach

Last winter, my family and I found ourselves in the heart of Delray Beach, at one point named the "Most Fun Small Town" in the United States. Occupying two miles of the east Florida coastline, the town of 67,000 people boasts a vibrant mix of restaurants, shops, and cultural activities and has a laid-back, artsy reputation. But it doesn't take a laissez-faire attitude to development. Fun, in its case, is carefully crafted, with architecture to match, thanks to a zoning code that sets forth the physical parameters for future growth.

Our stroll that day showed the results. After a dip in the Atlantic Ocean, we dried off, threw on clothes over our swimsuits, and walked westward on East Atlantic Avenue into town, crossing the barrier island protecting the Intracoastal Waterway, which the federal government created a century ago to provide an inland alternative to the high seas for coastline travel. With two vehicular lanes lined with sidewalks and palm trees, the avenue is the town's biggest draw. Boutiques and bistros sit alongside hotels and offices, in buildings between one and three stories tall. Together, these buildings create a continuous "wall" at the edge of the sidewalks. White predominates in the palette, while beachy yellows, pinks, and blues offer upbeat accents. Overhangs and awnings over the ground level alternate with arcades, shielding pedestrians from the sun. Every few buildings, wood Bermuda shutters protrude at a 45-degree angle, adding visual interest—while standing ready to cover windows during a tropical storm or hurricane. Short blocks typify the avenue, which mixes narrow storefronts with block-long buildings. Only one strip mall, Atlantic Plaza, mars the pedestrian experience, with about fifty parking spaces separating the sidewalk from shops and restaurants. Otherwise, most cars generally hide on side streets behind the avenue. The relative absence of the parked cars that clog so many American downtowns is just one of the features that make Delray so friendly and attractive, though for the Bronin family, the fact that we came upon five different ice-cream shops also ranks high.

While Delray Beach originally developed organically, the town has deployed its zoning code to ensure the same type of development continues in the future. This is a case where zoning doesn't have to correct so much as maintain. In 2015, the town adopted an ordinance that aims to preserve the scale of East Atlantic Avenue and the surrounding blocks, while encouraging pedestrian-friendly, mixed-use development. It's a form-based code, focused on architectural standards as much as on uses, in the same vein as such codes adopted in Nashville, Hartford, and Burlington, and seven hundred other American cities. Delray Beach likely drew inspiration from neighboring West Palm Beach, which adopted its form-based code in 1995, and from Seaside, in the Florida Panhandle, where the first American form-based code was written in 1982 by the founders of the "New Urbanism" planning movement. Nostalgic for the "traditional" neighborhoods of a century and more ago, New Urbanists love porches, pitched roofs, sidewalks, a set menu of building types and a mix of uses happening within them.

Along the avenue, the code permits every use that might reasonably fill out a downtown, including homes, shops, hotels, and offices. This inclusive use mix helps ensure both a diversity of businesses and a round-the-clock base of customers. The code goes further to ensure variety when it comes to housing. New apartment buildings with more than twelve units must have a "diverse unit" mix of studios, one-bedrooms, and apartments with two or more bedrooms. This mixing requirement counters the tendency of developers to overbuild studios and one-bedrooms, which provide a greater return on investment than larger units. While smaller units tend to attract single professionals and older individuals, larger units with more bedrooms allow larger households with families in them—and families typically require more amenities and services, another boost to area businesses. Again, a seemingly minor zoning requirement—in this case, for bigger apartments—can unloose cascading benefits.

Being a form-based code, it also outlines requirements for aesthetics. The town imposes height caps of about three stories along East Atlantic Avenue, with four stories allowed off the avenue. The more generous height caps for the surrounding blocks enable, but do not dictate, dense development. For a town wishing to incrementally increase its density, these caps make sense—and they do not hinder creativity, as architectural features such as spires, steeples, and cupolas may reach sixty-four feet, opening the door to inventive details. Delray Beach also imposes a height minimum of eighteen feet across the entire district, with a minimum of twelve-foot ground stories for shops. Like some other zoning code provisions, minimum height standards can increase a developer's initial costs. But a cohesive approach to the commercial spaces can also add value to the properties themselves, creating a more attractive shopping environment and boosting sales.

Frontage requirements, like height, help the town maintain continuity in the pedestrian experience. Walking along a sidewalk with gap-toothed development—say, a few charming brownstones next to a strip-mall parking lot—can be jarring. In Delray Beach, all buildings must sit within a tight range of the property line and must occupy between 75 and 100 percent of the width of the lot. Relatedly, the code eliminates side setbacks, meaning that each building can be as wide as the property itself, built from one side property line to the other. Together, these provisions prevent the incongruous development that we see in many other places, creating a parcel-by-parcel wall lining the street.

Importantly, the code also prevents the opposite: monolithic conditions can deaden a street. A building that exceeds 250 feet in length must provide a ten-foot-wide passageway for bikers and pedestrians to connect to alleys, streets, or parking lots behind the building. And it can't have large "blank walls," essentially exterior walls with no features, but rather must incorporate some kind of decoration or architectural detail—a vertical trellis with vines, say, or wall-mounted fountains, or public artwork. You might see these kinds of walls on the sides of a movie theater, performing arts space, or other large-interior volumes that repel the use of windows.

To add still more visual interest, Delray Beach delineates seven architectural styles after which property owners can model their buildings. This list captures the range of styles already on display in town and includes Art Deco, classical, Mediterranean, and "Florida Vernacular," among others. Architectural guidelines separate from the zoning code further articulate the features of each style. While the code prohibits mixing styles, it fosters creativity within them, giving designers many options for rooflines, materials, colors, and fenestration.

A great shopping and entertainment street will almost always have lots of windows. People are curious creatures who enjoy previewing retail wares, watching a salon-goer get a haircut, and spying into a restaurant to gauge its look and crowdedness. Most of the establishments on East Atlantic Avenue already have large storefront windows, but to prevent a contrarian developer from declining to install them, the zoning code requires storefront windows covering at least 20 percent of all ground-floor wall area in every building on the avenue. And these windows must be "transparent"—no tinted or mirrored glass.

In Florida, pedestrians aren't just looking for visual interest. They also seek shade. Delray Beach's code sets guidelines for the installation of both awnings and arcades on East Atlantic Avenue and requires parking lots,

plazas, and parking garage roofs be at least a third shaded. The code also
specifies other, subtle details that a visitor might not notice but that contribute to the vitality of the streetscapes, like the lively variety of building
widths. On East Atlantic Avenue, lots must be between twenty and seventy-
five feet wide, which replicates the widths of the small- and medium-width
lots already in place. These widths also effectively prevent big-box retail-
ers, whose retail siting formulas require more frontage, from gobbling up
the real estate on the avenue. In this way, zoning plays a defensive role for
existing downtown businesses.

Amid these beneficial code provisions lurks one questionable decree:
parking mandates. The city's code requires up to 1.75 parking spaces per
housing unit, plus one space for every 500 square feet of retail area, and
between six and twelve spaces per 1,000 square feet of restaurant. Delray
Beach would do well to delete this provision, strict enforcement of which
could single-handedly undermine the many provisions that foster such a
walk-friendly, mixed-use corridor.

Despite the onerous parking provision, the code appears to be working
well, creating an appealing environment that helps promote patronage of
local businesses. On our recent visit, we saw hordes of pedestrians brows-
ing at shops, and we dined at a café with sidewalk seating. New projects
seem to be fitting in nicely, too. The largest project to be permitted under
the new code is Atlantic Crossing, a block-length development that will
eventually contain six three- and four-story buildings, mostly in the Mediterranean and modern architectural styles. The development will include
343 housing units and roughly 80,000 square feet each of office and entertainment (shops and restaurants) space. The first phase of the project has
produced a three-story structure that boasts awnings, arcades, and balconies on the East Atlantic Avenue façade, and another building behind,
with two more nearing completion. Bermuda shutters and beachy colors
visually connect the new construction with its neighbors. Using the slogan
"Pedestrians Rule," the developers seem poised to reinforce the sense of
vibrant activity that Delray Beach's leaders and planners set out to foster.
Atlantic Crossing will bring hundreds of new people ready to stroll the

Pineapple Grove Arts District, eat Cuban cuisine, and wander over to the municipal beach where my family and I started our walk.

For those interested in zoning, Delray Beach presents a paradox that's important to understand. At first glance, its form-based code may seem to constrain creativity instead of unleashing it. But in reality it builds in flexibility, providing architects with limits within which they can inventively and fruitfully design. As Robert Frost once remarked in defense of traditional forms in poetry, you can't play tennis without a net. Architectural styles that set basic rules don't limit; they provide leeway for the creative mind. With clear guidelines, the form-based code has created a sense of certainty for property owners, raising property values. Most importantly, it creates a unifying sense of a place, one that is visually harmonious and easy to understand. Just as zoning can be crafted to ensure variety for commodity's sake, so too can we zone for visual interest, to create or capture a community's architectural essence.

Tracing the Intracoastal Waterway from the Florida coast westward to the Texas coast brings you eventually to Galveston, a city of 53,000 people fifty miles southeast of Houston. Unlike Delray Beach, where the zoning code attempts to encourage delightful and complementary new construction, Galveston's zoning code looks backward to preserve and enhance the old. The city occupies virtually all of Galveston Island, a slender barrier island in the Gulf of Mexico twenty-seven miles long and no more than two and a half miles wide. Incorporated in 1839, the "Queen of the Gulf" almost immediately boomed. Connected to railroads that crisscrossed Texas, Galveston's busy port saw trade in cotton, grain, flour, sugar, tea, and fruit as well as immigrants arriving to the United States and craftsmen, clergymen, and tourists simply traveling the Gulf Coast. By the late nineteenth century, cosmopolitan Galveston had become one of the world's wealthiest cities. Its primary commercial corridor, The Strand, hosted the most prominent businesses and earned the moniker "The Wall Street of the South."

On September 8, 1900, all this changed. A hurricane obliterated the island, resulting in the deaths of more than 6,000 people—the deadliest disaster in U.S. history. The city responded as best it could, building a large seawall, raising the streets, and reconstructing at least 2,000 homes. But it never regained its status. Ships shifted to the Port of Houston and, in time, the banks, merchants, and producers followed.

In the decades since, Galveston's fortunes have waxed and waned, but one constant has been its turn-of-the-century architecture, much of it intact to this day. Tourists frequent The Strand, five blocks of which are now designated a National Historic Landmark. The form nominating The Strand for this elite honor identifies forty-five buildings of interest, saying that "their preservation en masse . . . is of real architectural significance as a still extant visual segment of the business life of the latter third of the nineteenth century." The popular styles represented include Greek Revival, Italianate, Gothic, High Victorian, and Beaux Arts, expressed in stuccoed brick, red brick, cast iron, and stone. Galveston's annual Christmas festival, "Dickens on the Strand," which draws tens of thousands of visits each December weekend it runs, uses these buildings as a backdrop to evoke Victorian-era England.

Though The Strand receives a lot of attention, the neighboring East End has equal appeal. Sprawling across its more than fifty blocks are hundreds of Victorians and Greek Revivals, built between the 1840s and the 1910s. A primarily residential area, the East End boasts strong historical associations with Galveston's most prominent citizens. Even before the neighborhood became a National Historic Landmark, it earned the distinction (in 1970) of being the first historic district designated by the City of Galveston itself. The Strand followed, and many other sites in the city. This background is important because of where zoning comes in: the Historical Zoning District Ordinance provides not only the mechanism for the designation itself, but also for the protection of designated resources.

To trigger historic protection, Galveston's zoning code lays out a multistep rezoning process that starts with the city identifying landmarks to protect and ends with the assignment of these landmarks to a historic overlay district. The first step is typically initiated by the property owners, who apply for a district to the city's landmark commission. That commission reviews a variety of factors, including whether the site has an association with significant historical events or people, displays distinctive architectural characteristics, or contains important historical information. If the answer is yes, then the planning commission and city council review the application. Only after the council votes to proceed with the rezoning will the proposed district be assigned to the historic overlay district. Once this happens, the underlying district to which the land was originally assigned remains in effect. It controls the allowable uses, while the historic overlay introduces additional regulations for construction.

Before a property owner can change anything significant about a site in the historic overlay, she must ensure the change will work well with the historic architecture. And so she must apply for a "certificate of appropriateness": a written finding that the city has deemed any proposed alteration, relocation, or demolition appropriate considering all relevant factors. To help officials make this determination, the city has developed design standards, which generally track widely accepted national standards for the rehabilitation of historic properties. These standards offer specific suggestions for different types of buildings, including materials, proportion, roof pitch, and more. The landmark commission has allowed public comment to shape them through public meetings and revisions, with the result that, in general, the standards do not bar new ideas, but rather reward creativity within guardrails that ensure that the new honors the old.

Galveston's code does not merely provide for alterations. It also charts a path, albeit a difficult one, for property owners looking to demolish a structure. While the code bars demolitions of buildings that contribute to the historic significance of the district, it can make exceptions in cases where the owner would suffer an economic hardship from a denial. (Just over half of local governments with historic regulation have similar provisions.) The code specifies three necessary components of an economic hardship: the inability to realize a reasonable rate of return on the property, the inability to adapt it for a use that *would* offer a reasonable rate of return, and the failure over the last two years to find a buyer or ten-ants that would have enabled such a return. Owners must show the com-mission that they have tried to rehab, lease, and sell the property; they might also demonstrate that they pay high taxes, have outstanding liens (legal claims by creditors on the property), cannot afford required main-tenance, or have a mortgage that exceeds the value of the property. The applicant must provide evidence of "good faith efforts" to work with local preservation groups and other interested parties, and must provide evi-dence of these efforts to the commission. Property owners must also sign affidavits, submit financial information, obtain appraisals, and provide a documented rationale for the demolition. Owners only get one bite at the demolition apple each year: The city refuses to accept repeat applications for a demolition within a year of a denial.

Given these procedural hurdles, it's easy to see why so few buildings in Galveston's historic neighborhoods have been torn down. The East End has been preserved so well that I decided to celebrate my fortieth birth-day there, vainly hoping that I could remain so well preserved in years to come. My family rented a two-story charmer on Sealy Avenue. What delighted us as much as the surrounding architecture were the "tree sculp-tures" that artists have forged out of dead trunks. Across the neighbor-hood, squirrels, dogs, birds, warriors, and maidens emerge, in fairy-tale fashion, from random front and side yards. These sculptures are a meta-phor for the way Galvestonians treat their community. Honor what came before by bringing it new life.

Together, Delray Beach and Galveston illustrate how code drafters increasingly use zoning to guide the aesthetics of buildings using mea-sures that go well beyond zoning's baseline function of regulating land uses. Across the United States, other communities appear to be doing like-wise. The seven hundred places with form-based codes constitute about 2 percent of the 39,000 local governments around the country. As for historic preservation, I have published a census of over 3,500 localities—about 10 percent of all local governments—that regulate historic districts, either through zoning or through stand-alone historic preservation ordinances.

Both figures continue to rise, as more and more communities figure out how to harness land use controls to curate our experience.

At first glance, Las Vegas's glitzy, mid-century-mod Strip couldn't seem more unlike Galveston's East End. Infamous for its garish and colossal signage, a place where colors, lights, shapes, and sizes surprise and delight, the Las Vegas Strip is the West's sprawling answer to New York's Times Square. With four miles of hotels, casinos, performance venues, and restaurants on Las Vegas Boulevard, the Strip offers retirees, bachelor partiers, and conferencegoers alike an entertainment oasis in the desert. Unlike Times Square, which packs a compact, vertical punch of billboards and moving displays, the Strip metes out its trademark imagery in linear fashion, best seen by car. This assortment at first reads as visual chaos, with no semblance of order. Yet the order *is* the chaos, its motley elements collectively if somewhat haphazardly communicating an almost exuberant joy in the possibilities of expression. Zoning can—and does—play a role in perpetuating this joy and in protecting this type of bighearted expression. Like Galveston's charming historic neighborhood, Las Vegas's immortal, immoral Strip also turns out to make deft use of aesthetic zoning.

The Strip became a tourist destination in the 1940s, when the first casinos popped up. They offered an alternative to other gambling centers, like Atlantic City (and, incidentally, Galveston). As new casinos and hotels were constructed, each seemed to outdo the last in both architecture and signage. Creativity in signage design was at its peak in the 1940s through 1960s. Classics still standing include the futuristic Googie-style "Welcome to Fabulous Las Vegas" sign, the Hacienda Horse and Rider, and the Normandie Hotel's "Elvis Slept Here" sign. You can see many other remnants of the signage from this era at the Neon Museum, north of downtown.

For decades, cultural elites and aesthetes derided the Strip for its gaudy showiness. Then came *Learning from Las Vegas*, a seminal 1972 monograph by three architectural theorists. Chronicling and assessing the architecture, symbols, and signage of the Las Vegas Strip, it took the boulevard seriously as an urban form, even comparing it to the monuments of Rome and Greece. The study celebrated the Strip's appeal to the common man and encouraged the architectural community, and the world beyond, to reconsider their snobbish condemnation. At the time, Las Vegas was home to the longest and highest signs in the world—as well as some of the boldest. As the authors of *Learning from Las Vegas* explain, "Signs in Las Vegas use mixed media, words, pictures, and sculpture—to persuade and inform." And a sign in Vegas, they hardly needed to say, is also used to entertain—a multifunctional device that "revolves by day and becomes a play of lights at night." *Learning from Las Vegas* viewed the Strip hermeneutically, as the scene of competition between signs, or even signs and buildings, with some signs as large as buildings—and some buildings serving as signage. The book's publication burnished Vegas's image, encouraging readers to see the Strip not merely as tacky kitsch but as a uniquely American place, as fascinating as it is glitzy.

How exactly is this uniqueness managed and maintained? In its totality, Las Vegas Boulevard extends for close to fifty miles, weaving in and out of the city limits. The four miles of the boulevard with the highest concentration of character-defining signage actually sit not inside the City of Las Vegas but within unincorporated Clark County. The county's zoning map puts most of the Strip in the Limited Resort and Apartment District, which aims to "provide for the development of gaming enterprises, compatible commercial, and mixed commercial and residential uses." Some of the Strip sits within a district with general commercial purposes. In addition, as of 2019, county officials overlaid most of the Strip with the Mixed Use Overlay District, which aims to permit "a highly concentrated and intense development of mixed residential, commercial, employment, and recreational uses typical of high intensity central business districts." With three districts governing this stretch and its signage, the county does not make it easy to understand the Strip's desired outcomes.

It would seem natural for the zoning code to embrace the large, festive signage already existing on the boulevard, and in fact for freestanding signs, the code does enable larger sizes, allowing them to grow as linear street frontage grows. But the code limits other types of signs. For example, projecting signs max out at just 32 square feet in most districts. Animated signs are allowed in only a portion of the Strip, and only up to 150 square feet. A commercial complex or resort hotel can have only one revolving sign and must forgo constructing any other freestanding sign. Perhaps oddest of all, given the Las Vegas tradition, one portion of the code bans neon (other than "accent lighting limited to no more than 25% of a sign's area") as well as reflective lamps or bulbs. Some of the signs for which Las Vegas is best known probably couldn't be put up under the county's current zoning code.

The City of Las Vegas takes a much more permissive approach than the county in regulating its part of the Strip. Freestanding signs can reach up to forty feet high and up to eighty feet for signs that can be seen from the highways. In terms of their size, signs may be two square feet per linear foot of street frontage, meaning that signs can increase in size as lot size increases. Two hundred feet of streetside lot frontage, in other words, can yield a huge sign, forty feet long by ten feet high. What's more, a property owner can display up to three "supergraphic" (very large) signs on any building of nine stories or more, either incorporated into the building's façade or projected up to five feet from it, with no maximum size. And with the exception of signs near housing, internal and external illumination is allowed—so bring on the neon!

All these rules are very particular, and they follow the national trend of embedding signage regulation in zoning codes. To my mind, going too far to make Vegas's signage less garish aims to contradict the fundamental nature of the Strip: a bold, almost outrageous expression not found anywhere else. The U.S. Supreme Court in recent years has repeatedly struck down significant limitations on signage on free-speech grounds. In Las Vegas's case, over-regulation may not only be a violation of the Constitution, but also, from a design point of view, a violation of a unique and signature type of aesthetic expression—one that might be out of place in the average suburb, to be sure, but is perfectly at home in Sin City. Zoning codes that check free speech should balance the legal technicalities with the spirit of the place they're attempting to regulate, eschewing a one-size-fits-all approach and letting folks have a little fun.

All of this said, cool signs do not necessarily make a truly fulfilling public realm. I cannot argue that the Strip or Las Vegas Boulevard offers an ideal, or even tolerable, experience for all its visitors. At six (and sometimes ten) lanes wide, the boulevard itself can be characterized pejoratively as a "stroad": a fast-moving, car-prioritizing road that also attempts to function as a street lined with buildings and anticipating pedestrian activity. The term was coined by land use planner Charles Marohn, who called the stroad "the futon of transportation alternatives"—that is, made to serve as both a street and a road, as a futon is both couch and bed, but uncomfortable as either. That's funny, but humor can't obfuscate the Strip's unsafe reality as a place that has recently seen many pedestrians killed by errant or speeding drivers. Its sprawl, moreover, promotes the excesses of car-centric living, and thus greenhouse gas emissions, even as its carefully engineered allure injects millions of visitors into a fragile desert ecosystem. Recognizing these devastating flaws, I've chosen to focus on one positive aspect of an otherwise dysfunctional place, and the role of zoning in shaping it.

Zoning codes give us power to curate what we see, helping us more clearly articulate our cities and the relationship of the buildings within them to each other and to people, through mechanisms like the ones used by Delray Beach and Las Vegas. Yet very few places have harnessed the full legal power of such codes, and in most places the piecemeal approach still rules. Maximum building heights may bar overly tall structures, but they do little to foster aesthetic cohesion. Historic places are overlooked for new construction. Design particulars are absent from most codes. As a result, we often end up with a hodgepodge of buildings that don't "speak" to each other, and streetscapes that feel jarringly incoherent.

Architects do not leave their buildings to chance but affirmatively select materials, paint colors, and decor. If the façade of a building is intentional, you would think that the articulation of our cities would be too. But you'd be wrong. Worse yet, the problems in many codes are more than just errors of omission. The details they mandate can actually prevent us from making beautiful, coherent places. Few would say they love the look of their local strip mall, yet strip malls are what too many codes effectively require, through minimum parking mandates and market incentives for developers to maximize profits by building the least expensive construction available. We must become more intentional about our places, thinking more carefully and comprehensively about the built environments that zoning codes both preserve and produce. Each place requires something different. What makes sense for Delray may not make sense for Galveston. What happens in Vegas may need to stay in Vegas. But by thinking carefully and seriously about what makes a community unique and what's worthy of promotion or preservation, we can help write the rules that give us communities that enrich our everyday lives.

Conclusion

*Z*oning hides in plain sight. The home, workplace, learning environment, restaurant, corner store, nightlife venue: at every turn, behind whatever you are looking at—whatever you are doing—zoning is there, surreptitiously dictating our lives with its fateful rules. If we can understand its power, then we can also learn how to improve it.

It's easy to get caught up in the discouraging ways zoning gets things wrong. So many zoning codes make it hard for people to build the housing they need, walk safely, or enjoy nightlife. Zoning, coupled with street design manuals, has created car-centric neighborhoods that endanger pedestrians while sprawling out to damage our forests, deserts, and other ecosystems. Zoning disrupts the way we can grow and access the food we need to live healthy lives. It can neglect the very human need for visually appealing environments and meaningful experiences. Worst of all, zoning too often intrudes and imposes on deeply personal choices about where we live, how we live, and even who we live with.

Given these problems, it's not surprising that some have advocated for zoning's abolition. The roots of this laissez-faire, market-based approach come from the seductive work of economist Bernard Siegan, who lived in highly regulated La Jolla, California, but nonetheless wrote admiringly in the 1970s about Houston's lack of zoning. Siegan's admiration of my hometown has since been echoed by many contemporary commentators, other zoning minimalists and abolitionists who have studied and lauded it. While aspects of Houston's approach can be a model for overly restrictive cities, a total lack of land use controls can also trigger inequitable and unpleasant outcomes, as I've come to understand through my own Houston experiences—and those of my uncle the veterinarian, my grandparents the restauranteurs, my parents the condo-owners, and my sister, too, the perpetual passenger in the back seat of the family car. To ensure that our places are vibrant and fulfilling, and that the people who live in them find maximum enjoyment and opportunity, we need commonsense rules governing the way we use our land.

To realize zoning's broad power is to take the first step in understanding how to make it better, because for all the ways zoning can harm us, it can also benefit us. Through sensible reforms, we can end decades of policies that exalt the car. We can permit and even promote the flexibility that will help us deal with pandemics, climate change, and broadscale societal shifts. We can boost the diversity of local economies. And we can remove entrenched barriers to opportunity and improve racial and economic equality.

I am reminded of the power of zoning every time I step out of my front door. Over the course of writing this book, I moved from one capital—Hartford—to another, Washington, D.C., and set up my home in Georgetown, arguably the best neighborhood in the United States. While its evolution from industrial town to gentrified enclave was not sparked by zoning, the effects of zoning are all around, and the neighborhood serves as a primer for the principles I advocate in this book.

Georgetown's story is one of evolution, including periods of growth, decline, and revival, displacement, exclusion, and reform. Its history dates to 1751, nearly five decades before Washington was founded as the nation's capital. Georgetown's position on the bluffs of the Potomac River influenced its evolution as an active port for Maryland and Virginia tobacco, a hub for military suppliers during the Revolutionary War, and a center for a range of industries from paper mills and iron foundries to glass works and lime kilns. In the first half of the nineteenth century its prospects were boosted by public-works projects, among them the construction of a bridge across the Potomac, the lighting and paving of Pennsylvania Avenue, and the extension of the Chesapeake and Ohio Canal in 1831. Parallel to the river, the canal towpath that today serves as my running trail was once busy with boats carrying coal, tobacco, salt, sugar, and other commodities between the Alleghenies and the city.

In 1871, Georgetown became part of the District of Columbia, and around the same time its growing Black community, many employed in public service or other stable enterprises, purchased the area's more modest homes. By 1900, 4,000 of Georgetown's 15,000 residents were Black, and about 40 percent of them lived in barns, former quarters for enslaved persons, and alleys without electricity or plumbing. "Alley clearance" programs in the 1910s and 1920s removed hundreds of Black residents from the area, with devastating effects on the social and economic fabric of that community. Over the same period, as the canals silted up and flooding became a more serious problem, the area's maritime and industrial industries floundered, and Georgetown earned a reputation for being a gritty part of town. This reputation ensured that the neighborhood was ignored by developers—ironically advantageous, as the lack of interest spared its buildings from demolition and enabled the preservation-by-neglect of the laborers' rowhomes along the waterfront, the commercial buildings along Wisconsin Avenue and M Street, and the religious buildings and corner stores nestled among the homes north of M Street.

Washington, D.C.'s first zoning ordinance, adopted in 1924, established four distinct districts. Most of Georgetown was assigned to the residential district, but the lots on Wisconsin and the north side of M were relegated to the two commercial districts and the dozen or so blocks nearest the waterfront to the industrial district. Partly driven by the confidence in future growth patterns that the zoning code provided, young New Dealers began buying and fixing up Georgetown's Federal, classical, Georgian townhouses and mansions. Encouraged by rents lower than those in the newer streetcar suburbs, and by the presence of quaint urban dwellings full of character, up-and-coming families invested in restoring the physical integrity of the historic properties.

These residents took notice of local preservation ordinances that were adopted in several other cities, and they petitioned the city to follow suit. In 1950 Georgetown was deemed the city's first historic district, protecting it from further development, including urban renewal. An overhaul of the zoning code in 1958 kept the zoning designations more or less the same. Significantly, despite the collapse of industry in Georgetown, that version of the code preserved the waterfront blocks in industrial districts, which meant residents continued to be cut off from the Potomac as a potential recreational amenity—perhaps no loss given that the river was so polluted at the time. Only about fifty years later did the city rezone the waterfront for recreational uses; the waterfront was slowly redeveloped, including the expansion of a park, restaurants, and a promenade.

From one perspective, Georgetown's zoning code can be seen as a tool for simply locking in place what was there a century ago. But in truth, as is the case elsewhere, it's the code's flexibility—not its rigidity—that has helped make Georgetown what it is today. That flexibility ensures a mix of uses: I can walk from my house to three different places serving up chocolate croissants, or to get a haircut or a pair of shoes, while window-shopping for furniture and kitchen cabinetry. Tucked between my neighbors' homes are a local butcher shop, as well as a yoga studio, several pharmacies, and a few art galleries. That diversity of options isn't accidental; it's available because the D.C. zoning code, like Buffalo's, has a provision allowing "corner stores"—shops, arts, restaurants, and bars—in our neighborhood. Adding to the health of the neighborhood, the code requires that corner grocery stores devote a minimum of 20 percent of retail space to perishable goods (dairy, fresh produce, meat, and fish), instead of processed foods.

Housing options, too, vary far more than the area's tony reputation suggests it might: basement apartments for area college students, second-story apartments for young families who work in the shops, and multi-unit housing like the place I live now, mixed right in with single-family. While many housing units are unachievably expensive for most people, zoning allows some lots to be as small as 1,600 square feet—about the same size as Houston's much-lauded mini-parcels. Some older lots are smaller still; a cute rowhouse I can see from my bedroom window looks to be about eleven feet wide. In addition, the zoning code allows basement, over-store, and garage apartments for up to six people. It legalizes a wide variety of home-based occupations, so the barbers, small-scale food producers, tailors, doctors, and dentists in the neighborhood can see clients in their own homes. Agricultural uses, including both residential and institutional, are allowed, in case anyone wants to do a little (or a lot) of urban farming.

In terms of natural infrastructure, the neighborhood association and the city have partnered on a robust tree planting program, and the city's Green Area Ratio program, which resembles Seattle's, requires property owners to install and maintain landscaping. Meanwhile, now that the industrial areas have been rezoned, a massive engineering project has ensured that the new waterfront park can help manage flooding made worse by climate change. Adding to the health of the ecosystem, even in this urban location, between 20 and 50 percent of every lot must be permeable surface, allowing water to infiltrate the ground, rather than flood the streets.

As for transportation, the area is blessed with eight Metro bus lines running through it, ferrying passengers to downtown and other D.C. neighborhoods, and even to Virginia, with a couple of lines linking to subway stops. (The myth that residents blocked a Metro stop is urban legend.) I'm always dodging bikes and scooters. While there are nominal parking requirements (one space per single-family home or one for every two

apartments), they apply hardly anywhere in Georgetown because properties within a quarter-mile of Wisconsin Avenue are exempt, and no parking is required where it would infringe on the historic character of the
neighborhood or where the building has no access to a public alley. Only
the wealthiest residents have off-street parking, which means there aren't
many curb cuts, and walking is safe and pleasant. And it's pretty quiet,
too, except for a few occasional late-night cars, heading from a bar or jazz
club, windows open and music blasting—racing home, I'm guessing to
the suburbs.

Not every place should become Georgetown, and many would not want
to. Every place has its own unique history, one that continues to shape the
present in profound ways. But Georgetown demonstrates the way that sensitive zoning can help build a neighborhood, in the fullest sense of the word.

Zoning's many tools—use tables, minimum lot sizes, parking minimums, tree-canopy coverages, accessory buildings, transferable development rights, dispersion radii, turf mandates, inclusionary mandates,
transit-oriented zones, street designs, height caps, stepbacks, setbacks, and
signage—all shape outcomes, for better and for worse. Recoding zoning's
rules means not only knowing what the tools are, but where these tools
are being deployed—and where they need to be deployed.

In most places, harnessing the power of zoning requires tedious work:
demystifying lengthy codes filled with opaque jargon, filling out endless
forms, making applications, working with city staff, and appearing at
public hearings. But there are already people out there doing the work.
My latest project, the National Zoning Atlas, is working in nearly every
state to collect information about how local zoning codes work. It seeks
to decipher complicated codes and accessibly display this information in
an online interactive map. As the Atlas expands, it will offer a much richer
understanding of all the levers of zoning that influence a broad array of
social and economic outcomes. For the first time, it will illuminate local
zoning code across state and regional lines. With any luck, it will lead to a

collective rethinking not only of how we write zoning codes, but of what level of government should administer them.

As we work to use zoning's power for good in its second century, I hope that we'll begin to see zoning not as a boring and bureaucratic chore, but as a tool that can be used creatively, imaginatively, and carefully to build community in an ethical and intentional way. Zoning allows us to see and to develop a relationship between rules and plans, aspirations and outcomes. It calls for a keen awareness of the yin and yang of flexibility and guidance in making those outcomes a reality. Finding the critical balance between encouraging growth and setting limits; between the enthusiastic "yes!" and the prudent "maybe not here": that is the art of zoning. Engaging with zoning means applying design thinking on a neighborhood scale, curating built environments just like our art galleries—in the hope of inspiring joy and reaching our collective human spirit.

In that sense, we would do well to follow the thinking of famed Roman architect Vitruvius, who wrote that every great building must have three features: *utilitas*, *venustas*, and *firmitas*, usually translated to mean utility, delight, and firmness. A building that isn't useful or doesn't function well for its occupants is a waste; its configuration of walls, entrances, and windows must ensure that people can use it for its intended purpose. A building that isn't beautifully expressed will never delight us, even if it manages to stand up and serve a purpose. And a building without structural integrity—without a strong foundation, and with faulty or insecure components among its steel, concrete, and timber—will collapse.

Like a great building, our places, too, need to be useful, beautiful, and well-structured. In function, they must thrive with activities that meet the needs of a mix of residents, workers, and visitors alike. In experience, they must be visually appealing, elicit a sense of order and calm, and be scaled to the human body. And in overall structure, they must deploy thoughtfully designed public systems, from transportation to open space, for the benefit of all who use them.

Unfortunately, too many places lack these qualities—as Denise Best's Upper Albany neighborhood in Hartford lacked them, for far too long. In failing to offer the types of establishments she and other residents need and desire, the neighborhood doesn't—yet—deliver on its promise. Denise knew she wanted a more well-balanced place, and so do we all. Zoning can create that balance—or in Upper Albany's case, restore it. In time, the changes we made together on Albany Avenue will help re-create the neighborhood that residents want. The process is incremental and takes time. But despite zoning's sometimes impenetrable language, its promise is simple enough: reducing harm while promoting healing—and, step by step, closing in on our vision of how we want to live.

To be sure, zoning is not the only tool that matters. History, time, wealth, geography, and countless other factors will shape how communities evolve and develop. But while good zoning is not sufficient, it is necessary. Most important, it's something that we control. And that makes it the key to building the cities and towns that we long for.

Acknowledgments

This book is about the importance of understanding our power to improve the places where we live: the places that can—that should—sustain and fulfill us. So I'd first like to recognize the places that have shaped the way I think, write, and live. First and foremost, Houston: the unzoned city that still today both frustrates and surprises me. Then Crosby, the rural town chasing the American suburban dream. Austin, where I joyously wandered and wondered, and learned about architecture from the best. Oxford, England, where I spent two glorious years dreaming under the spires. Tokyo and St. Petersburg, where spectacular summers offered enough inspiration for many lifetimes. New York City, whose Morningside Heights hosted me for an all-too-short time before I packed up for Connecticut. And now Georgetown, the nearly perfect place in which I'm grateful every day to live—and walk. These places fill my life's atlas, and I will forever be in dialogue with them.

Of them all, the city of Hartford sits largest in my heart and has taught me most. I have dedicated this book to its people because they embarked with me on a journey to shape and reshape our future. I'm grateful to every Hartford resident who graciously introduced me to their neighborhood, who shared their aspirations about the way the city should evolve, and who put their trust in me and my fellow planning and zoning commissioners to do our best as we served them. Those commissioners, especially my two vice-chairs, Aaron Gill and Tony Koos, and my successor as chair, Josye Utick, deserve my gratitude for collaborating every step of the way to make bold changes for the city we loved. And we couldn't have done it without the support of numerous city staff—especially Jaime Brätt, Sean Fitzpatrick, Sandy Fry, Jonathan Mullen, and Caitlin Palmer—or consultant Leslie Oberholzer, who labored over zoning code drafts. It's no exaggeration to say that every minute I spent over those seven years—the meetings, the line edits, the walk-and-talks—was an honor and privilege. I hope we made some things right, and I hope we did some good.

And now to my family. To my dad, thanks for taking me to job sites and giving me your drafting table, parallel bar, mechanical eraser, and French curves and making me feel that I could be a creator, just like you. To my mom, thanks for letting me take home more books from the library any kid should have been allowed to take—and for encouraging me to see the world. To my sisters, Kathleen and Eva, thanks for talking to me nearly every day and loving me unconditionally. To my husband, Luke, thanks for reading every word of this draft, and for inspiring me with all you've done for Hartford, and beyond. You've given me the full and challenging life you promised me, and I love you for that. To my kids—the three best to have ever lived—thanks for being good sports as I've dragged you to all kinds of places, making endless commentary about their Vitruvian attributes, and for letting me bring my zoning maps to your classroom show-and-tells. And to my in-laws, Andy and Elaine, thank you for being loving grandparents to those kids, which made it easier for me to write this book.

This book interrogates the decisions—some intentional, some thoughtless—that cumulatively impact what we see and how we live. I only thought to ask these questions because my professors in college, grad school, and law school asked them of me. Jeff Chusid, Richard Cleary, Bob Ellickson, David Heymann, Avner Offer, Carol Rose, Bob Solomon, and Larry Speck: thank you for encouraging me to explore the links between law, design, and built reality.

This book's production would not have been possible without an incredible amount of help. Cornell University—through my wonderful faculty colleagues and through the City and Regional Planning Department, the Law School, the Libraries, and the Clarence S. Stein Institute—provided critical support that helped power this book. Deborah Berke and Phil Bernstein invited me to teach a "Curating Cities" course at the Yale School of Architecture, which allowed me to test some of my ideas and introduced me to a spectacular crop of budding architects. Rand Cooper provided invaluable editorial assistance, and Luke Reynolds—my tireless deputy at Desegregate Connecticut—offered ideas and encouragement. Thanks also go to the students, among them Giacomo Cabrera, Emma Cotnoir, Duncan Grimm, Jessica Kim, and Danny Woods, who pitched in to fact-check and assemble sources. Finally, thank you to Margo Beth Fleming, my agent, and Huneeya Siddiqui, my lead editor, who not only skillfully shepherded this book through many rounds of edits, but also wrote to me from vacation spots with their zoning queries—and to Matt Weiland, for picking up the book in the first place. You've collectively taught me as much about writing as anyone, and you've managed to sharpen the wonky first drafts into something that I hope people will actually enjoy reading.

Notes

Introduction

4 **the asthma capital of Connecticut:** DataHaven, Connecticut City Neighborhood Profiles 2020, www.ctdatahaven.org/.

4 **the worst such health outcomes:** DataHaven, Health Equity in Connecticut 2023 (2023), noting that adults in Hartford are twice as likely as adults in suburbs to say they have asthma, 6.

4 **Upper Albany is predominantly Black:** DataHaven, Health Equity, 6.

4 **income of about $23,000:** University of Hartford, Upper Albany Main Street Area Demographics, www.upperalbany.com/.

4 **income of about $131,000:** DataHaven, Avon 2021 Health Equity Profile (2021), www.ctdatahaven.org/.

6 **The earliest maps we've discovered:** John Noble Wilford, *The Mapmakers* (New York: Vintage Books, 1981), 7–14.

6 **new multifamily "tenement" dwellings:** As one example, the city of New Haven had individual ordinances on noxious uses, aesthetics, and tenement housing decades before it adopted zoning in 1926. Andrew J. Cappel, "A Walk Along Willow: Patterns of Land Use Coordination in Pre-Zoning New Haven (1870–1926)," *Yale Law Journal* 101, no. 3 (1991).

6 **rife with semicovert, racially invidious action:** In 1880, San Francisco required

laundry operators to obtain a hard-to-get permit before they could establish a laundry facility in a residential neighborhood. See Charles J. McClain, *In Search of Equality: The Chinese Struggle Against Discrimination in Nineteenth-Century America* (Berkeley: University of California Press, 1994), 101–4. Laundry operators had to get the signatures of a dozen people on the block; no signatory could be of Chinese origin. Nearby Stockton went further, banning laundries except in uninhabitable marshland. These seemingly neutral laws, ostensibly designed to banish "nuisance" enterprises and promote public safety, were in fact motivated by anti-Chinese sentiment: Chinese immigrants owned and operated many local laundries. Invalidating both cities' laws, a federal appeals court sarcastically dismissed "the miserable pretense that the business of a laundry . . . is against good morals or dangerous to the public safety," In Re Quong Woo, 13 F. 229, 233 (9th Cir. 1882). In a later case, the same court added that cleanliness was "necessary to civilization—necessary to the health, comfort, and happiness of a civilized people." In Re Tie Loy, 26 F. 611, 613 (9th Cir. 1886). These and other similar legal decisions did little to deter municipal leaders from embedding discrimination in zoning laws. They just became a little more careful to establish a credible pretense.

7 **factory workers daring to use Fifth Avenue:** Gregory F. Gilmartin, *Shaping the City: New York and the Municipal Arts Society* (New York: Clarkson Potter, 1995), 190–91.

7 **a map and a thirteen-page-long text:** NYC, Building Zone Resolution (1916).

7 **Zoning Enabling Act:** U.S. Department of Commerce Advisory Committee on Zoning, *A Standard State Zoning Enabling Act* (Washington, DC: Government Printing Office, 1926).

7 **"purpose of promoting health, safety, morals":** U.S. Department of Commerce, *A Standard State Zoning Enabling Act*, § 1. It offered few definitions or specifics, explaining: "Definitions are generally a source of danger. They give to words a restricted meaning."

8 **425 municipalities with zoning:** U.S. Department of Commerce, *A Standard State Zoning Enabling Act*, iii nn.1 and 2.

8 **1926 Supreme Court decision:** Village of Euclid v. Ambler Realty Company, 272 U.S. 365, 394 (1926).

8 **can't ordinarily be applied retroactively:** One exception to this general rule is that in some cases, states give local governments the power to use zoning to amortize, or phase out, certain types of previously legal existing activities. Often, state law requires local governments to make a finding that the activity being phased out is a nuisance before the activity can be regulated out of existence. Amortization of adult uses is discussed in Chapter 5.

10 **only two dozen large cities:** Sara C. Bronin, "Comprehensive Rezonings," *Brigham Young University Law Review* 2019, no. 3 (2020): 725–68, 737. These two dozen cities were among the 350 U.S. cities with over 100,000 people.

Chapter 1: The Goldilocks Zone

15 **Houston's population exploded:** Joe R. Feagin, *Free Enterprise City: Houston in the Political-Economic Perspective* (New Brunswick: Rutgers University Press, 1988).

15 **new apartments, about 15,000:** The Rice University Kinder Institute for Urban Research recently found Gulfton to have the second-highest percentage of multifamily units of all Houston neighborhoods (93.2 percent). Kinder Institute analysis referenced in these notes can be found on its "Houston Community Data Connections" dashboard, aggregating neighborhood-level data from a variety of sources (including the Census and the American Community Survey) and online at www.datahouston.org.

16 **advertisements toward young professionals:** Susan Rogers, "Superneighborhood 27: A Brief History of Change," *Places* 17, no. 2 (2005): 36, 37.

16 **U.S. Submarine Sandwiches:** The address is 5422 Chimney Rock Road, currently occupied by Mauricio Express, Tienda Salvadoreña, an El Salvadorean clothing and general-goods store.

16 **Romy's Hamburgers:** The address is 6817 Bissonnet, currently occupied by El Pupusodromo, an El Salvadorean restaurant.

16 **Seeking a new clientele:** Lisa Taaffe and Robert Fisher, "Public Life in Gulfton: Multiple Publics and Models of Community Organization," *Journal of Community Practice* 4, no. 1 (1997): 31, 35.

16 **Gulfton quickly shifted:** According to Census data analyzed by the Kinder Institute, of 143 Houston neighborhoods, Gulfton has the highest population of foreign-born residents (58.5 percent), and only 15 percent have a high school education.

16 **the "Gulfton Ghetto":** In 1999, the Gulfton Comprehensive Strategy Planning Team, consisting of representatives from the city and county, local schools, the Houston Police Department, and area nonprofits, developed the *Gulfton Community Five Year Plan*, which summarized the issue as follows: "Economic downturns in the 1980's, out-of-state investors, poor housing construction and substandard infrastructure, and mass immigration of unskilled blue-collar workers transformed this once safe and appealing neighborhood into one of Houston's most crime-ridden and dangerous areas." See also Kim Cobb, "Drugs, Neglect Transform 'Single Scene' to Slums," *Houston Chronicle*, July 17, 1988, indicating that "the once fashionable apartment communities in the area . . . are now referred to as the 'Gulfton Ghetto.'"

16 **crime skyrocket:** The increase in crime made national news. See, for example, Wayne King, "New Police Chief Battles Crime Boom in Houston," *New York Times*, January 14, 1983, section A, 8, noting that at the time, Houston's "population, area and crime rate are all growing faster than anywhere else in the country" and that one in every thirty-two Houston residences was burglarized in 1980.

17 **employed covenants:** In most cases, developers creating a subdivision incorpo-

rated such covenants into the deeds for each new home. But property owners may also add a covenant to their own deeds after homes are constructed, sold, or occupied, by recruiting like-minded neighbors who agree to be bound by the terms of the covenant.

17 **historic house my uncle Rich owns:** The address is 1631 West Alabama.

17 **the Supreme Court deemed:** Shelley v. Kraemer, 334 U.S. 1 (1948).

18 **"runs with the land" forever:** In addition to those methods of expunging a racially restrictive covenant, some states have changed their laws to give property owners the ability to petition for the removal of such covenants from the land records. In 2021, the Texas legislature enacted Senate Bill 30, which allows for property owners to apply to the county deed recorder for removal. Texas Property Code § 5.026(a). That provision was not in place at the time of my uncle's lawsuit.

18 **had to file a lawsuit:** The procedural posture of this lawsuit differs from most. In general, covenants can be enforced in court by any property owner subject to them—say, a neighbor in a subdivision seeking to shut down a nonresidential use. In Houston, there is an additional (and highly unusual) option for enforcement: the city attorney's office. Houston, TX, Code of Ordinances §§ 10-551 to 10-555 (hereinafter the "Houston Code"). After the city proceeded to exercise its power to enforce the covenant on my uncle's land, he sued the city for relief. Dylan McGuinness, "Montrose Vet Sues Over 99-Year-Old Deed Restriction Blocking New Clinic," *Houston Chronicle*, February 4, 2001.

19 **one that Gulfton lacks:** The only part of Gulfton with deed restrictions is the original 1950s-era subdivision Shenandoah, which retains its single-family covenants today.

19 **second lowest of Houston's 143 neighborhoods:** Median home value is $66,493, according to Kinder Institute analysis.

19 **population grew:** The population grew from 26,855 in 1980 to 47,431 in 2015, with a net decrease of approximately 173 housing units over that period. Rogers, "Superneighborhood 27," 37 n. 3; City of Houston, Gulfton Complete Community Data Snapshot, www.houstoncc.org.

20 **Euclidean refers to zoning:** While the term "Euclidean zoning" now refers to distinct, use-based regulation of districts, the scheme at issue in the Supreme Court combined uses in a slightly different way than zoning is generally practiced today. At the time of the case, Euclid's zoning was actually pyramidal in nature, meaning that as zoning districts became more intense (i.e., moving from single-family residential to industrial), each more intense district allowed all of the uses in every less-intense zoning districts. Today, pyramidal zoning schemes are rare.

20 **special districts and "overlay" districts:** Special districts might be tailored for mobile homes, entertainment venues, correctional facilities, quarries, technology parks, and assisted-living facilities, among many other uses. These special districts tend to be small, often just a single block or a few plots of land. Sometimes a district

will be fashioned as an "overlay," meaning that it can be layered over another district and that it changes some, but not all, of the rules of the underlying district. For example, a historic preservation overlay might be applied to historic buildings in any zoning district. The overlay may add a new use, require a design review, or eliminate parking mandates, leaving the other rules the same.

20 **a brazenly anti-apartment sentiment:** Village of Euclid v. Ambler Realty Company, 394.

21 **Economists agree:** Chang-Tai Hsieh and Enrico Moretti, "Housing Constraints and Spatial Misallocation," *American Economic Journal: Macroeconomics* 11, no. 2 (2019), reviewing data from 220 metropolitan areas and finding that local legal constraints, including zoning, lowered aggregate growth in the United States by 36 percent from 1964 to 2009; Kyle F. Herkenhoff, Lee E. Ohanian, and Edward C. Prescott, "Tarnishing the Golden and Empire States: Land-Use Restrictions and the U.S. Economic Slowdown," *Journal of Monetary Economics* 93 (2018), asserting as much as a 10 percent loss in labor productivity.

21 **United States is unique internationally:** Sonia A. Hirt, *Zoned in the USA: The Origins and Implications of American Land-Use Regulation* (Ithaca: Cornell University Press, 2014), 7.

23 **"to incubate small businesses and artisans":** Buffalo, NY, Unified Development Ordinance § 6.1.1.F (hereinafter "Buffalo Development Ordinance").

23 **to bring dozens of old gems:** Bernice Radle, "The Magic of Legacy Shops Comes Back to Life in Buffalo," *Strong Towns*, May 17, 2022.

23 **more than doubled in population:** According to the Census, the city grew from 203,341 in 1940 to 573,224 in 1960.

24 **proponents of the rezoning made the case:** City of San Diego, Meeting Minutes of the Regular Meeting of the Council, June 26, 1958.

24 **"If we build another central city":** Richard F. Pourade, *City of the Dream, 1940–1970* (San Diego: Copley Press, 1977).

24 **urged city leaders to punt:** Hamilton Marston became the city's most ardent proponent of comprehensive planning, creating parkland and promoting mass transit. North County Times Wire Services, "San Diego County Pioneer Ham Marston Dies," *San Diego Union-Tribune*, January 29, 2006.

25 **Marston building was demolished:** The demolition occurred eight years after Marston sold the store to a larger company.

25 **departure of Saks:** Jennifer Davies, "Fashion Valley Saks Fifth Avenue Closing," *San Diego Union-Tribune*, May 4, 2010.

25 **reportedly attracted only a few:** Roger Showley, "Last Days of Macy's in Mission Valley: Not Much Left but Mannequins," *San Diego Union-Tribune*, March 17, 2017.

25 **"infill" development:** For example, the city's 2019 "Mission Valley Community Plan" called for mixed-use developments "either through total redevelopment of existing sites, or the creation of new uses coupled with existing buildings of different uses."

25 **two mixed-use districts:** The minimum lot size for these districts is 20,000 square feet, which is a little less than half an acre. San Diego, CA, Municipal Code, tbl. 131.07B (hereinafter "San Diego Code").

25 **the purpose for these districts:** The San Diego Code (at section 131.0701) also calls for the zones "to provide housing and jobs near commercial centers and corridors[,] to reduce dependency on the automobile, to promote access to transit and multi-model [*sic*] transportation systems, and to provide for a walkable, pedestrian-oriented setting, including infill of existing development."

25 **allows for office, industrial, and retail uses:** San Diego Code § 131.0706 (Employment Mixed-Use District).

26 **Together, these guidelines:** All of these provisions can be found in San Diego Code §§ 131.0702, 131.0713, 131.0714, and 131.0716.

26 **website for her last reelection campaign:** "The San Diego Housing Shortage," Vivian Moreno City Council District 8, https://vivianmorenosd.com/2021/12/13/social-equity-in-housing/.

27 **site-specific master plan:** The Riverwalk Specific Plan (Draft September 2020), drafted by the developers of the site, received the endorsement of the city council in November 2020.

27 **an executive order that suspended local zoning:** Office of Governor Ned Lamont, State of Connecticut, Executive Order No. 7MM, May 12, 2020.

Chapter 2: The Magic of Makers

30 **In Remington, stone quarries:** Greater Remington Improvement Association, Remington Neighborhood Plan (2017), 2.2.

30 **Around World War I:** "Remington Historic District," National Register of Historic Places—Registration Form, 2015.

30 **a resident whose home business:** The address is 1513 Park Avenue, a mile and a half from Charm City Cakes.

30 **Maryland's supreme court agreed:** Goldman v. Crowther, 128 A. 550 (Md. 1925).

31 **state supreme court struck down the law:** Tighe v. Osborne, 131 A. 801 (Md. 1925).

31 **second challenge:** Tighe v. Osborne, 133 A. 465 (Md. 1926).

31 **zoners in Charm City:** Maryland's adoption of the State Standard Zoning Enabling Act in 1927 would further solidify zoning's legal standing.

31 **the effects of regulatory stagnation:** See, e.g., Robert C. Ellickson, *America's Frozen Neighborhoods* (New Haven: Yale University Press, 2022), studying the Austin, Silicon Valley, and New Haven regions.

31 **Remington had fallen on particularly hard times:** Kathleen C. Ambrose, *Remington: The History of a Baltimore Neighborhood* (Charleston: History Press, 2013).

32 **property values rose:** Greater Remington Improvement Association, Remington Neighborhood Plan, 2.4.

32 **mixed-use zoning would benefit Baltimore:** Rachel L. Johnson Thornton et al., "Achieving a Healthy Zoning Policy in Baltimore: Results of a Health Impact Assessment of the TransForm Baltimore Zoning Code Rewrite," *Public Health Reports* 128, no. 6 (2013).

32 **"Mixed-use districts":** Johnson Thornton et al., "Achieving a Healthy Zoning Policy in Baltimore."

32 **a comprehensive rezoning:** It was one of just twenty-six cities that undertook a comprehensive rezoning that decade. Sara C. Bronin, "Comprehensive Rezonings," 737.

33 **the industrial mixed-use zone:** Baltimore, MD, Zoning Ordinance § 11-204(a) (hereinafter "Baltimore Zoning Ordinance").

33 **industrial and nonindustrial uses:** Baltimore Zoning Ordinance § 1-308(b).

33 **The zone enables:** Baltimore Zoning Ordinance, tbl. 11-301.

33 **No public hearing:** My one quibble is that the city maintains minimum parking mandates that may not be able to be satisfied on-site. Baltimore Zoning Ordinance, tbl. 16-406.

33 **number of housing units:** City of Baltimore, Census 2010–2020 Population and Demographic Changes (Excel Spreadsheet), showing 1,250 housing units and 2,458 residents in 2010 and 1,386 units and 2,678 residents in 2020.

33 **A plan developed:** Greater Remington Improvement Association, Remington Neighborhood Plan, 2.4.

34 **more than 10,000 brewers:** The Brewers' Association maintains a directory of breweries, www.brewersassociation.org/directories/breweries.

35 **"craftsman industrial" uses:** Hartford, CT, Zoning Regulations § 3.3.7.B (hereinafter "Hartford Zoning Regulations").

35 **many allowable uses:** Hartford Zoning Regulations, fig. 3.3-E.

37 **the Rolling Stones:** Barbara Carlson, "Stones Roll Off Midst Shoving, Yelling, Kicking, Tugging Teens," *Hartford Courant*, June 28, 1966, 33.

Chapter 3: Cultivating Creativity

39 **the neighborhoods of South Shore:** Many of Gates's projects are located in the western portion of the South Shore neighborhood, but they share more demographic characteristics with Greater Grand Crossing and Woodlawn.

40 **the Supreme Court struck down:** Buchanan v. Warley, 245 U.S. 60 (1917).

40 **St. Louis:** Richard Rothstein, The Making of Ferguson, Economic Policy Institute Report, October 15, 2014.

40 **a "Negro invasion":** Nancy Cambria et al., *Segregation in St. Louis: Dismantling the Divide* (St. Louis: Washington University in St. Louis, 2018).

40 **twenty-two pages of text:** Chicago, IL, Zoning Ordinance (April 16, 1923).

40 **tied demographic and land use records:** Allison Shertzer, Tate Twiman, and

Randall P. Walsh, "Race, Ethnicity, and Zoning: The Case of Chicago's First Comprehensive Land Use Ordinance" (working paper, National Bureau of Economic Research, 2014).

41 **a house with a racially restrictive covenant:** The address is 6140 South Rhodes Avenue.

41 **to the U.S. Supreme Court:** Lee v. Hansberry, 311 U.S. 32 (1940).

41 **the invalidation of all racially restrictive covenants:** Shelley v. Kraemer.

41 **Parkway Garden Homes:** "Parkway Garden Homes Historic District," National Register of Historic Places—Registration Form, 2011. Parkway Garden Homes sits many blocks west from Gates's interventions but is still considered part of Greater Grand Crossing.

41 **remain racially homogeneous:** Chicago Metropolitan Agency for Planning (CMAP), "Community Data Snapshot: South Shore," July 2023 (93 percent Black residents); CMAP, "Community Data Snapshot: Greater Grand Crossing," July 2023 (95 percent Black residents); CMAP, "Community Data Snapshot: Woodlawn," July 2023 (80 percent Black residents). CMAP data snapshots are all available at www.cmap.illinois.gov.

41 **Unemployment tops three times the regional average:** CMAP data snapshots show 15 percent unemployment for South Shore, 19.6 percent for Greater Grand Crossing, and 18.5 percent for Woodlawn.

41 **purchased a home:** The address is 6918 South Dorchester Avenue.

42 **ceremonially sweeping the home:** Theaster Gates, "How to Revive a Neighborhood," filmed by TEDTalk, March 26, 2015, www.ted.com.

42 **the Archive House:** The address is 6916 South Dorchester Avenue.

42 **the Black Cinema House:** The address is 6901 Dorchester Avenue.

43 **a primarily residential zone that allows:** Chicago, IL, Zoning Ordinance §§ 17-2-0103, 17-0207 (hereinafter "Chicago Zoning Ordinance"). This flexibility has not necessarily been applied to retail establishments. In September 1986, for example, prior owners of the Listening House property applied for a zoning variance for a grocery and liquor store, but the Chicago Zoning Board of Appeals denied their application.

43 **"There are city policies":** Gates, "How to Revive a Neighborhood."

43 **a zone intended to accommodate manufacturing:** Chicago Zoning Ordinance § 17-5-0102.

43 **a long-abandoned neoclassical bank building:** The address is 6758 South Stony Island Avenue.

44 **provisions enabling city planning staff:** Chicago Zoning Ordinance § 17-3-0207.

44 **"cultural exhibits and libraries":** Chicago Zoning Ordinance § 17-10-0207-F.

44 **within 1,320 feet of Stony Island Avenue:** Chicago Zoning Ordinance § 17-10-0102-B.2.

44 **"contribute[d] to the comfort":** Chicago Zoning Ordinance § 17-9-0201-B.

45 **a national organization:** Tina El Gamal, "Artists and Sacred Spaces: A Natural Fit on Chicago's South Side," *American Theater*, December 21, 2023.

46 **"Projects like this":** Diana Budds, "The Stony Island Arts Bank Brings 'Redemptive Architecture' to Chicago's South Side," *Fast Company*, October 16, 2015.

46 **could bring long-lasting benefits:** Allison Shertzer, Tate Twinam, and Randall P. Walsh, "Zoning and the Economic Geography of Cities" (working paper, National Bureau of Economic Research, 2016).

47 **the city decided to use zoning:** PBS, "Music Row: Nashville's Most Famous Neighborhood," aired August 17, 2017.

48 **blew out the first floor:** Jeremy Hill, *Country Comes to Town: The Music Industry and the Transformation of Nashville* (Amherst: University of Massachusetts Press, 2015).

49 **over 3,200 residential units:** Metropolitan Government of Nashville and Davidson County Planning Department, Music Row Vision Plan, 2019, 18, 22.

49 **property values increased by 176 percent:** Metropolitan Government of Nashville, Music Row Vision Plan, 18.

49 **saw the shuttering of the last live music venue:** Margaret Renkl, "The Day the Music Died," *New York Times*, January 21, 2019.

50 **conservation overlay district:** City of Nashville, Neighborhood Conservation Zoning Design Guidelines for Turn-of-the-20th Century Districts (Parts I and II) (2021).

50 **buildings were demolished:** Historic Nashville, "Save Music Row!" www.historic nashvilleinc.org/get-involved/save-music-row/.

50 **half of the remaining businesses are music-related:** Metropolitan Government of Nashville, Music Row Vision Plan, 10.

50 **especially in the northern portion:** The southern portion has some "conservation"-type zoning protections that make such exemptions harder.

51 **zoning code could offer TDRs:** Metropolitan Government of Nashville, Music Row Vision Plan, 29.

Chapter 4: Rock Around the Clock

54 **"and it was the last east-west street":** "Sixth Street Historic District," National Register of Historic Places Inventory—Nomination Form, 1970.

55 **area thrived as a commercial mecca:** "Sixth Street Historic District," National Register of Historic Places Inventory—Nomination Form, 1970.

55 **multiple-venue performing arts extravaganza:** South by Southwest, "History of South by Southwest," www.sxsw.com/about/history/.

56 **pushed some zoning boundaries:** In 1994, the city rezoned the airport land from rural residential to an aviation services zone, extending that zone in 2002. Austin, TX, Ord. No. 940210-C (February 10, 1994); Austin, TX, Ord. No. 020801-56 (August 12, 2002). The code does not expressly allow live-music stages, either as principal or as accessory uses, in the airport zoning district. See Austin, TX, Municipal Code § 25-2-142, allowing "major

public airport facilities"; § 25-2-622, allowing "commercial or industrial uses that provide services to airport customers," and § 25-13-44, allowing "[c]hurches, auditoriums, and concert halls" and "recreational uses" as principal uses (hereinafter "Austin Code").

57 **generated 45,500 hotel-room night reservations:** South by Southwest, Analysis of the Economic Benefit to the City of Austin of SXSW (2022).

57 **"embarrassed that so many out-of-towners":** Andy Langer, "It's Time to Talk About Sixth Street in Austin," *Texas Monthly*, August 2016.

57 **central business district zone:** Austin Code § 25-2-491.

58 **the code also allows:** Separate from the zoning code, city rules prohibit alcohol sales within three hundred feet of a church, school, or hospital except as provided under state law or unless the city council issues a waiver. Austin Code §§ 4-9-4 to 4-9-5. There do not appear to be any churches, schools, or hospitals within three hundred feet of the Sixth Street businesses discussed here.

58 **constraints appear to be cosmetic:** Austin Code §§ 25-2-643, 25-2-586, 25-2-591 to 25-2-594.

58 **requires bars to undergo a public hearing:** Hartford Zoning Regulations § 3.3.5.I.

58 **Stores selling beer, wine, or liquor:** Hartford Zoning Regulations § 3.3.4.C.

59 **Downtown Austin Alliance:** Chad Swiatecki, "Safer Sixth Street Push Includes Call to Rezone Portions of Entertainment District," *Austin Monitor*, November 30, 2021.

60 **"vacant upper stories":** "Printer's Alley Historic District," National Register of Historic Places Inventory—Nomination Form, 1977.

60 **a large number of vacant buildings:** "Fifth Avenue Historic District," National Register of Historic Places Inventory—Nomination Form, 1984.

60 **"physical decay, unsightly signs":** "Broadway Historic District," National Register of Historic Places Inventory—Nomination Form, 1980.

60 **Ryman Auditorium itself was renovated:** Ryman Auditorium, "1975–1994: Explore the Ryman Timeline," https://ryman.com/history/1975-1994/.

60 **spurring hope among local businesses:** One business, Robert's Western World, documented this 1990s-era optimism on its website, chronicling how its owner added "a jukebox, beer, and cigarettes" and then a stage to the store as things improved.

61 **code was so restrictive:** Metropolitan Nashville and Davidson County Code of Ordinances § 17.37.1: "In recent years, nearly all projects in Downtown have sought rezoning or variances to existing zoning."

61 **"[e]nsure that Downtown remains the civic":** Metropolitan Nashville Code § 17.37.1.

61 **multifamily apartments, hospitals, concert halls:** Metropolitan Nashville Code § 17.08.030.

61 **Bars, nightclubs, and liquor stores:** Metropolitan Nashville Code § 17.08.090.A.1.a.i, exempting the DTC zoning district from dispersion requirements required for "on-sale" beer permits for on-site consumption. Beer is defined to include any beverage with an alcoholic content of not more than 8 percent by weight (§ 7.08.010).

61 **eliminates minimum parking requirements:** Metropolitan Nashville Code § 17.37.4.

62 **now has only about a dozen:** Nashville Downtown Living Initiative, "A Report on the Current State of and Possibilities for Housing in Downtown Nashville" (2003), 8: "[I]n the approximate 80-block area, 134 parcels are currently used as surface parking lots. These parcels represent over 38 acres of property in the heart of a major urban center."

62 **nearly septupled its downtown housing stock:** In 2000, downtown had 1,500 dwelling units. City of Nashville, Nashville Next: A Plan for Nashville and Davidson County (2022). In 2022, it had 9,917 units. Nashville Downtown Partnership, "Midyear Residential Update 2022."

63 **a special committee convened by the city council:** City of Baltimore Joint Special Committee, "Report of the Board of Engineers Upon Changing the Course of Jones' Falls with a View to Prevent Inundations" (1868), 33.

64 **banning them altogether:** See Schad v. Borough of Mount Ephraim, 452 U.S. 61 (1981), holding unconstitutional a zoning law excluding live entertainment, including "non-obscene" nude dancing.

65 **"sexually explicit materials":** Baltimore Zoning Ordinance § 1-302(i)(1).

65 **adult use overlay district:** Baltimore, MD, Zoning Map (2023). The adult use overlay district is one of nine used overlays in the C-5 district, each with different rules.

65 **extra requirements, like design review:** Baltimore Zoning Ordinance §§ 4-405(a)(6)-(7).

65 **exemption from the code's parking mandates:** Baltimore Zoning Ordinance § 10-503(a).

65 **To establish an adult use:** Baltimore Zoning Ordinance § 12-1204(b).

65 **so long as they make their case:** Austin Code § 25-2-801. Austin uses the term "churches" instead of listing other types of religious buildings or using the nondenominational terms "religious institutions" or "houses of worship."

65 **Hartford's code stipulates they may be:** Hartford Zoning Regulations § 3.3.6.E.(1): the placement of an "adult establishment" within 1,000 feet of any building or lot "used for any household living [residential] use; religious institution, medical clinic, medical office, hospital, school, facility attended by persons under the age of 18 (including but not limited to school programs, children's museums, camps, and athletic leagues), park, or other adult establishment."

65 **a statewide thousand-foot-radius dispersion:** N.J. Rev. Stat. § 2C:34-7.

65 **a 1976 decision by the U.S. Supreme Court:** Young v. American Mini Theaters, Inc., 427 U.S. 60 (1976).

66 **upheld a Renton, Washington, dispersion requirement:** City of Renton v. Theaters, Inc., 475 U.S. 41 (1986).

66 **a 1991 study done in Garden Grove:** Richard McCleary and James W. Meeker, "Final Report to the City of Garden Grove: The Relationship Between Crime and Adult Business Operations on Garden Grove Boulevard," October 23, 1991.

66 **crime rises in a statistically significant manner:** McCleary and Meeker, "Final Report to the City of Garden Grove," section IV, page 4.

66 **regulations dispersing "adult entertainment businesses":** Garden Grove Code § 9.16.020.070.

67 **a 1986 study of adult-oriented businesses:** City of Austin Office of Land Development Services, "Report on Adult Oriented Businesses in Austin," May 19, 1986.

67 **either a dispersal or a concentration approach:** See Young v. American Mini Theaters, Inc.: "It is not our function to appraise the wisdom of its [Detroit's] decision to require adult theaters to be separated rather than concentrated in the same areas."

68 **behaviors and practices:** Party buses and "pedal taverns" carrying drunken revelers topped his list of initial priorities, not zoning concerns.

Chapter 5: Making It Home

72 **an excellent location:** West U is one of just three independent municipalities "inside the Loop" surrounded by Houston. The other two are Southside Place and Bellaire.

72 **conceived as a suburb of country homes:** June A. Begeman, *Stepping Back in Time, History of West University Place* (Houston: D. Armstrong, 1999), 23–24, describing the area as "a low-lying, poorly drained swamp . . . streets and yards [flooded] each time there was a heavy rain. . . . Snakes floated in with the floods."

73 **pool their resources to pay for better flood infrastructure:** Begeman, *Stepping Back*, 25–27, documenting two incorporation votes taking place in 1923 and 1924.

73 **first land use ordinance:** West U adopted Ordinance #36, restricting disorderly and bawdy houses, in 1929 and Ordinance #44, restricting fowl, in 1931. See Begeman, *Stepping Back*, 54, explaining these and other early ordinances. Chapter 7 explains that many American cities banned agricultural uses during that period. In 2003, the city's code was amended with a provision that allows up to twelve fowl. City of West U., Tex., Ordinance § 14-8.

73 **adopted a zoning code:** Courts heard several early challenges to the city's zoning code. While two decisions limited the applicability of the code, none resulted in a complete rejection of the code. See, e.g., City of West University Place v. Ellis, 134 Tex. 222 (S.W.2d 1940), holding a two-classification zoning ordinance invalid when applied to business owner's proposed commercial use; West University Place v. Martin, 113 S.W.2d 295 (Tex. Civ. App. Ct. 1938), cause dismissed, 132 Tex. 354 (S.W.2d 1939), invalidating incorporation of fire prevention rules.

73 **its population peaking:** U.S. Census Bureau, 1950 Census of Population, September 14, 1950, documenting 17,053 people living in West University Place.

73 **5,200 homes:** Begeman, *Stepping Back*, 53.

73 **among the fastest-growing cities:** The population increase can also be attributed,
in part, to the city's annexation of extraterritorial land to expand its borders. Unlike
many East Coast cities, Houston remains surrounded by land not incorporated into
any municipality. City government has powers granted by the legislature to over-
take unincorporated areas and, in some instances, incorporated areas belonging to
another municipality. But Houston's growth does not exclusively result from its outward sprawl; it gains more through in-migration within its existing borders.

73 **land development rules are also found in zoning:** See, e.g., Teddy M. Kapur,
"Land Use Regulation in Houston Contradicts the City's Free Market Reputation,"
Environmental Law Reporter News & Analysis 34 (2004). See also Bernard H. Siegan,
"Non-Zoning in Houston," *Journal of Law & Economics* 13, no. 1 (1970), documenting
minimum lot sizes at the time of 5,000 square feet for sewered lots and 7,000 square
feet for nonsewered lots, along with 25-foot front setbacks for single-family dwellings, and 20-foot front and 10-foot side setbacks for apartment buildings, and off-
street parking requirements for housing, 76–77.

73 **subdivision ordinance:** Houston Code ch. 42 ("Subdivisions, Developments, and
Platting"); § 42-186 (requiring two parking spaces for most single-family dwellings).

74 **these ordinances are not zoning:** Powell v. City of Houston, 628 S.W.3d 838 (Tex.
2021). In 2021, two disgruntled Houston homeowners wishing to avoid having to
comply with the historic district ordinance argued before the court that the city's
preservation ordinance constituted zoning in disguise, and that the city's adoption
process for the preservation ordinance failed to comply with legal requirements to
adopt a zoning ordinance. (Full disclosure: I wrote an amicus brief supporting the
city, differentiating the preservation ordinance from zoning. Brief for Historic Preservation Organizations and Legal Scholars as Amici Curiae in Support of Respon-
dents, Powell v. City of Houston, 628 S.W.3d 838 [Tex. 2021].) The court rejected
the homeowners' claim. To paraphrase the ruling: Houston's land use rules do not
divide the whole city into districts and regulate land uses and land development
holistically, and thus Houston lacks zoning as the term is normally understood.

74 **wealthier homeowners who historically have:** William A. Fischel, *The Homevoter
Hypothesis: How Home Values Influence Local Government Taxation, School Finance, and
Land Use Policies* (Cambridge: Harvard University Press, 2005).

74 **80 percent of the state's residential land:** National Zoning Atlas, "Connecticut
Zoning Atlas," www.zoningatlas.org/connecticut.

74 **only 15 percent of the state's buildable land:** National Zoning Atlas, "New Hampshire Zoning Atlas," www.zoningatlas.org/new-hampshire. The lots counted in
the 15 percent figure are those allowed to have less than two hundred feet frontage, defined as the length of land abutting the street. See also Jason Sorens, "The
New Hampshire Zoning Atlas" (working paper, American Institute for Economic

Research, 2023), for a description of methodology in comparison to the methods used on the Connecticut Zoning Atlas.

74 **if Connecticut's lot sizes were reduced by half:** Jae-Hee Song, "The Effect of Residential Housing in U.S. Markets" (working paper, 2021) .

75 **even moderate lot-size mandates resulted in underproduction:** M. Nolan Gray and Salim Furth, "Do Minimum Lot-Size Regulations Limit Housing Supply in Texas?," Mercatus Center at George Mason University (2019).

75 **there is more demand for small lots:** Paul D. Gottlieb et al., "Determinants of Local Housing Growth in a Multi-Jurisdictional Region, Along with a Test for Nonmarket Zoning," *Journal of Housing Economics* 21, no. 4 (2012).

75 **required a minimum size:** Siegan, "Non-Zoning in Houston."

75 **city has reduced those mandates:** Houston Code §§ 42-181–42-184.

75 **minimum lot-size change alone significantly increased:** M. Nolan Gray and Adam A. Millsap, "Subdividing the Unzoned City: An Analysis of the Causes and Effects of Houston's 1998 Subdivision Reform," *Journal of Planning Education and Research* 43, no. 4 (2020).

75 **Houston has issued more permits:** U.S. Department of Housing and Urban Development, State of the Cities Data Systems.

76 **the resulting units were affordable:** Jake Wegmann, Aabiya Noman Baqai, and Josh Conrad, "Here Come the Tall Skinny Houses: Assessing Single-Family to Townhouse Redevelopment in Houston, 2007–2020," *Cityscape* 25, no. 2 (2023), referring to households at 105 percent area median income.

76 **for every additional acre:** Glaeser and Ward, "The Causes and Consequences of Land Use Regulation," 273.

76 **almost three times the number of housing units:** In 2021, Houston (2.3 million people) issued permits for 15,429 housing units, while New York City (8.5 million people) issued permits for 19,923 units. U.S. Department of Housing and Urban Development, State of the Cities Data Systems, https://socds.huduser.gov/permits/.

76 **"more than twice as well":** Michael Kimmelman, "How Houston Moved 25,000 People from the Streets into Homes of Their Own," *New York Times*, June 14, 2022.

76 **supply of housing:** See, e.g., Edward L. Glaeser and Bryce A. Ward, "The Causes and Consequences of Land Use Regulation: Evidence from Greater Boston," *Journal of Urban Economics* 65, no. 3 (2009); Alex Horowitz and Ryan Canavan, "More Flexible Zoning Helps Contain Rising Rents," Pew Charitable Trusts, April 17, 2023, showing zoning changes in Minneapolis, New Rochelle, Portland (Oregon), and Tysons (Virginia) have resulted in an increase in market-rate housing whose existence has curtailed rent growth to far less than the 31 percent rent growth across the country between 2017 and 2023.

76 **minimum lot-size requirements of 8,250 square feet:** West University Place, TX, Zoning Ordinance, tbl. 5-1.

76 **prohibits multifamily housing:** All forty-eight building permits issued in 2021 by the municipality were for single-family homes. U.S. Department of Housing and Urban Development, State of the Cities Data Systems.

77 **constraints dampen production:** Edward L. Glaeser and Joseph Gyourko, "The Impact of Building Restrictions on Housing Affordability," *FRBNY Economic Policy Review* 9, no. 2 (June 2003); Edward L. Glaeser, Joseph Gyourko, and Raven Saks, "Why Is Manhattan So Expensive? Regulation and the Rise in Housing Prices," *Journal of Law & Economics* 48, no. 2 (2005); Keith R. Ihlanfeldt, "The Effect of Land Use Regulation on Housing and Land Prices," *Journal of Urban Economics* 61, no. 3 (2007); John M. Quigley and Steven Raphael, "Regulation and the High Cost of Housing in California," *American Economic Review* 95, no. 2 (2005).

77 **its comprehensive plan:** City of West University Place, Comprehensive Plan (2017).

77 **city has achieved this narrow goal:** A 1989 study of 1978 single-family home prices in West University Place, another independent city within Houston with zoning (Bellaire), and the City of Houston revealed that buyers paid 7 percent more for houses with zoning and deed restrictions. Janet Furman Speyrer, "The Effect of Land-Use Restrictions on Market Values of Single-Family Homes in Houston," *Journal of Real Estate Finance and Economics* 2, no. 2 (1989). The study included 230 home sales and covered a three-mile radius. That said, the study did not control for neighborhood quality or proximity to undesirable uses.

77 **for just $60,000:** I looked at realtor.com in February 2024 for condominiums in their complex.

78 **problematic aspects of Houston's anarchic siting procedures:** Robert D. Bullard, *Invisible Houston: The Black Experience in Boom and Bust* (College Station: Texas A&M University Press, 2000); Robert D. Bullard, *Dumping in Dixie: Race, Class, and Environmental Quality* (Boulder: Westview Press 1990).

79 **that 25 percent of racial segregation:** Jonathan T. Rothwell, "Racial Enclaves and Density Zoning: The Institutionalized Segregation of Racial Minorities in the United States," *American Law & Economics Review* 13, no. 1 (2011).

79 **Connecticut suburbs and towns had more zoning constraints:** Yonah Freemark, Lydia Lo, and Sara C. Bronin, "Bringing Zoning into Focus," Urban Institute Report, June 2023.

79 **for every year a low-income child:** Raj Chetty and Nathaniel Hendren, "The Impacts of Neighborhoods on Intergenerational Mobility I: Childhood Exposure Effects," *Quarterly Journal of Economics* 133, no. 3 (2018), analyzing the trajectories of children growing up in families at the 25th percentile of the income distribution.

80 **one of the most segregated:** John R. Logan and Brian J. Stults, "Metropolitan Segregation: No Breakthrough in Sight" (working paper, U.S. Census Bureau Center for Economic Studies, 2022).

80 **This segregation costs an estimated:** Metropolitan Planning Council, "The Cost of Segregation," 2017.

80 **residential segregation in the 209 largest cities:** Stephen Menendian, Samir Gambhir, and Arthur Gailes, "The Roots of Structural Racism Project: Twenty-First Century Racial Residential Segregation in the United States," Othering and Belonging Institute at UC Berkeley, June 30, 2021.

80 **rushed to record:** University of Minneapolis, Mapping Prejudice Project, https://mappingprejudice.umn.edu.

81 **highest Black-White homeownership gap:** Jung Hyun Choi et al., "Explaining the Black-White Homeownership Gap: A Closer Look at Disparities Across Local Markets," Urban Institute, 2019.

81 **legislative mandate that requires the city:** Minn. Stat. Ann. § 473.864.

82 **the final plan:** City of Minneapolis Department of Community Planning and Economic Development, Minneapolis 2040—The City's Comprehensive Plan (2020).

82 **eliminate single-family zoning:** Minneapolis, MN, Code of Ordinances § 546.30 (hereinafter "Minneapolis Code").

82 **Minneapolis a wild outlier within the Twin Cities metro:** Mary Jo Webster and Michael Corey, "How Twin Cities Housing Rules Keep the Metro Segregated," *Star Tribune*, August 7, 2021.

82 **YIMBY-style change requires three groups:** Hearing on Housing Supply and Innovation Before the U.S. Senate Committee on Banking, Housing, and Urban Affairs Subcommittee on Housing, Transportation, and Community Development, 118th Cong. D864 (2023) (statement of Janne Flisrand on behalf of Neighbors for More Neighbors).

82 **a mere seventy-six units:** Alex Schieferdecker, "The Reality and Myth of the Minneapolis 2040," *streets.mn* (blog), June 20, 2022.

83 **a "floor-to-area ratio":** Minneapolis Code § 535.90(a).

83 **For accessory apartments:** Minneapolis Code §§ 537.60, 537.110.

83 **code also sets design standards:** Minneapolis Code § 537.110(6)e.

83 **under-the-radar restrictions:** Sara C. Bronin, "Zoning by a Thousand Cuts," *Pepperdine Law Review* 50 (2023).

83 **subject to so many hidden requirements:** Bronin, "Zoning by a Thousand Cuts," 755–57.

83 **94 percent of Connecticut districts:** Bronin, "Zoning by a Thousand Cuts," 763.

83 **may also introduce bias:** Most people who speak and participate in land use meetings in Massachusetts are White, male, older homeowners. Katherine Levine Einstein, David Glick, and Maxwell Palmer, *Neighborhood Defenders: Participatory Politics and America's Housing Crisis* (Cambridge: Cambridge University Press, 2019).

83 **puts the public participation at the wrong time:** Anika Singh Lemar, "Overparticipation: Designing Effective Land Use Public Processes," *Fordham Law Review* 90, no. 3 (2021).

84 **"segregation of the affluent":** Michael C. Lens and Paavo Monkkonen, "Do Strict Land Use Regulations Make Metropolitan Areas More Segregated by Income?," *Journal of the American Planning Association* 82, no. 1 (2016): 12: "Particular types of regulation, such as density restrictions, more independent reviews for project approval and zoning changes, and a greater level of involvement by local government and citizenry in the permitting process are significantly associated with segregation overall and of the affluent, specifically when we control for a range of metropolitan areas characteristics."

84 **"mere parasite[s]":** Village of Euclid v. Ambler Realty Company, 394.

84 **In Connecticut, just 2 percent:** National Zoning Atlas, "Connecticut Zoning Atlas."

85 **roughly nine hundred:** Emily Thaden and Ruoniu Wang, "Inclusionary Housing in the United States: Prevalence, Impact, and Practices," Lincoln Institute of Land Policy, September 2017. The authors identified 1,379 housing policies (sometimes several in one jurisdiction) across studied jurisdictions.

85 **argue that inclusionary zoning could:** Robert Damewood, "Building Inclusive Communities: A Review of Local Conditions, Legal Authority, and Best Practices for Pittsburgh," Regional Housing Legal Services, January 2022.

85 **no research has shown:** Emily Hamilton, "Inclusionary Zoning Hurts More Than It Helps," Mercatus Center at George Mason University, February 2021.

86 **inclusionary zoning actually increases overall prices:** Jenny Schuetz, Rachel Meltzer, and Vicki Been, "Silver Bullet or Trojan Horse? The Effects of Inclusionary Zoning on Local Housing Markets in the United States," *Urban Studies* 48, no. 2 (2011).

86 **in California jurisdictions:** Tom Means and Edward P. Stringham, "Unintended or Intended Consequences? The Effect of Below-Market Housing Mandates on Housing Markets in California," *Journal of Public Finance and Public Choice* 30, no. 1–3 (2015).

86 **recommended that the city pilot:** Grounded Solutions Network, "Memorandum to City Officials Re: Inclusionary Housing and Incentive Zoning Exploratory Committee Recommendations," October 30, 2017.

86 **area median household income:** The Census calculates area median income to be the household income for a region's median household. (This is the same measure used by the Department of Housing and Urban Development to assess eligibility for programs like Section 8 subsidies.)

86 **provisions apply to developments:** Pittsburgh, PA, Code of Ordinances § 907.04.A.5 (hereinafter "Pittsburgh Code"), requiring 10 percent if the units are provided on the same lot as the permitted activity and 12 percent if the units are provided somewhere else.

86 **many jurisdictions with such ordinances:** Thaden and Wang, "Inclusionary Housing in the United States."

86 **code requires a developer to record:** Pittsburgh Code § 907.04.A.6.

86 **with 90 percent requiring affordability periods:** Thaden and Wang, "Inclusionary Housing in the United States," 7.

86 **644 units of housing:** U.S. Department of Housing and Urban Development, State of the Cities Data Systems.

87 **filed a federal lawsuit:** Builders Association of Metropolitan Pittsburgh v. City of Pittsburgh, No. 2:22-cv-706 (W.D. Pa.), filed May 12, 2022. In April 2023, the court mostly rejected the city's motion to dismiss, finding the plaintiff association had standing to sue and that certain arguments were ripe for adjudication. The case remains pending.

87 **remain an unproven mechanism:** The particular provisions of inclusionary zoning ordinances, alongside market dynamics, can make a big difference in the success of such ordinances. See Claudia Aiken, "Evaluating Inclusionary Zoning Policies," New York University Furman Center, July 2023.

88 **definition of "family":** Sara C. Bronin, "Zoning for Families," *Indiana Law Journal* 95, no. 1 (2020).

88 **40 percent of the city's housing stock:** State of Connecticut Department of Housing, "2021 Affordable Housing Appeals List—Exempt Municipalities."

Chapter 6: A Bigger Menu for Movement

90 **"A wonderful welcome to you":** Bobby Schuller, *Hour of Power*, first episode, February 8, 1970, www.youtube.com.

92 **only White veterans:** Richard Rothstein, *The Color of Law: A Forgotten History of How Our Government Segregated America* (New York: Liveright, 2017).

93 **over three trillion annually:** U.S. Bureau of Transportation Statistics, U.S. Vehicle-Miles Dataset Table.

93 **28 percent of such emissions:** U.S. Environmental Protection Agency, Sources of Greenhouse Gas Emissions: Total U.S. Greenhouse Gas Emissions by Economic Sector in 2021, showing a total of 6,340 million metric tons of CO_2 equivalent.

93 **have 35 percent higher vehicle miles traveled:** Desegregate Connecticut, "The Environmental Case for Zoning Reform," 2021.

93 **In Connecticut, for instance:** Justin Sears and Leslie Badger, "Mapping Household Energy & Transportation Affordability in Connecticut," Vermont Energy Investment Corporation for CT Green Bank, 22–23 (2020).

93 **affordability gap primarily burdens Connecticut's poor:** Sears and Badger, "Mapping Household Energy," 24–25.

93 **14 percent overall and about a quarter of urban residents:** DataHaven, 2023 Community Wellbeing Index (2023). A quarter of the state's Black residents and a third of Latino residents are food insecure, far more than the 11 percent of White residents with food insecurity.

93 **nearly a quarter of all adults:** Alix Gould-Werth, Jamie Griffin, and Alexandra K. Murphy, "Developing a New Measure of Transportation Insecurity: An Exploratory Factor Analysis," *Survey Practice* 11, no. 2 (2018).

93 **those affected are disproportionately people of color:** Alexandra K. Murphy, Karina McDonald-Lopez, and Alix Gould-Werth, "Transportation Insecurity in the United States: A Descriptive Portrait," *Socius: Sociological Research for a Dynamic World* 8, no. 10 (2022).

95 **the bank purchased adjacent properties:** Aaron Qualls, "One Line of Your Zoning Code Can Make a World of Difference," *Strong Towns*, January 31, 2019.

95 **$50 million a year:** Bryan P. Blanc et al., "Effects of Urban Fabric Changes on Real Estate Property Tax Revenue: Evidence from Six American Cities," *Transportation Research Record* 2543, no. 1 (2014).

95 **it costs a jaw-dropping:** Donald Shoup, "The High Cost of Minimum Parking Requirements," *Parking: Issues and Policies, Transport and Sustainability Series* 5 (2014).

95 **Developers pass these costs on to tenants or buyers:** Allen Greenberg, "How New Parking Space May Effectively Increase Typical U.S. Urban Housing Total Unit Costs by $52,000 to $117,000" (working paper, Federal Highway Administration Office of Policy, 2005); C. J. Gabbe and G. Pierce, "Hidden Costs and Deadweight Losses: Bundled Parking and Residential Rents in the Metropolitan United States," *Housing Policy Debate* 27, no. 1 (2017) (garage parking adds $1,700 to annual housing rents); Wenyu Jia and Martin Wachs, "Parking Requirements and Housing Affordability: Case Study of San Francisco," *Transportation Research Record* 1685, no. 1, (1999) (off-street parking in San Francisco increases home prices by 10 percent, or about $40,000, for both single-family housing and condominiums).

96 **reduce the developer's incentive to build smaller:** Lewis Lehe, "Minimum Parking Requirements and Housing Affordability," *Journal of Transport and Land Use* 11, no. 1 (2018).

96 **cost of parking is "bundled" with the price of housing:** Michael Manville, "Bundled Parking and Vehicle Ownership: Evidence from the American Housing Survey," *Journal of Transport and Land Use* 10, no. 1 (2017).

96 **an increase in parking from 0.1 to 0.5 spaces:** Christopher T. McCahill et al., "Effects of Parking Provision on Automobile Use in Cities, Inferring Causality," *Transportation Research Record: Journal of the Transportation Research Board* 2543, no. 1 (2016).

96 **directors generally establish parking standards:** Richard Wilson, "Local Jurisdiction Parking Requirements: A Survey of Policies and Attitudes" (working paper, Department of Urban and Regional Planning, California State Polytechnic University, 1996) (surveying 144 planning directors).

97 **voted to incorporate:** The city was sued for not following proper procedures, but prevailed. People v. City of Garden Grove, 165 Cal. App. 2d 794 (1958).

97 **sued by a disgruntled property owner:** Garden Grove Congregation v. City of Garden Grove, 176 Cal. App. 2d 136 (1959).

97 **zoning code requires four parking spaces:** Garden Grove, CA, Municipal Code § 9.12.040.180.A.1.a (hereinafter the "Garden Grove Code").

97 **a tenth of a lot:** Two outdoor parking spaces typically occupy about 320 square feet, with a buffer for a curb cut about the length of the car, while a two-car garage occupies about 550 square feet. That could mean 1,200 square feet or more paved for cars.

98 **zoning code requires 2.75 parking spaces:** Garden Grove Code § 9.12.040.180.A.2.a. Oddly, the code reduces these requirements by 0.25 spaces when the housing is not located on a "principal, major, primary, or secondary arterial street."

98 **one parking space for every three fixed seats:** Garden Grove Code § 9.16.040.150.

99 **a poor city struggling:** In 2020, the U.S. Census said that Buffalo had the sixth-highest rate of childhood poverty, at 42.3 percent.

100 **one provision gave me pause:** Buffalo Development Ordinance §§ 8.4.1, 8.4.2. Exempt from these provisions are single-family homes and duplexes.

101 **board can require off-street parking:** Buffalo Development Ordinance § 8.4.1.

101 **suggests several strategies:** Buffalo Development Ordinance § 8.4.2.B. The full list includes:

1. Walking, cycling, ridesharing, and transit promotion and education.
2. Parking cash-out programs or unbundled parking/market rate pricing.
3. Shared parking arrangements.
4. Enhanced bicycle parking and services (above the minimum required).
5. Support for car-share and bike-share services and facilities.
6. Carpooling or vanpooling programs or benefits.
7. Free or subsidized transit passes, transit-to-work shuttles, or enhanced transit facilities (such as bus shelters).
8. Guaranteed-ride-home programs.
9. Provision for alternative work schedules (i.e., flextime, compressed work week, staggered shifts, telecommuting).
10. Promotion of "live near your work" programs. Roadway improvements adjacent to the site that will help encourage transportation alternatives.
11. Roadway improvements adjacent to the site that will help encourage transportation alternatives.
12. Designation of an on-site employee and/or resident transportation coordinator.
13. Membership in a Transportation Management Association.

101 **The Green Code specifically:** Buffalo Development Ordinance § 8-1.

101 **must provide long-term and short-term bicycle parking:** Buffalo Development Ordinance tbl. 8A: Bicycle Parking.

102 **study of fourteen mixed-use projects:** Daniel Baldwin Hess and Jeffrey Rehler,

"Minus Minimums: Development Response to the Removal of Minimum Parking Requirements in Buffalo (NY)," *Journal of the American Planning Association* 87, no. 3 (2021).

102 **also repealed parking minimums:** Sandpoint, ID, City Code § 9-5-1(F-H) (hereinafter "Sandpoint Code").

102 **allowed a local taqueria:** Qualls, "One Line of Your Zoning Code."

102 **allowed nearby properties:** Sandpoint Code § 9-5-3.

102 **first major city to completely eliminate:** Hartford Zoning Regulations, fig. 7.2-A. There is one exception: car dealers, where on-site parking for the unregistered and unsold cars seems an obvious necessity.

103 **must include a shower and changing facility:** Hartford Zoning Regulations § 7.2.2.

103 **Flisrand has hinted:** Jake Blumgart, "How Important Was the Single-Family Zoning Ban in Minneapolis?" *Governing*, May 26, 2022.

103 **San Francisco repealed:** San Francisco, CA, Planning Code § 151 (hereinafter "San Francisco Planning Code"). Oddly, the code singled out mortuaries, which must provide eight off-street parking spaces; no reasoning was provided for this exception.

103 **provides a cap of 0.5 parking spaces:** San Francisco Planning Code § 151

103 **identifies fifteen districts:** San Francisco Planning Code §§ 151, 151.1 (applying to "NCT, RC, RCD, RTO, Mixed Use, M-1, PDR-1-D, PDR-1-G, and C-3 Districts, and to the Broadway, Excelsior Outer Mission Street, Japantown, North Beach, Polk, and Pacific Avenue Neighborhood Commercial Districts").

103 **a broad range of smaller-scale reforms:** All of these provisions can be found at Sacramento, CA, City Code §§ 17.608.020(F)-(K).

104 **same proportion of people drive:** Compare County of Los Angeles Open Data, *Commute Mode Share in LA County* (2005–2017), with Sacramento Area Council of Governments, *Sacramento Regional Transportation Study* (2018).

104 **"one line of your zoning code":** Qualls, "One Line of Your Zoning Code."

105 **its density bonus program:** San Diego Code § 143.0720; see also § 143.1001.

105 **program produced 3,283 homes:** Mott Smith, Anthony Dedousis, and Michael Manville, "Parking Requirements Are Not a Useful Bargaining Chip for Increasing Affordable Housing," *Streetsblog California*, May 19, 2021.

105 **enacting a law:** MA General Laws ch. 40A § 3A.

106 **"shall be without age restrictions":** MA General Laws ch. 40A § 3A(a)(1).

107 **lacks typical zoning authority:** Until 2023, the land on which Disney World sits was managed by the Reedy Creek Improvement District, a special-purpose government created by the state legislature in 1967, whose five-member board consisted of Disney executives. But the district was dissolved by the state legislature, seemingly in retaliation by Florida political leadership for Disney's stance on LGBTQ rights.

Chapter 7: You Reap What You Zone

110 **one in ten Americans:** U.S. Department of Agriculture Economic Research Service, "Food Security and Nutrition Assistance," 2022.

110 **state's food insecurity is worse than the national average:** DataHaven, 2023 Community Wellbeing Index.

110 **more than 6,500:** Paula Dutko, Michele Ver Ploeg, and Tracey Farrigan, "Characteristics and Influential Factors of Food Deserts," U.S. Department of Agriculture Economic Research Report No. 140 (August 2012).

111 **Boston Common, used as a pasture:** "Boston Common," National Register of Historic Places Inventory—Nomination Form, 1985.

111 **among many cities that passed laws:** Catherine Brinkley and Domenic Vitiello, "From Farm to Nuisance: Animal Agriculture and the Rise of Planning Regulation," *Journal of Planning History* 13, no. 2 (May 2014).

111 **mayor banned cows:** "Boston Common" National Register Nomination.

111 **dispersion requirements for dairies:** Brinkley and Vitiello, "From Farm to Nuisance."

111 **"redefined the economic geography and opportunities":** Brinkley and Vitiello, "From Farm to Nuisance."

112 **food-producing land has diminished:** Brian Donahue, *Food Solutions New England, A New England Food Vision* (Durham: University of New Hampshire, 2014).

112 **Lloyd bent the ear:** U.S. Green Building Council, "Article 89 Gives Boston a New Lease on Urban Agriculture," April 9, 2015.

112 **in 2012 the mayor convened:** Laurie Beyranevand et al., "Using Urban Agriculture to Grow Southern New England," *Connecticut Planning*, 2015 Special Edition, 18.

112 **"agricultural activists, farmers":** Glynn Lloyd, *Resilience*, December 20, 2017.

113 **review focuses on design issues:** Boston, MA, Code of Ordinances §§ 89-2.8; 89-6 (hereinafter "Boston Code").

113 **allows ground-level farms:** Boston Code § 89-4.

113 **allows roof-level farms:** Boston Code § 89-5.

113 **farmers can now retail their produce:** Boston Code § 89-2.13. These stands can be tables, stalls, or tents up to 200 square feet in area.

113 **farmers' markets as of right:** Boston Code § 89-12.

113 **set back five feet:** Boston Code § 89-8.

113 **"washable and sanitizable material":** Boston Code § 89-9.

113 **must keep honeybees:** Boston Code § 89-10.

114 **"Boston's rapidly growing reputation":** Oset Babur, "Is Boston the Next Urban Farming Paradise?" *The Guardian*, April 16, 2017.

115 **"craftsman industrial":** Hartford Zoning Regulations, fig. 3.3-E.

117 **currently produce 50 percent:** Doug Gurian-Sherman, *CAFOs Uncovered: The Untold Costs of Confined Animal Feeding Operations* (Cambridge: UCS Publications, 2008).

117 **defines a CAFO to include:** U.S. Environmental Protection Agency, Regulatory Definitions of Large CAFOs, Medium CAFOs, and Small CAFOs, 2015. The Clean Water Act includes CAFOs in its definition of "point source" pollution and regulates the largest CAFOs accordingly. See 33 U.S.C. § 1362(14).

117 **distribute fecal matter:** Sierra Club, "Why Are CAFOs Bad?" www.sierraclub.org/ michigan/why-are-cafos-bad.

118 **an array of health problems:** Carrie Hribar and Mark Schultz, "Understanding Concentrated Animal Feeding Operations and Their Impact on Communities," National Association of Local Boards of Health, 2010.

118 **have adopted "right-to-farm" laws:** National Agricultural Law Center, "Right-to-Farm Statutes," https://nationalaglawcenter.org/state-compilations/right-to-farm/. Right-to-farm laws often exempt CAFOs from nuisance liability only for a period of time. Iowa's right-to-farm law is the most protective of CAFOs, because it exempts CAFOs from liability without limitation. See Iowa Code Ann. § 657.11, which states that an "animal feeding operation . . . shall not be found to be a public or private nuisance under this chapter or under principles of common law."

118 **CAFOs there have grown fivefold:** Environmental Working Group, "EWG Study and Mapping Show Large CAFOs in Iowa Up Fivefold Since 1990," 2020; U.S. Environmental Protection Agency, NPDES CAFO Permitting Status Report: National Summary, Endyear 2022, May 16, 2023.

118 **empowered a new state board:** Wisconsin Stat. Ann. § 93.90.

118 **ruled in favor of the CAFO:** Adams v. State Livestock Facilities Siting Review Board, 820 N.W.2d 404 (Wis. 2012).

118 **2,800 milking cows:** Larson Acres, "The Larson Family History," www.larsonacres .com/Our_family.html. According to the 2020 Census, there were 742 people living in Magnolia.

118 **now has 337:** U.S. Environmental Protection Agency, NPDES CAFO Permitting Status Report. Impressively, given its small size and long winters, Iowa is second only to California in receipts, employing nearly 20 percent of the state's workers. U.S. Department of Agriculture Economic Research Service, Farm Sector Financial Indicators, State Rankings, 2021.

119 **topping 21,500:** U.S. Environmental Protection Agency, NPDES CAFO Permitting Status Report, May 2023.

119 **sang the same song:** Setlist.Fm, George Jones setlist September 22, 1985.

Chapter 8: The Force of Nature

123 **"Chief Justices and Reverend Doctors":** "The Charter Oak Is Prostrate," *Hartford Daily Courant* (1856), 1.

124 **one that I frequently visit at the Wadsworth:** Charles DeWolf Brownell, *The Charter Oak*, 1857.

124 **lost much of its canopy:** The Dutch elm disease around a century ago felled the city's elm trees, and today's emerald ash borer is tackling its ash trees.

124 **prohibits the removal:** Hartford Zoning Regulations § 6.6.1.B; City of Hartford and TO Design, *Hartford Connecticut's Tree Canopy Action Plan* (2020), 30 (noting that 10 percent of trees constitute half of the tree canopy, because they are older and more mature).

124 **must protect trees:** Hartford Zoning Regulations § 6.6.2.

125 **requires tree planting:** Hartford Zoning Regulations § 6.4.1.

125 **requirements are flexible:** Hartford Zoning Regulations § 6.4.1.D.

125 **trees annually generate nearly $5.5 million in benefits:** City of Hartford and TO Design, *Hartford Connecticut's Tree Canopy Action Plan*, 11.

125 **improve property values by up to 20 percent:** Erin House et al., *Outside Our Doors: The Benefits of Cities Where People and Nature Thrive* (Seattle: Nature Conservancy, 2016), 22–25.

126 **vision of Broadacre City:** Frank Lloyd Wright, *The Disappearing City* (New York: W. F. Payson, 1932).

126 **the "garden city":** An originator of this concept was Ebenezer Howard. See Ebenezer Howard, *To-morrow: A Peaceful Path to Real Reform* (London: Swan Sonnenschein & Co., 1898).

126 **reserving the vast majority of zoned land:** Hirt, *Zoned in the USA*, 7.

127 **lots the size of at least one and a half football fields:** National Zoning Atlas, "Connecticut Zoning Atlas." The Atlas logs minimum lot sizes between 0.92 and 1.84 acres or more, because many jurisdictions had minimum lot sizes of 40,000 square feet, which is 0.92 acres (an acre is 43,560 square feet). Similarly, many jurisdictions used 80,000 square feet, about 1.84 acres.

127 **state even has large-lot zoning:** Desegregate Connecticut, "Get on Board for Transit-Oriented Communities," 2021.

127 **resulted in 4.5 percent of the state being converted:** Emily Wilson, Chester Arnold, and John Volin, "Connecticut's Changing Landscape," University of Connecticut CLEAR Story Map Gallery, https://clear.uconn.edu/storymaps/.

129 **regulates air quality and atmosphere composition:** Intergovernmental Panel on Climate Change, *IPCC Fourth Assessment Report: Climate Change* (2007) § 4.4.2.

129 **precipitation has dropped 40 percent:** Defenders of Wildlife, "Climate Change and the Sonoran Desert Region." Temperatures in the desert have risen 1.5 degrees Fahrenheit over that time period.

130 **minimum lot sizes of about an acre:** Scottsdale, AZ, Basic Zoning Ordinance §§ 5.104 and 5.204 (hereinafter "Scottsdale Zoning Ordinance"), specifying lot sizes of 43,000 and 35,000 square feet for the zoning districts R1-43 and R1-35.

130 **require more than four acres:** Scottsdale Zoning Ordinance § 5.014, specifying a lot size of 190,000 for the R-190 district.

130 **more than 31 million acres:** Rebecca Lindsey, "Looking for Lawns," Nasa Earth Observatory, November 8, 2005; Ted Steinberg, *American Green: The Obsessive Quest for the Perfect Lawn* (New York: W. W. Norton, 2006).

130 **mandating that landscaped areas be finished with:** Scottsdale Zoning Ordinance §§ 10.302.A., 10.303.A.

130 **landscaping be well-maintained:** Scottsdale Zoning Ordinance § 10.700.B.2.

130 **in fact 70 percent of the water:** City of Scottsdale, "Residential Water Use," 2022, www.scottsdaleaz.gov/water/residential-water-use.

130 **yards tend to be cooler than the desert:** Chris A. Martin, "Landscape Sustainability in a Sonoran Desert City," *Cities and the Environment* 1, no. 2 (2008), 7.

131 **nearly thirty times as large:** Tucson, AZ, Unified Development Code tbl. 6.3-2.A (hereinafter "Tucson Development Code"); Scottsdale Zoning Ordinance § 5.014 (the R-1-190 district).

131 **must plant native vegetation or drought-tolerant plants:** Tucson Development Code § 7.6.4.

131 **incorporate water-conserving designs:** Tucson Development Code §§ 7.6.5, 7.7.5. In Scottsdale there is a provision protecting certain existing mature native vegetation, such as saguaros, from uprooting. Scottsdale Zoning Ordinance §§ 7.500–7.506.

131 **caps the amount:** Tucson Development Code § 7.6.4.A.4.c.

131 **submit a rainwater harvesting plan:** A technical manual adopted with the zoning code provides additional guidance for both active and passive rainwater harvesting. Tucson, AZ, Technical Standards Manual § 4.

131 **must also plant one tree:** Tucson Development Code § 7.6.4.B.1.

131 **around three decades:** The 1995 Tucson, AZ, zoning code includes such provisions, Tucson Zoning Code § 3.7 (1995).

132 **down 32 percent:** "Residential Water Use in Tucson, Arizona MSA," University of Arizona, 2017.

132 **mere 40 percent of the water:** Drew Beckwith et al., *Arizona Water Meter: A Comparison of Water Conservation Programs in 15 Arizona Communities* (Boulder: Western Resources Advocates, 2010), 95, 105.

132 **increased 30 percent:** U.S. Environmental Protection Agency, "Climate Change Indicators: U.S. and Global Precipitation," fig. 3, August 1, 2022.

132 **can also earn points:** Seattle, WA, Land Use Code § 23.86.019, tbl. A. The requirement does not apply to single-family homes or some industrial or downtown zones.

132 **requires property owners to maintain:** Seattle, WA, Municipal Code, § 23.86.019.

132 **wrote about installing a green roof:** Frank Lloyd Wright, *The Natural House* (New York: Horizon Press, 1954).

133 **reduce stormwater runoff by 60 percent:** A. M. Hathaway, W. F. Hunt, and Gregory D. Jennings, "A Field Study of Green Roof Hydrologic and Water Quality Performance," *Transactions of the ASABE* 51, no. 1 (2008).

133 **are 30–40 percent cooler:** U.S. General Services Administration, *The Benefits and Challenges of Green Roofs on Public and Commercial Buildings* (Suitland, MD: U.S. General Services Administration, 2011).

133 **building code mandates that developers:** Denver, CO, Code of Ordinances § 10-301.

133 **offers property owners density bonuses:** Austin Code § 25-2-586(E)11.

133 **at least half of the water:** Austin, TX, Environmental Criteria Manual, Appendix W (2022).

133 **fifty-eight green roofs:** Alex von Rosenberg, "The Green Roof Landscape of Austin, Texas: A Contemporary Inventory of Green Roof Systems," master's thesis (Texas State University, 2018), 14.

134 **better health outcomes:** Marcia P. Jimenez et al., "Associations Between Nature Exposure and Health: A Review of the Evidence," *International Journal of Environmental Research in Public Health* 18, no. 9 (2021), analyzing many studies to show positive associations between exposure to nature and increased physical activity, reduced incidence of cardiovascular disease, and reduced depression, anxiety, and cognitive function.

134 **and feel like they do, too:** Mathew P. White et al., "Spending at Least 120 Minutes a Week in Nature Is Associated with Good Health and Wellbeing," *Scientific Reports* 9, no. 1 (2019).

Chapter 9: Completing the Street

136 **"Bays are defined by fluted pilasters":** "City Hall Park Historic District," National Register of Historic Places Inventory—Nomination Form, 1984.

137 **Pearl Street spans:** City of Burlington, Great Streets BTV: Downtown Street Design and Construction Standards, 64 (2022).

139 **first "complete streets" policy:** 19 Vt. Stat. Ann. §§ 10b(c)(2)(A), 309d. There are a few reasonable exceptions to this policy, including unpaved highways and situations where pedestrians and bikers are prohibited from using a particular transportation facility, as they might be on an active high-speed highway.

140 **one of thirty-seven states:** Smart Growth America, "Complete Streets Policies," 2023.

140 **identifying six different types of neighborhoods:** Vermont Department of Health, *Complete Streets: A Guide for Vermont Communities* (Montpelier: State of Vermont, 2012).

140 **its streets must accommodate:** As another example, streets in a smaller-town with a village feel (category "C4") would need to accommodate purposeful walkers, confident and recreational road bikers, and the same buses and trucks as the C6 district, as well as tractor trailers.

141 **the Environmental Protection Agency required:** Vermont Agency of Natural Resources, *Lake Champlain Phosphorous TMDL* (2002).

141 **federal officials decided:** Letter from H. Curtis Spaulding, EPA Regional Administrator, to Secretary Deborah Markowitz, January 24, 2011.

141 **a design and construction manual:** City of Burlington, Greet Streets BTV.

142 **complementary form-based zoning code provisions:** Burlington, VT, PlanBTV Downtown Code, art.14.

142 **range is now:** Burlington, VT, Zoning Code §§ 14.3.4-C, 14.3.5-C (hereinafter "Burlington Zoning Code").

143 **a 100 percent frontage requirement:** Burlington Zoning Code §§ 14.3.4-C, 14.3.5-C.

143 **must be between three and fourteen stories:** Burlington Zoning Code §§ 14.3.4-D, 14.3.5-D. The code sets a maximum of fourteen stories in the primary core and ten stories in the outer area.

143 **step back every few stories:** These stepbacks cap building height along the sidewalk at three, four, or six stories depending on the street width, with more stories allowed for wider streets.

143 **smaller buildings may have porches:** Burlington Zoning Code, tbl. 14.5-A.

143 **Awnings and canopies:** Burlington Zoning Code §§ 14.3.5-G, 14.4.13(h).

144 **reaching beyond the buildings:** These provisions can all be found in Burlington Zoning Code §§ 14.3.6, 14.6.4, 14.6.6, 14.6.7, and 14.6.9.

144 **art in the park:** City of Burlington Parks, Recreation & Waterfront, "City Hall Park FAQs," 2021.

145 **"lessen[ing] congestion in the streets":** U.S. Department of Commerce, *A Standard State Zoning Enabling Act*, § 3.

146 **dismissed her lawsuit:** Fabiano v. Boston Redevelopment Authority, 806 N.E.2d 128 (Mass. App. Ct. 2004).

146 **university acted within its governmental authority:** Montclair State University v. County of Passaic, 191 A.3d 614 (N.J. 2018).

146 **"zone lots":** Denver, CO, Zoning Code §§ 1.2.1, 1.2.2 (hereinafter "Denver Zoning Code"): "The purpose of a Zone Lot is to provide a boundary for a defined area of land to which this Code's regulations for both land uses and structures apply."

147 **in its "campus" zone:** Denver Zoning Code § 1.2.3.2.B.

147 **85th percentile speed of traffic:** Sara C. Bronin and Gregory H. Shill, "Rewriting Our Nation's Deadly Traffic Manual," *Harvard Law Review Forum* (2021).

148 **disrupts animal habitat:** Ben Goldfarb, *Crossings: How Road Ecology Is Shaping the Future of Our Planet* (New York: W. W. Norton, 2023).

148 **granted immunity to governments:** Some state statutes lift immunity where a local government has not maintained traffic control devices (like lights) required by the MUTCD. See, e.g., Ohio Rev. Code § 2744.02(B)(3), a statute at issue in Slane v. City of Hilliard, 59 N.E.3d 545 (Ohio Ct. App. 2016).

148 **"where such plan or design":** Ga. Code Ann. § 50-21-24(10).

148 **partly dismissed a lawsuit:** Steele v. Georgia Department of Transportation, 609 S.E.2d 715 (Ga. App. 2005). The appeals court found sufficient evidence that the slope

of the shoulder at the intersection where the crash occurred was steep, and not com-
pliant with the Green Book, so it remanded that part of the case back to the trial court.

148 **well-known alternative manual:** National Association of City Transportation
Officials, *Urban Street Design Guide* (Washington, DC: National Association of City
Transportation Officials, 2013).

149 **street-design chapter:** Hartford Zoning Regulations, ch. 9.

150 **a catchall reference:** Hartford Zoning Regulations § 9.1.4.

151 **"a beautiful green belt":** Gates, "How to Revive a Neighborhood."

Chapter 10: A Curatorial Approach

153 **adopted an ordinance:** Delray Beach, FL, Land Development Regulations §
4.4.13(A)(1) (hereinafter "Delray Beach Regulations"), aiming "to result in development that preserves the downtown's historic moderate scale, while promoting a bal-
anced mix of uses . . . [and] to foster compact, pedestrian oriented growth that will
support downtown businesses."

153 **seven hundred other American cities:** Hazel Borys, Emily Talen, and Matthew
Lambert, "The Codes Study," PlaceMakers, 2019.

153 **permits every use:** Delray Beach Regulations, tbl. 4.4.13(A).

154 **must have a "diverse unit" mix:** Delray Beach Regulations § 4.4.13(D)(1).

154 **height caps:** Delray Beach Regulations § 4.4.13(D)(1)(a).

154 **height minimum:** Delray Beach Regulations § 4.4.13(D)(1)(a)4.

154 **increase a developer's initial costs:** Jan K. Brueckner and Ruchi Singh, "Stringency
of Land-Use Regulation: Building Heights in U.S. Cities," *Journal of Urban Economics*
116 (2020); Alain Bertaud and Jan K. Brueckner, "Analyzing Building-Height Restrictions: Predicted Impacts and Welfare Costs," *Regulatory Science and Urban Economics*
35 (2005).

154 **must sit within a tight range:** Delray Beach Regulations, tbl. 4.4.13(C).

155 **must provide a ten-foot-wide passageway:** Delray Beach Regulations § 4.4.13(D)(2).

155 **can't have large "blank walls":** Delray Beach Regulations § 4.4.13(F)(4)(e): blank
walls cannot exceed the lesser of fifty feet, or 20 percent of the length of the building.

155 **seven architectural styles:** Delray Beach Regulations § 4.4.13(F)(3)(a).

155 **requires storefront windows:** Delray Beach Regulations § 4.4.13(F)(5).

155 **sets guidelines for:** Delray Beach Regulations, tbls. 4.4.13(I) and 4.4.13.(J) and §
4.4.13(F)(9).

156 **lots must be:** Delray Beach Regulations, tbl. 4.4.13(C).

156 **requires up to 1.75 parking spaces:** Delray Beach Regulations, tbl. 4.4.13(L) and
§ 4.4.13(I)(3)(a). The code allows for the planning board to approve off-site or even
valet parking as an alternative to on-site parking lots.

157 **occupies virtually all of Galveston Island:** The exception is Jamaica Beach, a small
subdivision incorporated as a distinct city in 1975.

158 **"their preservation en masse":** "The Strand Historic District," National Register of Historic Places Inventory—Nomination Form, 1976.

158 **Sprawling across its more than fifty blocks:** "Galveston—East End Historic District," National Register of Historic Places Inventory—Nomination Form, 1976.

159 **The first step:** Galveston, TX, Code of Ordinances § 10.104.

159 **then the planning commission and city council:** Galveston, TX, Code of Ordinances, tbl. 10.105.

159 **"certificate of appropriateness":** Galveston, TX, Code of Ordinances § 10.106.A.2.

159 **demolish a structure:** Galveston, TX, Code of Ordinances § 10.107.

159 **Just over half:** Sara C. Bronin and Leslie R. Irwin, "Regulating History," *Minnesota Law Review* 108, no. 1 (2023): 306–8.

159 **components of an economic hardship:** Galveston, TX, Code of Ordinances § 10.107.E.

160 **refuses to accept repeat applications:** Galveston, TX, Code of Ordinances § 10.107.G.

160 **the 39,000 local governments:** U.S. Census Bureau, 2017 Census of Governments: Organization Component Estimates, tbl. 3 (2021).

160 **over 3,500 localities:** Bronin and Irwin, "Regulating History."

161 **With four miles:** Although the Strip's boundaries have changed, and other parts of Las Vegas Boulevard boast similar entertainment facilities, I focus on its length roughly between Sahara Avenue and Russell Road.

161 **a seminal 1972 monograph:** Robert Venturi, Denise Scott Brown, and Steven Izenour, *Learning from Las Vegas* (Cambridge: MIT Press, 1972).

162 **"Signs in Las Vegas":** Venturi, Scott Brown, and Izenour, *Learning from Las Vegas*, 52.

162 **"revolves by day":** Venturi, Scott Brown, and Izenour, *Learning from Las Vegas*, 52.

162 **viewed the Strip hermeneutically:** Venturi, Scott Brown, and Izenour, *Learning from Las Vegas*, 35: "[H]ere, the imagery is heated up by the need to compete in the surroundings."

162 **"provide for the development of gaming enterprises":** Clark County, NV, Unified Development Code § 30.40.320 (hereinafter "Clark County Code").

162 **"a highly concentrated and intense development":** Clark County Code § 30.48.760.b.1.

162 **the code does enable larger sizes:** Clark County Code, tbl. 30.72-1.

163 **bans neon:** Clark County Code § 30.48.760.b.9.

163 **much more permissive:** This portion of the city is also subject to a form-based code overlay, which covers most of the downtown core, through which the northern part of the boulevard runs. Las Vegas, NV, Unified Development Code § 19.09 (hereinafter "Las Vegas Code"). Like Delray Beach's code, the City of Las Vegas code sets out building forms and articulates frontage requirements, window and door treatments, and other aspects of design. However, it has no pertinent provisions on signage that would override the underlying C-2 district zoning.

163 **Freestanding signs:** Las Vegas Code, tbl. 12.

163 **up to three "supergraphic":** Las Vegas Code § 19.08.120.H. Note that supergraphic signage is disallowed in the Las Vegas Boulevard Scenic Byway Overlay District, which encompasses a portion of the boulevard.

163 **illumination is allowed:** Las Vegas Code § 19.08.120.C.

163 **struck down significant limitations on signage:** See, e.g., Reed v. Town of Gilbert, 135 S. Ct. 2218 (2015), finding unconstitutional content-based regulations stricter for temporary directional signs to an event than for other types of signage; City of Ladue v. Gilleo, 512 U.S. 43 (1994), finding unconstitutional an ordinance prohibiting a woman from displaying a "For Peace in the Gulf" sign on her residence; Metromedia, Inc. v. City of San Diego, 453 U.S. 490 (1981), finding unconstitutional a total ban on outdoor advertising signage that exempted on-site commercial signs and noncommercial signs.

163 **a violation of the Constitution:** For example, it offers different rules on height, typeface, and location for "subdivision development," "real estate," "political," "garage sale," "directory," and "house of worship directional" signs—content-based regulation that the U.S. Supreme Court has said is illegal. Las Vegas, NV, Unified Development Code §§ 19.06.140, 19.08.120.

164 **"the futon of transportation alternatives":** Charles Marohn, "Shared Space," *Strong Towns,* January 30, 2012.

Conclusion

167 **wrote admiringly in the 1970s about Houston's lack of zoning:** Bernard H. Siegan, *Land Use Without Zoning* (Lanham, MD: Lexington Books, 1972).

168 **influenced its evolution:** U.S. Commission of Fine Arts and U.S. Department of the Interior Office of Archeology and Historic Preservation, *Georgetown Historic Waterfront* (Washington, DC: U.S. Government Printing Office, 1968).

168 **became part of the District of Columbia:** DC Organic Act of 1871, conclusion 16 Stat. 419.

168 **By 1900, 4,000 of Georgetown's 15,000 residents:** Eileen Zeitz, *Private Urban Renewal: A Different Residential Trend* (Lexington, MA: Lexington Books, 1979), 34.

169 **was assigned to the residential district:** All the historic zoning maps that I discuss in this chapter are available on the Washington, DC, Office of Zoning website.

169 **up-and-coming families invested:** Historian Constance Green described the change: "Tiny fenced-off patches of ground at the rear, recently littered with rubbish, again turned into gardens and patios with lilac bushes and crepe myrtle nursed back to vigor by pruning and feeding. Every rejuvenated spot inspired the redemption of others, while real estate brokers hastily played down their decades-old argument that once a neighbourhood had become part-Negro, it deteriorated with inexorable rapidity." Green, *Washington: A History of the Capital, 1800–1950* (Princeton: Princeton University Press, 1976), 399–400.

169 "corner stores": DC Zoning Code, Subtitle U, § 254.

170 as small as 1,600 square feet: DC Zoning Code, Subtitle D, § 1202.1.

170 allows basement, over-store, and garage apartments: DC Zoning Code, Subtitle U, § 253.

170 a wide variety of home-based occupations: DC Zoning Code, Subtitle U, § 251.

170 Agricultural uses: DC Zoning Code, Subtitle D, § 1211; Subtitle U, § 202.1.

170 the city's Green Area Ratio program: DC Zoning Code, tit. 11.C, § 606.1.

170 between 20 and 50 percent of every lot: DC Zoning Code, Subtitle D, § 1208.

170 myth that residents blocked a Metro stop: Zachary Schrag, *The Great Society Subway: A History of the Washington Metro* (Baltimore: Johns Hopkins University Press, 2006).

170 nominal parking requirements: DC Zoning Code, Subtitle C, §§ 700–701.

171 Not every place: The neighborhood must also continue to reflect on its past, as it does through historical markers throughout the neighborhood about some of the stains on our history—including markers exposing the auctions selling people into slavery that happened in a theater-turned coffee shop on Wisconsin Avenue.

172 *utilitas, venustas,* and *firmitas*: *Vitruvius: The Ten Books on Architecture*, vol. 1, trans. Morris Hicky Morgan (Mineola, NY: Dover Publications, 1960).

Index

streets and roads (*continued*)
  curb extensions (bulb-outs), 149, 150
  measuring a road's success, 147
  megablocks, 26
  narrowing existing, 141
  "neighborhood streets," 149, 150
  right-of-way, 138, 143–44
  traffic management, 2, 24, 44, 58, 65, 108,
    137–39, 146–47, 204
  See also automobiles; bicycling; pedestrians
strip malls, 3, 15, 44, 153, 154, 165
Sublime (band), 98
suburbs, 3–5, 21
  American sprawl, 19, 25, 92–93, 126–28,
    129, 134, 158, 161
  flight, 60
  health outcomes, 178
  lawns, 126, 128, 130, 142
  Levittown, 92
  malls, 24–27
  office districts in the, 28
  stagnation of the, 31
  "streetcar suburbs," 47, 169
  swimming pools, 15, 16, 87, 130
  "vehicle miles traveled," 93, 101
  See also automobiles; single-family housing
subways, 6, 104, 170
Sullivan, Louis, 99, 102
"supergraphic" (very large) signs, 163, 207
Swift, Taylor, 49
swimming pools, 15, 16, 87, 130

Taliesin West, 128–30
tax revenues, 3, 18, 95, 160
TDRs (transferable development rights),
  51–52, 171
"tenement" dwellings, 6, 63, 111–12, 178
Tennessee. *See* Nashville, TN
"Tennessee Whiskey" (song), 119
Texas
  Crosby, 17, 34, 71–73
  Dallas, 104
  Newport, a subdivision in Crosby, 19–20, 28
  Senate Bill 30 (to remove racially restric-
    tive covenants), 181
  Shenandoah, 181
  Supreme Court of, 74–75
  weather in, 72, 133

  See also Austin, TX; Galveston, TX; Hous-
    ton, TX
Texas Monthly, 57
"third places," 50–52
Thomas Hooker Brewery, Hartford, 35–37
Times Square, 67, 161
topography, 54
tourism, 24–25, 62, 64, 65, 68, 88, 90–91, 157,
  158, 161
  hotels, 47, 54–55, 57–58, 64, 68, 101, 152–54,
    161–63
traffic management, 2, 24, 44, 58, 65, 108,
  137–39, 146–47, 204
transferable development rights (TDRs),
  51–52, 171
"transit-oriented development," 12, 104–7, 171
transportation, 90–108
  building Austin's new airport, 56, 186–87
  call for a new infrastructure of "active
    transportation," 101, 104
  carpooling, 101, 197
  Disney Transport, 107
  security, 10, 93–94
  "transit-oriented" development, 12, 101,
    104–7, 171
  transportation security, 94
  walking distance and access to, 106, 127
  See also automobiles; bicycling; pedestri-
    ans; public transportation
Tucson, AZ, 11, 130, 131, 132, 134–35, 202
Twain, Mark, 2–3, 10

U.S. Submarine Sandwiches, 16, 180
uncertainty, 19, 51, 61, 83
underwriting guidelines for mortgages, 92
unemployment, 41, 110, 185
unincorporated land, 162, 190
United States federal government
  Census, 19, 77, 101, 110, 180, 194
  Congress, 36, 82, 119–20. *See also* legisla-
    tion and law
  Environmental Protection Agency, 117,
    141, 195, 200
  Federal Highway Administration, 147–49,
    196, 204
  Federal Housing Administration, 92
  federally funded "urban renewal," 137, 369
  Mint, 124